ICN 2019

The Eighteenth International Conference on Networks

March 24 - 28, 2019

Valencia, Spain

ICN 2019 Editors

Pascal Lorenz, University of Haute Alsace, France
Eugen Borcoci, University "Politehnica" of Bucharest (UPB), Romania
Vasilis Ververis, Humboldt University Berlin, Germany
Marios Isaakidis, University College London, UK
Gunnar Wolf, Universidad Nacional Autónoma de México, Mexico

Printed from e-media with permission by:

Curran Associates, Inc.
57 Morehouse Lane
Red Hook, NY 12571

CURRAN ASSOCIATES INC. proceedings.com

Some format issues inherent in the e-media version may also appear in this print version.

Printed by Curran Associates, Inc. (2019)

International Academy, Research, and Industry Association (IARIA)
412 Derby Way
Wilmington, DE 19810

Phone: (408) 893-6407
Fax: (408) 527-6351

petre@iaria.org

Additional copies of this publication are available from:

Curran Associates, Inc.
57 Morehouse Lane
Red Hook, NY 12571 USA
Phone: 845-758-0400
Fax: 845-758-2633
Email: curran@proceedings.com
Web: www.proceedings.com

Table of Contents

ICN 2019

Forward

The Eighteenth International Conference on Networks (ICN 2019), held between March 24, 2019 and March 28, 2019 in Valencia, Spain, continued a series of events organized by and for academic, research and industrial partners.

We solicited both academic, research, and industrial contributions. We welcomed technical papers presenting research and practical results, position papers addressing the pros and cons of specific proposals, such as those being discussed in the standard fora or in industry consortia, survey papers addressing the key problems and solutions on any of the above topics short papers on work in progress, and panel proposals.

The conference had the following tracks:

- Communication
- Networking
- Advances in Software Defined Networking and Network Functions Virtualization
- Next generation networks (NGN) and network management
- Computation and networking
- Topics on Internet Censorship and Surveillance

We take here the opportunity to warmly thank all the members of the ICN 2019 technical program committee, as well as all the reviewers. The creation of such a high quality conference program would not have been possible without their involvement. We also kindly thank all the authors who dedicated much of their time and effort to contribute to ICN 2019. We truly believe that, thanks to all these efforts, the final conference program consisted of top quality contributions.

We also thank the members of the ICN 2019 organizing committee for their help in handling the logistics and for their work that made this professional meeting a success.

We hope that ICN 2019 was a successful international forum for the exchange of ideas and results between academia and industry and to promote further progress in the field of networks. We also hope that Valencia, Spain provided a pleasant environment during the conference and everyone saved some time to enjoy the historic charm of the city.

ICN 2019 Chairs

ICN 2019 General Chair
Jaime Lloret Mauri, Universitat Politecnica de Valencia, Spain

ICN Steering Committee
Pascal Lorenz, University of Haute Alsace, France
Carlos Becker Westphall, University of Santa Catarina, Brazil
Tibor Gyires, Illinois State University, USA
Iwona Pozniak-Koszalka, Wroclaw University of Technology, Poland

ICN 2019
Committee

ICN 2019 General Chair

Jaime Lloret Mauri, Universitat Politecnica de Valencia, Spain

ICN Steering Committee

Pascal Lorenz, University of Haute Alsace, France
Carlos Becker Westphall, University of Santa Catarina, Brazil
Tibor Gyires, Illinois State University, USA
Iwona Pozniak-Koszalka, Wroclaw University of Technology, Poland
Carlos T. Calafate, Technical University of Valencia, Spain
Calin Vladeanu, University Politehnica of Bucharest, Romania
Gary Weckman, Ohio University, USA
Yenumula B. Reddy, Grambling State University, USA
Eric Renault, Institut Mines-Télécom - Télécom SudParis, France
Sherali Zeadally, University of Kentucky, USA

ICN Industry/Research Advisory Committee

Marc Cheboldaeff, Deloitte Consulting GmbH, Germany
Megumi Shibuya, The University of Electro-Communications, Japan
Arslan Brömme, Vattenfall GmbH, Berlin, Germany
Cristian Anghel, Politehnica University of Bucharest, Romania / Pentalog, France
Abdelmajid Khelil, Landshut University of Applied Sciences, Germany

ICN 2019 Technical Program Committee

Alireza Abdollahpouri, University of Kurdistan, Sanandaj, Iran
Hussein Al-Zubaidy, KTH Royal Institute of Technology, Sweden
Cristian Anghel, Politehnica University of Bucharest, Romania / Pentalog, France
Imran Shafique Ansari, Texas A&M University at Qatar (TAMUQ), Qatar
Suayb S. Arslan, MEF University, Istanbul, Turkey
Jocelyn Aubert, Luxembourg Institute of Science and Technology (LIST), Luxembourg
Mehdi Bahrami, Fujitsu Laboratories of America, Sunnyvale, USA
Harald Baier, Hochschule Darmstadt / CRISP, Germany
Katherine Barabash, IBM, Israel
Alcardo Alex Barakabitze, University of Plymouth, UK
Alvaro Barradas, University of Algarve, Portugal
Carlos Becker Westphall, University of Santa Catarina, Brazil
Luis Bernardo, Universidade Nova de Lisboa, Portugal
Robert Bestak, Czech Technical University in Prague, Czech Republic
Patrick-Benjamin Bök, Weidmüller Group, Germany
Fernando Boronat Seguí, Universitat Politecnica de Valencia, Spain

Feng Lin, University at Buffalo, SUNY, USA
Jaime Lloret Mauri, Universitat Politecnica de Valencia, Spain
Pascal Lorenz, University of Haute Alsace, France
Ahmed Mahdy, Texas A&M University - Corpus Christi, USA
Zoubir Mammeri, IRIT - Paul Sabatier University, France
Christopher Mansour, Mercyhurst University, Erie, USA
Antonio Martín-Montes, Sevilla University, Spain
Boris Miller, Institute for Information Transmission Problems - Russian Academy of Sciences, Moscow, Russia
Mario Montagud Climent, Universitat de València (UV) & i2CAT, Spain
Shintaro Mori, Fukuoka University, Japan
Masayuki Murata, Osaka University, Japan
Mort Naraghi-Pour, Louisiana State University, USA
Giovanni Nardini, University of Pisa, Italy
Carla Osthoff, National Laboratory for Scientific Computing (LNCC), Brazil
Constantin Paleologu, University Politehnica of Bucharest, Romania
Paulo Pinto, Universidade Nova de Lisboa, Portugal
Agnieszka Piotrowska, Silesian University of Technology - Gliwice, Poland
Marcial Porto Fernandez, Universidade Estadual do Ceara (UECE), Brazil
Iwona Pozniak-Koszalka, Wroclaw University of Science and Technology, Poland
M. J. Shankar Raman, Indian Institute of Technology Madras, India
Yenumula B. Reddy, Grambling State University, USA
Eric Renault, Institut Mines-Télécom - Télécom SudParis, France
Karim Mohammed Rezaul, Glyndwr University, Wrexham, UK
Ruben Ricart-Sanchez, University of the West of Scotland, UK
Imed Romdhani, Edinburgh Napier University, UK
Mohand-Yazid Saidi, L2TI - University of Paris 13, France
Rodrigo Sanches Miani, Universidade Federal de Uberlândia, Brazil
Panagiotis Sarigiannidis, University of Western Macedonia, Greece
Masahiro Sasabe, Nara Institute of Science and Technology, Japan
Narasimha K. Shashidhar, Sam Houston State University, USA
Mohammad Abu Shattal, The Ohio State University, USA
Megumi Shibuya, The University of Electro-Communications, Japan
Dimitrios N. Skoutas, University of the Aegean, Greece
Andrew Snow, Ohio University, USA
Kostas Stamos, University of Patras, Greece
Cristian Stanciu, University Politehnica of Bucharest, Romania
Aaron Striegel, University of Notre Dame, USA
Karthikeyan Subramaniam, Samsung R & D Institute, Bangalore, India
Bruno Tardiole Kuehne, Federal University of Itajuba, Brazil
Giorgio Terracina, Università della Calabria, Italy
Manabu Tsukada, University of Tokyo, Japan
Muhammad Mahboob Ur Rahman, Information Technology University (ITU), Lahore, Pakistan
Muhammad Usman, University of Trento, Italy

Copyright Information

Performance of LoRaWAN Networks in Outdoor Scenarios

[1,2]Pablo Romero-Díaz, [3,4]Laura Garcia, [1,2,3]Sandra Sendra, [1,2]Jorge Navarro-Ortiz
[1] Dep. of Signal Theory, Telematics and Communications (TSTC), Universidad de Granada, Granada, Spain.
[2]Research Centre for Information and Communications Technologies of the University of Granada.
[3]Instituto de Investigación para la Gestión Integrada de Zonas Costeras, Universitat Politècnica de València, València, Spain.
[4]University of Haute Alsace, Mulhouse-Cedex, France.

Emails: pabloromerodiaz@ugr.es, laugarg2@teleco.upv.es, ssendra@ugr.es, jorgenavarro@ugr.es

***Abstract*—The growing interest in Internet of Things (IoT) has facilitated the appearance of applications which use Low-Power Wide Area Networks (LPWAN). Networks based on the Long Range Wide Area Network (LoRaWAN) standard highlight among these. This paper presents a wide overview of this recent technology and some practical experiments. The developed LoRaWAN devices that compose the network as well as the server used to collect data are presented. Based on this testbed, some experiments are performed in two different scenarios to check the performance in terms of coverage, Signal-to-Noise Ratio (SNR) and Received Signal Strength Indicator (RSSI). Results show that LoRaWAN networks can be a useful solution to implement monitoring networks.**

Keywords-Internet of Things (IoT); LPWAN; LoRa; LoRaWAN; LoraServer: Highway; Rural; SNR; RSSI.

I. INTRODUCTION

The evolution of technologies and the ability to interconnect different devices have led to the existence of networks capable of communicating and acting together, creating what is known as Internet of Things (IoT) [1]. Thanks to sensors and actuators, it is possible to measure our environment and share data which, collected by platforms, allows the developers to create useful applications for the society [2]. The critical point in many scenarios resides in the energy consumption due to the batteries which feed these things. This is why so-called LPWAN technologies, which permit low power transmission, have been developed. In return, the transmission data rate is reduced (e.g., hundreds of kbps) but it is still enough for many IoT applications. Because of their standardization and the usage of non-licensed spectrum, these technologies have become serious competitors of solutions based on cellular networks, such as Long Term Evolution-Category M (LTE-M) or NarrowBand-IoT (NB-IoT) [3]. The most popular LPWAN technologies are Sigfox, LoRaWAN, Ingenu TPMA, and nWave. Their main characteristics and differences, assuming European parameters, are shown in Table I.

In this paper, we present the LoRaWAN technology and its main features to be considered for deploying this kind of networks. The paper also presents the devices we develop that compose our network and the server used to collect the data. Finally, practical experiments are carried out in two different scenarios to check the actual performance of this kind of networks.

TABLE I. CHARACTERISTICS OF LPWAN TECHNOLOGIES

Parameter	*Standard*			
	LoRa	*Sigfox*	*RPMA*	*nWave*
Frequency Band	868/915 MHz ISM	868/902 MHz ISM	2.4 GHz ISM	Sub-GHz ISM
Bandwidth	Ultra NB	8x125kHz Mod: CSS	1 MHz 40 channels	Ultra NB
Range	2-5k urban 15k rural	30-50k r. 1000k LoS	500k LoS	10k u. 20-30k r.

The remainder of this paper is organized as follows. Section II presents some related work. Fundamentals of the LoRaWAN standard are explained in Section III. Section IV depicts our LoRaWAN network prototype. Section V describes the performance evaluation experiments and results. Finally, Section V draws the main conclusions and future work.

II. RELATED WORK

In this section, we present the related work on LoRa and LoRaWAN performance evaluations and LoRa implementations.

A performance analysis of the LoRa FABIAN network protocol stack for IoT, that employs protocols, such as CoAP, HTTP and DNS, was performed by Tara Petrić et al. in [4]. Authors evaluated the Packet Error Rate (PER), the Received Signal Strength Indicator (RSSI) and the Signal to Noise Ratio (SNR) of three LoRa stations deployed over Rennes, France. They highlighted the importance of the location and elevation of the antenna on the performance. Results showed frame losses of 3% under the best conditions. Authors concluded that SNR could be the best metric as RSSI did not present strong correlations.

A performance analysis of LoRa over critical noise conditions was performed by L. Angrisani et al. in [5]. For the transmitter, a LoRa STM32 Nucleo pack comprised of a SX1272 low-power RF shield and a NUCLEO-L073RZ board was utilized. The testbed utilized a master-slave configuration between the transmitter and receiver and employed LabView to perform the measurements. Results showed worse communication with larger bandwidth configurations. High SF (Spreading Factor) values achieve better performance. Finally, higher CR (Coding Rate) values obtained lower improvements in packet loss.

LoRa servers have been implemented in order to be utilized for different types of applications. Jaeyoung So et al. implemented in [6] a LoRa server on OpenStack called LoRaCloud. Authors employed four virtual machines to implement the functions of LoRaCloud. These functions were the application server agent, the gateway agent, LoRa data and LoRa control. The gateway was implemented employing the SK-iM880A and the LoRa device was implemented with the 868 IoT station (Kerlink), using Semtech's HAL as software.

T. Hirata et al. presented in [7] a rice field management system employing LoRa servers. The servers were comprised of an AVR microcontroller, an SD card module, a LoRa module and a battery. The master was implemented utilizing a Raspberry Pi. Experiments were performed for seven days employing seven field servers. Results showed a power consumption of 75.36 mW per day providing the system with a 995-day continuous operation time.

Lastly, W. Zhao et al. implemented in [8] a smart irrigation system that utilized LoRa as the communication protocol. The system was comprised of a LoRa server for validation, description and data analysis, a cloud server for data storage and, as an interface between the applications and the LoRa server, the irrigation nodes and the gateway. Real experiments were performed measuring SNR and RSSI every 500 meters. Results showed that the SNR decreased 20 dBm and the RSSI presented a sharp decrease in the first kilometer. However, the SNR presented a slow decrease and RSSI remained stable in the last 7 km. Moreover, a communication distance of 8 km was achieved between node and gateway.

Other papers have studied performance analysis of LoRa or have used LoRa for diverse IoT systems. In this paper, we focus on the performance analysis of LoRaWAN with the implementation of TTN (The Things Network).

III. LoRaWAN Overview

This section presents some of the most important issues to be taken into account for deploying a LoRaWAN netwotk.

A. *LoRa Modulation*

LoRa® (Long Range) is a proprietary modulation of Semtech. It is based on CSS (Chirp Spread Spectrum) and aims at increasing the communication range while keeping the same low power characteristics of the FSK modulation. This modulation uses the full channel bandwidth to send signals, making a distinction between 'up-chirp' and 'down-chirp'. 'Up-chirp' refers to transmissions in which the frequency changes from the lowest to the highest value, and 'down-chirp' refers to the opposite situation. This technique allows LoRa to modulate its symbols in 'up-chirps' with a bandwidth of 125 kHz, 250 kHz or 500 kHz and with different Spreading Factors (SF) depending on the required data rate and channel conditions [9][10].

B. *LoRaWAN Networks*

The LoRaWAN standard, which is managed by the LoRa Alliance, defines a protocol architecture (specifying the Medium Access Control layer or MAC) and a system architecture. This standard allows devices to use either FSK or LoRa as modulations on the physical layer.

Regarding its architecture, it uses a star topology with a central device known as gateway. End- nodes communicate directly with the gateway through the radio interface. The gateway uses a normal network interface (e.g., Ethernet or Wi-Fi) to communicate with an application server through a network server. The usage of a star topology, instead of mesh network architecture, increases the lifetime of batteries, network capacity, security and quality of service (QoS), among other characteristics. In a mesh network, each node would act as an end-node and as a gateway (router) [11], which causes a greater number of hops and their corresponding packet forwarding, hence producing higher power consumption.

Nodes are not associated with specific gateways. Instead of this, any message received by a gateway will be forwarded to its network server, and these, in turn, will forward it to its application server.

Bi-directional communication between nodes and gateways are allowed by LoRaWAN. In particular, there are three classes of end-nodes named A, B and C [10]. Class A must be implemented by all the nodes, and all the classes are able to coexist in the same network. The characteristics of each class, whose transmission is depicted in Figure 1, are defined below:

- Class A: It is the class that consumes the lowest possible power. It is used in applications with unidirectional communication (from nodes to gateway), allowing a transmission in the downlink direction just after the node has finished its transmission. It is suitable for battery-based sensors.
- Class B: It is characterized by the possibility of opening extra reception windows at certain moments, in order to increase transmissions from the gateway to the nodes. For this reason, the consumption is higher than that of class A. This class is suitable for battery-powered actuators.
- Class C: The devices that implement this class are able to receive data from the gateway at any time (except when the device is transmitting). It is suitable for nodes connected to the electricity grid.

The prototype presented in this paper will employ class A devices.

C. *LoRaWAN Security*

LoRaWAN uses two security layers characterized by protecting data at the link layer as well as at the application layer. As for the application layer, data is encrypted between the node and the application server, which implies end-to-end confidentiality. As for the link layer, a field (MIC), which allows guaranteeing data integrity between the node and the network server, is included. Figure 2 summarizes LoRaWAN security, which is explained below:

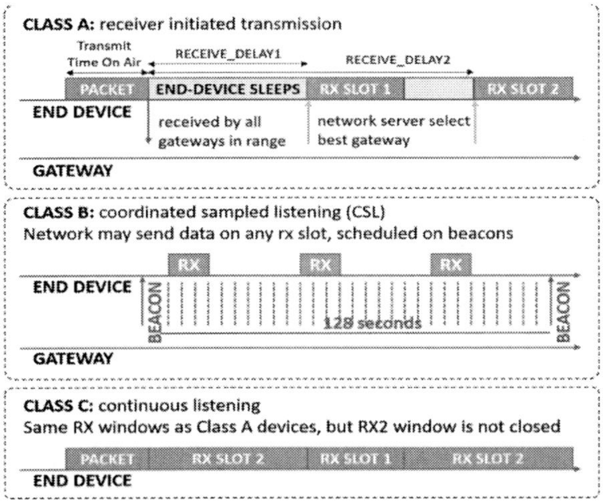

Figure 1. LoRaWAN Device Classes and Packet Transmission.

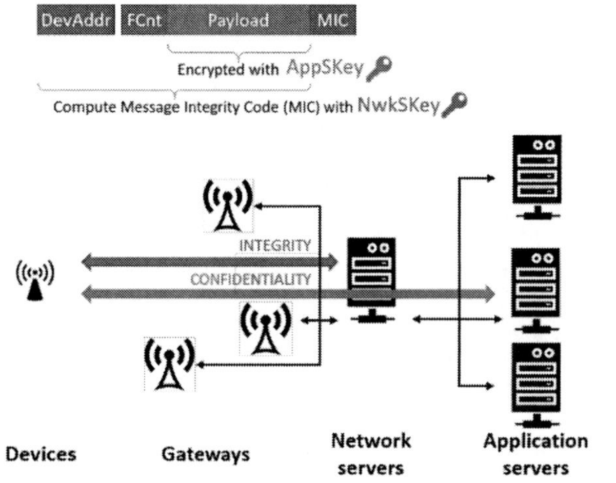

Figure 2. LoRaWAN Security.

- Authentication: A shared key is known by the node and the network, and it is used by AES-CMAC algorithms which are employed when a node joins the network. Two keys named AppSKey and NwkSKey, which are used for the data encryption and data integrity, are derived from the previous key.
- Integrity and confidentiality: The previous session keys are used for protecting all the traffic in a LoRaWAN network. Therefore, the NwkSKey is used for the end-to-end encryption between the node and the application server. Similarly, the AppSKey key is used to calculate a Message Integrity Code (MIC) in order to guarantee the integrity between the node and the network server. Finally, a sequence frame counter is included to prevent replay attacks.

There are two activation methods for initiating the connection: Over the Air Activation (OTAA) and Activation By Personalization (ABP). OTAA uses the parameters JoinEUI (Application ID), DevEUI (Device ID), NwkKey and AppKey (end-nodes specific keys). The previous session keys are obtained from these parameters. On the other hand, using ABP, these parameters must be previously personalized in both the node and the servers.

IV. LoRaWAN Network Prototype

In this section, the implemented prototype is presented. This prototype will be used for the performance assessment in several scenarios.

The first components of a LoRaWAN network are the end-nodes and the gateway. The components are shown in Figure 3 and are described below:

- DIY multi-channel Raspberry Pi Gateway: the chosen gateway is composed of a Raspberry Pi 3 Model B, an IMST ic880A concentrator with a maximum transmission power of 20 dBm and an 868 MHz antenna with 2 dBi gain.
- End-Device: the used end-device is based on the development board 'WeMos D1 Mini', which uses the ESP8266 chip. A shield with the RN2483A chip (up to 14 dBm of TX power), which implements both the physical and the MAC layers of the LoRaWAN standard, is connected to the WeMos board. These are supplied by a external power bank.

As shown in Figure 4, the gateway is connected to a network server by an Ethernet, WiFi or 3G/4G connection. The most popular LoRaWAN network infrastructure is called The Things Network [12]. This infrastructure is an open and collaborative LoRaWAN network. There are also other network infrastructures which allow creating a private environment, such as the LoRa Server [13]. The main characteristics of those servers are described below.

A. *The Things Network (TTN)*

TTN is a community which offers open source software projects to its users to make possible the connectivity between different elements in a LoRaWAN network. One of its main strengths is the capability of connecting any LoRaWAN gateway to its network servers, so no extra infrastructure is required. In addition, it allows the configuration and data gathering through a simple but complete graphical user interface. Even if TTN offers a simple and scalable solution for servers, they are still external and therefore data is shared with the organization.

B. *LoRa Server*

LoRa Server (LS) project provides open-source components for building LoRaWAN networks. It provides the necessary and MIT licensed software components. Those are depicted in Figure 4, which shows the architecture of this project.

Packets are sent to the "LoRa Gateway Bridge". This component could be installed both on the gateway and on the server environment, and it is in charge of the transformation of the packet-forwarder UDP protocol into messages over MQTT. The Broker will forward packets received by the Lora Gateway Server to the LoRa Server. This last component is in charge of the control and management of the network state as well as of the knowledge of active devices and their uplink/downlink frames.

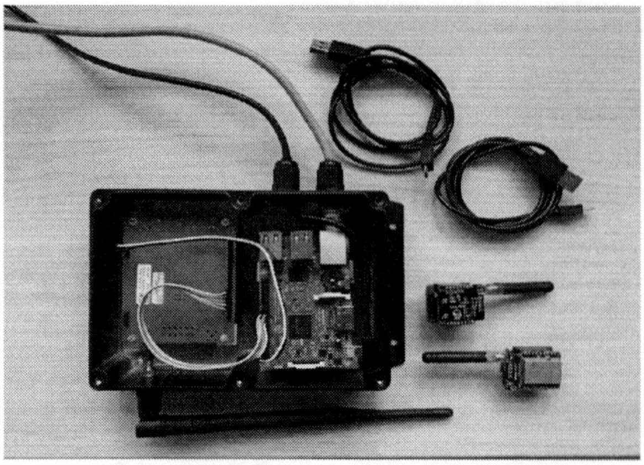
Figure 3. LoRaWAN Components: Gateway and End-node.

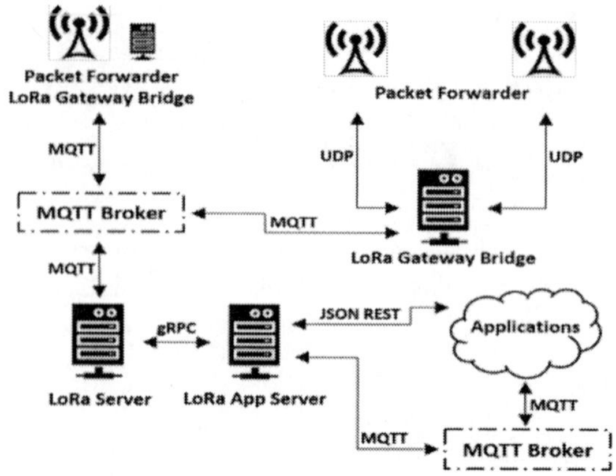

Figure 4. LoRa Server Architecture.

Lastly, LS project provides an application server called LoRa App Server, which allows the configuration of users, devices and applications by a graphical user-friendly interface. It is also responsible for handling of join-request and the handling and encryption of application payloads.

The main difference between both projects is the privacy. Using TTN you are able to create a collaborative network which allows you to use other gateways to reach your network and application server. However, if you are running a commercial solution and data is sensitive, you may create your own private solution with LoRa Server.

Although TTN has been used for the deployment done in this article, we have deployed a private environment using Ubuntu 16.08 Xenial EC2 instances of Amazon Web Services. This server will be used for future works.

V. Results

This section shows the results of the network performance registered in our test bench. In order to evaluate the received signal strength by the nodes, an obstacle-free scenario and a coast rural scenario have been chosen.

A. *Highway Scenario*

The selected scenario is a road environment very similar to a highway (See Figure 5). It has three lanes in each side and also, pedestrian and bike lanes which lets us walk to take the measurements. Measurements have been taken while walking. The evaluated parameters have been the SNR, the RSSI, the packets loss ratio and the coverage of the end-device.

This road joins together the road named A-4006 on the north area of Granada with the street named *Camino Nuevo* at the entrance of Maracena. The route has approx. 3.3 km with 74 m of gradient. The gateway, whose location is in (37.2136373, -3.5951833) geographical point, is placed on a bridge which crosses the road as shown in Figure 5. It is almost a straight route without buildings or obstacles.

Figure 5. Gateway Placed.

Figure 6 shows the results obtained as a function of the distance, taking the gateway as reference point. The X axis of Figure 6a and 6b represents the distance from the end-device to the gateway. By performing an analysis of the results (Table II), it is possible to split them into four distance ranges. As shown, at 1000 m from the gateway, the average and maximum SNR values are 8.56 dB and 11 dB, respectively. In addition, Table II shows the 5 and 95 percentiles of the SNR, showing e.g., that 95% of the measurements are above 5.53 dB. The SNR decreases as the distance from the gateway increases. At 2.5 km, we can observe negative SNR values, which indicate that the noise level is higher than the received signal. Despite this, LoRa modulation robustness lets the gateway receive the packets correctly up to 3.3 km (see Figure 6c). It should be pointed out that the urban area of Maracena starts at this point, so the presence of buildings significantly reduces the SNR and the level of the RSSI.

Finally, Table II also shows the percentage of packet losses as a function of the distance to the gateway. As shown, the number of wrong packets received by the gateway increases as the distance to the gateway increases, being these losses more problematic for the last range (from 3 to 3.3 km).

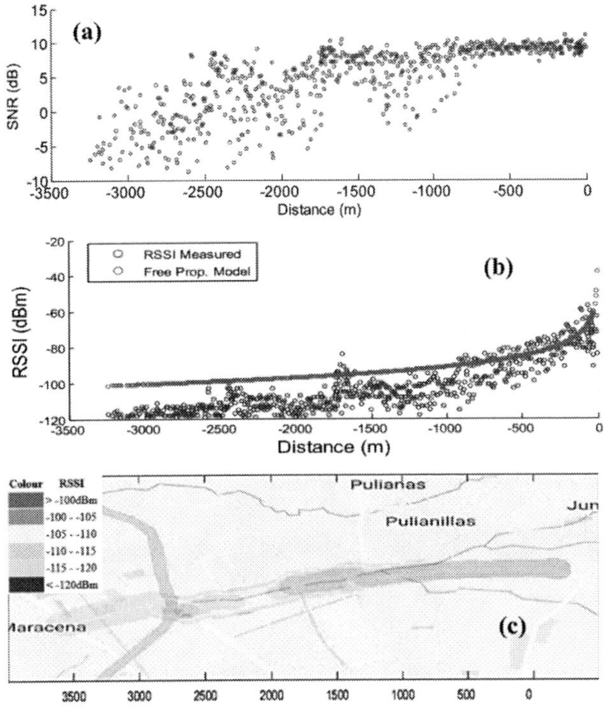

Figure 6. Measurement results of scenario 1. (a) SNR vs. Distance; (b) RSSI vs. Distance; (c) coverage map.

TABLE II. AVERAGE VALUES AND PERCENTILES IN SCENARIO 1

Dist. (km)	*Average Values, percentiles and packet loss in scenario 1*						
	SNR (dB)	*P5 (dB)*	*P95 (dB)*	*RSSI (dBm)*	*P5 (dBm)*	*P95 (dBm)*	*% of Packet Loss*
0-1	8.6	5.53	10.2	-89.4	-107	-68	4.72
1-2	4.82	-2	8.66	-108.3	-116	-99	9.84
2-3	-0.54	-7.33	6	-114.5	-118	-108	28.35
3-3.3	-5.14	-8.2	-0.5	-118.1	-119	-117	71.42

B. *Coast Rural Scenario*

In this case, the gateway with coordinates (38.932457, -0.099974) is placed on the terrace of a second floor house (~9m of height). The building is found at Oliva, a coast village of Valencia (Spain). The path followed and the coverage map is shown in Figure 7. The maximum measured distance is about 615 meters. As we can observe, this scenario has very different conditions. The scenario is composed by several small houses and the climate conditions are also different (higher humidity).

Taking the position of the gateway as the reference point, the measurements show the SNR (see Figure 8a) and RSSI (see Figure 8b) values as a function of the distance. It is remarkable how those values decrease with respect to the highway scenario. This is due to the presence of different obstacles like houses and vegetation. Table III summarizes the performance results. These results can be split into three distance sections. First one ranges from the first 200 meters and it includes the urban core. Considering the height of the gateway, there is practically direct vision with the end-node. The average SNR is 5 dB and the highest value is 8.2 dB.

According to the 5 percentile and Figure 8a, we observe that a 95% of the measurements are over 0.1 dB.

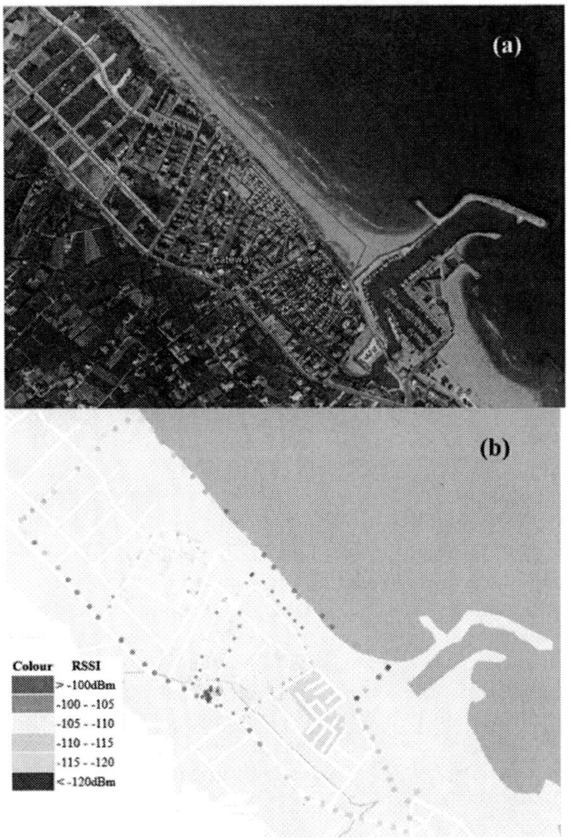

Figure 7. Oliva Map Coverage. (a) aerial map;(b) TTN map results

TABLE III. AVERAGE VALUES AND PERCENTILES IN SCENARIO 2

Dist. (km)	**Average values, percentiles, and packet loss in scenario 2**						
	SNR (dB)	***P5 (dB)***	***P95 (dB)***	***RSSI (dBm)***	***P5 (dBm)***	***P95 (dBm)***	***% of Packet Loss***
0-0.2	4.97	0.1	7.5	-85.77	-111.1	-61.9	50
0.2-0.4	2.75	-7.78	6.8	-105.31	-122.3	-87	48
0.4-0.6	0.52	-9.88	6.39	-112.15	-120	-101	57

The rest has a negative SNR value due to the non-direct vision with the gateway. The second section ranges from 200 to 400 meters. In this area, we find the beach (in front of the gateway), a nautical port (right) and houses with empty parcels (left). As we can see, SNR and RSSI values start to decrease because of the distance and the different nature of the environment. The average RSSI decreases by 20 dBm, which implies that the strength of the signal worsens considerably.

Last section ranges from 400 to 615 meters approximately. The majority of those measurements are taken in the left area of the gateway. This part includes empty parcels so the measurements improve with respect to the total of measurements in the second area.

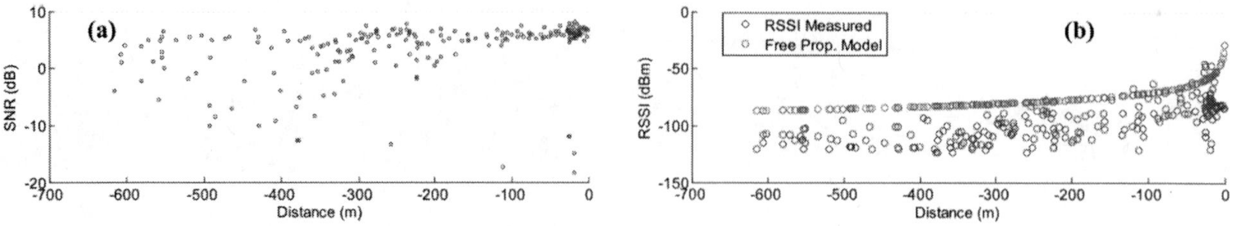

Figure 8. Measurement results of scenario 2. (a) SNR vs. Distance; (b) RSSI vs. Distance.

As shown in Table III, the average SNR is still positive and the 95% of the SNR measurements is over and above -9.8 dB, two points lower than in the second area. Even so, the 95% of the RSSI measurements are two points better than in the previous section. Regarding the percentage of packet losses, the RSSI and SNR are more affected by the presence of buildings, reaching values of 57% for distances of 600 m.

VI. CONCLUSIONS

The aroused interest in LoRaWAN networks and the lack of practical experimental studies have generated the need of deploying these networks in several scenarios to get valuable information regarding aspects of maximum coverage and network performance. This article has presented the main characteristics of the LoRaWAN architecture and how these networks work, including as well, a real experimental study performed in two different scenarios. From the analysis of the results, we can conclude that a LoRa network based on our devices could be cover a distance higher than 3 km, in free-obstacle scenarios, since our gateway is still capable of receive packets correctly. Thus, LoRa networks would be an interesting solution for getting data in scenarios, such as crops or rural areas where we want to cover a very large area. As future work, we would like to test new networks and application servers which allow us to deploy completely private environments. The different power options will be also measured. Finally, we will perform real experiments in urban and indoor environments in order to compare the LoRa performance in several scenarios, such as agricultural holdings [14].

ACKNOWLEDGMENT

This work has been partially supported by the European Union through the ERANETMED (Euromediterranean Cooperation through ERANET joint activities and beyond) project ERANETMED3-227 SMARTWATIR, by the "Ministerio de Economia, Industria y Competitividad", through the "Convocatoria 2016 - Proyectos I+D+I - Programa Estatal De Investigación, Desarrollo e Innovación Orientada a los retos de la sociedad" (Project TEC2016-76795-C6-4-R) and (Project UNGR15-CE-3311), through the "Convocatoria 2017 - Proyectos I+D+i - Programa Estatal de Investigación, Desarrollo e Innovación, convocatoria excelencia" (Project TIN2017-84802-C2-1-P), by the "Ministerio de Ciencia, Innovación y Universidades" through the "Ayudas para la adquisición de equipamiento científico-técnico, Subprograma estatal de infraestructuras de investigación y equipamiento científico-técnico (plan Estatal I+D+i 2017-2020)" (project EQC2018-004988-P) and through the Research Contracts of Youth Employment of the University of Granada, through its operative program of Youth Guarantee of the Regional Government of Andalusia and the European Social Fund.

REFERENCES

[1] L. Garcia, J.M. Jiménez, M. Taha, and J. Lloret, "Wireless Technologies for IoT in Smart Cities", *Network Protocols and Algorithms*, vol.10, no.1, pp.23-64,2018.

[2] J. Gubbi, R. Buyya, S. Marusic, and M. Palaniswami, "Internet of Things (IoT): A vision, architectural elements, and future directions,"in Future Generation Computer Systems. vol.29, no. 7, pp. 1645-1660, Apr. 2013.

[3] J. Navarro-Ortiz, S. Sendra, P. Ameigeiras, and J. M. Lopez-Soler, "Integration of LoRaWAN and 4G/5G for the Industrial Internet of Things,",IEEE Communications Magazine, vol.56, no. 2, pp. 60-67, 2018.

[4] T. Petrić, M. Goessens, L. Nuaymi, L. Toutain, and A. Pelov, "Measurements, Performance and Analysis of LoRa FABIAN, a real-world implementation of LPWAN", IEEE 27th Annual Int. Symp on Personal, Indoor and Mobile Radio Communications (PIMRC). Valencia, Spain, Sep. 4-8, 2016. pp. 1-7.

[5] L. Angrisani, P. Arpaia, F. Bonavolontà, M. Conti, and A. Liccardo, "LoRa Protocol Performance Assessment in Critical Noise Conditions", IEEE 3rd Int. Forum on Research and Technologies for Society and Industry, Modena, Italy, Sep. 11-13, 2017, pp. 1-5.

[6] J. So, D. Kim, H. Kim, H. Lee, and S. Park, "LoRaCloud: LoRa Platform on OpenStack", 2016 IEEE NetSoft Conf, and Workshops (NetSoft), Seoul, South Korea, Jun. 6-10, 2016, pp. 431-434.

[7] T. Hirata et al., "Proposal of a Power Saving Network for Rice Fields Using LoRa", IEEE 6th Global Conference on Consumer Electronics, Nagoya, Japan, Oct 24-27, 2017, pp. 1-4.

[8] W. Zhao, S. Lin, J. Han, R. Xu, and L. Hou, "Design and Implementation of Smart Irrigation System Based on LoRa", IEEE Globecom Workshops, Singapore, Dec. 4-8, 2017, pp. 1-6.

[9] S. Ghoslya, "All about LoRa and LoRaWAN,"(2018, April 12th) Available at: https:// goo.gl/ACxaxx. [Last Accessed: Dec. 3, 2018]

[10] N. Sornin, M. Luis, T. Eirich, T. Kramp, and O.Hersent, "LoRa Specification 1.1,"LoRa Alliance Std Spec., Available at: https://www.lora-alliance.org/. [Last Accessed: Dec. 3, 2018]

[11] I. F. Akyildiz,X. Wang and W. Wang, "Wireless mesh networks: a survey,"in Computer Networks, vol.47, no. 4, pp. 445-487, 2005.

[12] W. Giezeman, "The Things Network,"(2018, April 13th), Available at: https://www.thethingsnetwork.org [Last Accessed: Dec. 3, 2018]

[13] O. Brocaar, "LoRa Server,"(2018, Abril 12th), Available at:https://www.loraserver.io [Last Accessed: Dec. 3, 2018]

[14] C. Cambra, S. Sendra, J. Lloret and L. Garcia, "An IoT service-oriented system for agriculture monitoring, 2017 IEEE Int. Conf. on Communications (ICC'17), Paris, France. May 21-25, 2017. pp.1-6.

Investigation in Communication Behavior of Ionosphere Regions

Kareem AbdulAmeer Difar
Department of Telecommunication Engineering
Faculty of Electronic Telecommunication and Information Technology
Politehnica University of Bucharest
Bucharest, Romania
e-mail: Kaad1983@gmail.com

Antonio Sorin Tasu
Department E119
Faculty of Electronics and Telecommunications
Maritime University of Constanta
Bucharest, Romania
e-mail: sorin.tasu@gmail.com

***Abstract*—The Ionosphere is the region from 80 to 1000 km altitude above the Earth and it contains free electrons and ions that disturb the electromagnetic waves when the waves pass through it. The larger electrons density in the Ionosphere disturbs the GPS (Global Position System) signal that passes through it. The Ionosphere is a variable medium and its frequency behaviour cannot be predicted accurately. One issue arises because the Ionosphere near the equatorial region causes more electromagnetic signal errors compared to the North and South Poles. In this article, it has been proved that the GPS signals transmitted in equatorial regions are more refracted than the ones crossing the Ionosphere in the North and South Poles regions. The refraction index will decrease as the electron density increases. This subject is important, because if, for instance, a satellite is not working in military events, then there is an alternative communication solution, which employs Ionosphere as a reflector for long-distance terrestrial communication around the world. The free electrons in the Ionosphere create a high conductivity layer, which could be used as a perfect reflector for short waves in long-distance terrestrial communication. Two models, namely IRI (The International Reference Ionosphere)-Plas 2017 model and VOACAP model (The Voice of America Coverage Analysis Program), have been used in our simulations. These models were used to evaluate the quality of the Ionosphere in different regions for reflecting shortwaves frequencies and the perturbations for GPS signals. The selected regions for the simulations were Iraq, Romania, and Ukraine. The conclusion was that the Ionosphere efficiency of reflecting frequencies for Iraq region is better than the one for Romania and Ukraine regions.**

Keywords- IRI-Plas 2017; VOACAP; Refraction index.

I. INTRODUCTION

The Ionosphere is the region between 80km to 1000km of the Earth's atmosphere. The attentiveness in this region of free electrons is so great that it affects radio waves [1]. The Ionosphere was discovered when it was detected that radio waves can transmit over great spaces and therefore one then must adopt the existence of an electrically conductive layer in the upper atmosphere which could reflect the waves [2][3]. The electrically conductive region extends from about 50km to 500km above the ground and the10^6 m^3 at 50km to a maximum of 10^{12} particles per m^3 at 250-300 km [3][4]. The challenges of our work were the mathematical equations that cover the derivatives of these equations compatible with the three regions studied in this paper: Iraq, Romania and Ukraine. We had chosen five parameters together: phase and group velocity, plasma frequency, and error distance for the first and second order. All these parameters together prove that the equatorial region has an influence on the GPS signal more than other places on Earth, like the North Pole. In this paper, we have focused on evaluating the disturbances of the lower and upper regions of the Ionosphere from 80km to 1000km. Section II explains the state of art of this paper. In Section III, the related work is presented. In Section IV, the adopted model is described. Section V presents the effects of Ionosphere on the microwave signal with extended numerical examples in Section VI, including approaches for Ionosphere disturbances. The simulation and analysis of the refraction index of the GPS signal are illustrated in Section VII. Finally, Section VIII concludes and hints to future work.

II. STATE OF ART

In [5], the distance error of GPS signal that propagates through the Ionosphere at equatorial is computed by using total electron content (TEC) which disturbs the radio wave propagation. In [6], two models, IRI-Plas 2017 and NeQuick, are used for computing the discrepancies of the Ionosphere. Here, the Ionosphere disturbance at high latitudes was investigated. The output parameters of these models are electron density and total electron content. The electron density is like TEC which disturb the radio wave propagation. In our paper, we used IRI-Plas 2017 model and we computed the refraction index that represents the strength of the signal in the Ionosphere medium depending on the electron density, for both Iraq and Romania regions. This parameter could be used as an indicator of the reflection capabilities of Ionosphere for long distance communications. VOACAP model was used by us provided by free professional high-frequency (HF) propagation prediction software to determine the quality for long distance communications, using the Ionosphere as a reflector [7]. This model is based on frequency. The parameter frequency is used to evaluate the Ionosphere disturbance at low and high latitudes by using VOACAP model. The range of reflected frequencies that can be used for long distance communication provided by VOACAP online model gives an indicator about Ionosphere capacity to reflect the communication signals.

VOACAP provides the observer with more accurate results than IRI-Plas 2017 and NeQuick models, determining the highest usable frequency for the long-distance communications, using the Ionosphere as a reflector.

III. RELATED WORK

In Gsponer [8] showed that Maxwell equations can be used for many applications in Ionosphere for electron density, or another component in the atom that constitutes the plasma frequency. In M. K. Mardan and K. A. Hadi [3] used Baghdad, the capital of Iraq, to test the Ionosphere features, like the energy of an electron. In this paper, the group velocity of the signal that gives the accurate description of the medium of the disturbance of Ionosphere at Iraq space and Romania space was computed. By using VOACAP as in Fig. 1, several different latitudes have been chosen and compared from the point of view of real plasma frequency, instead of electron density. The VOACAP model provides us with the best frequencies reflected from Ionosphere which have good SNR. Based on these frequencies, it is possible to determine the Ionosphere disturbance can be evaluated.

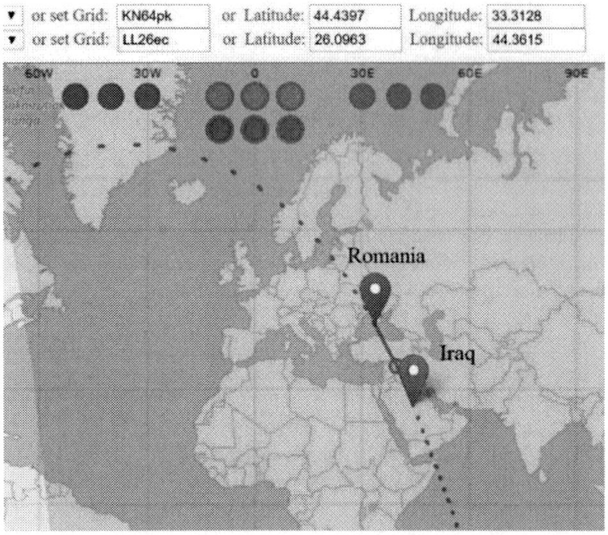

Figure 1. The coordinates of Romania and Iraq [5]

IV. THE APPLETON–HARTREE EQUATION

IRI-Plas 2017 model has been used in the Appleton–Hartree equation (13). This is a general formula for the Appleton–Hartree equation that comprises all the effects in Ionosphere that could happen and affect the electrometric signal and may disturb the transmission [9].

$$n^2 = f(variables) general\ formula \quad (1)$$

$$n^2 = 1 - \frac{X}{1-jZ-\frac{Y_T^2}{2(1-X-jZ)}\pm\left(\frac{Y_T^4}{4(1-X-jZ)^2}+Y_L^2\right)^{\frac{1}{2}}} \quad (2)$$

$$X = \frac{\omega_0^2}{\omega^2} \quad (3)$$

$$Y = \frac{\omega_H}{\omega} \quad (4)$$

$$Z = \frac{\nu}{\omega} \quad (5)$$

$$\omega_0 = 2\pi f_0 = \sqrt{\frac{N_e e^2}{\epsilon_0 m_e}} \quad (6)$$

$$\omega_H = 2\pi f_H = \frac{B_0 e}{m_e} \quad (7)$$

TABLE I. ALL CONSTANTS ARE ILLUSTRATED BY THEIR MEANING

θ	Angle between the direction of propagation and the magnetic field.
Ne	Electron density.
$\omega = 2\pi f$	(Radial frequency).
f	Wave frequency.
ω_0	Electron plasma frequency.
ω_H	Electron gyrofrequency.
ε_0	Permittivity of free space.
B_0	Magnitude of the magnetic field vector.
m_e	Mass of electron.
ν	Collision frequency.

By neglecting the frictional force, assuming that we are in a cold, collisionless, magnetized plasma such as the Ionosphere, the refractive index for the carrier phase, n_P, can be expressed by the Appleton expression, for both ordinary (upper sign) and extraordinary (lower sign) waves.

Equation (2) can be simplified by neglecting the parameter Z that represents the ratio between the collision frequency and signal frequency, being dimensionless.

$$n_P^2 = 1 - \frac{X}{1-\frac{Y_T^2}{2(1-X)}\pm\left(\frac{Y_T^4}{4(1-X)^2}+Y_L^2\right)^{\frac{1}{2}}} \quad (8)$$

V. EFFECTS OF IONOSPHERE IN MICROWAVE SIGNAL

For signals with frequencies $\omega >> \omega_P$ (and hence $\omega >> \omega_g$), as in satellite communication for higher frequencies, equation (2) could be represented into a second-order Taylor approach which can be obtained in terms only up to (f^-4), similarly to [10].

$$n_P^2 = 1 - \frac{1}{2}X \pm XY_L - \frac{1}{8}X^2 - \frac{1}{4}X.Y^2(1+\cos^2\theta) \quad (9)$$

$$Y^2 = Y_L^2 + Y_T^2 = (\frac{\omega_g}{\omega})^2 \quad (10)$$

$$Y_L = -\frac{\omega_g}{\omega}\cos\theta \quad (11)$$

$$Y_T = -\frac{\omega_g}{\omega} \sin\theta \quad (12)$$

Here, the positive sign signifies ordinary wave and the minus sign extraordinary wave. It is possible to identify the equation (8) by real parameters that describe the Ionosphere state in:

$$n_P^2 = 1 - \frac{a_1}{f^2} - \frac{a_2}{f^3} - \frac{a_3}{f^4} \quad (13)$$

Wherea_1, a_2, $a_3$and a_4 are constants. All these constants comprise the physical constants m_e, q, ϵ_0 , their units being in SI. The simulated data are provided by [7][11].

VI. Numerical Approaches for Ionosphere Disturbances

After inserting the physical contents and proceed with numerical calculations, the constants $a_1, a_2, and\ a_3$ can be expressed as follows:

$$a_1 = 40.3 \int_{T_X}^{R_X} N_e\, dl \quad (14)$$

$$a_2 = 1.1284.10^{12} \int_{T_X}^{R_X} N_e\, B\, \cos\theta\, d \quad (15)$$

$$a_3 = 812.42 \int_{T_X}^{R_X} {N_e}^2 + 1.5793.10^{22} \int_{T_X}^{R_X} B^2\, N_e\, (1 + \cos^2\theta) dl \quad (16)$$

n_P^2 , Y^2 ,a_1 ,a_2 ,$a_3$and n_P as shown in [9][12][13]

These parameters $a_1, a_2, and\ a_3$ will determine the error distance for all electromagnetic waves that propagate in the Ionosphere. In this paper it has been used GPS signals. The GPS signals are in microwaves frequencies. These waves usually refract tens of meters in the ionosphere. But shortwaves will be refract hundreds of meters. The free electrons and ions are responsible of these error distance and especially the free electrons because they are lighter than ions. This error distance is significant in the Equatorial region because they highly concentrated there. The most important parameters is a1 because it depends mainly on the electron density and no other factor. The second parameter depends on magnetic field that is very weak in Equatorial regions and mid-latitudes. But in the Poles the magnetic field is very large. This work is specifically employed for low latitudes that comprises Iraq region and mid latitude that comprises Romania and Ukraine.

VII. Simulations and Analysis

A. The simulations and analyses in Iraq and Romania regions by using IRI-Plas 2017 model.

Fig. 2 and Fig. 3 show that the refraction index in Iraq is smaller than the one in Romania. In Fig. 4 and Fig. 5, the group velocity of GPS signals for Romania region is larger than in the Iraq region. The results are mentioned in Table II and Table III.

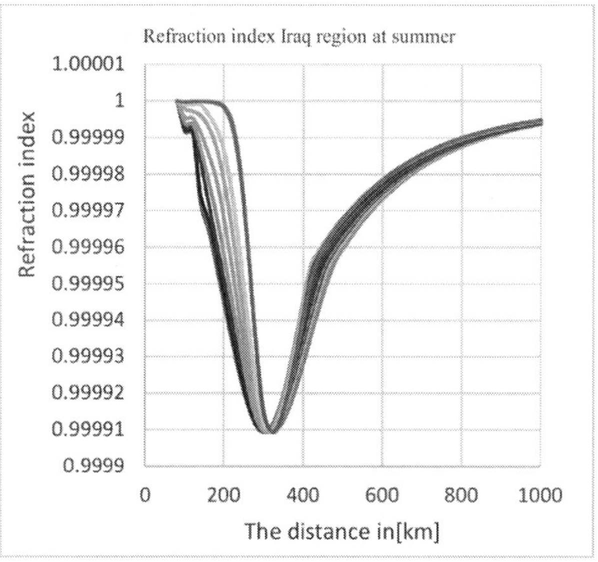

Figure 2. Refraction index Iraq region at summer

TABLE II. REFRACTION INDEX IN IRAQ REGION AT SUMMER.

Index	Refraction index distance [km]	value
1	350	0.99991
2	400	0.99992
3	600	0.99997
4	1000	1.00000

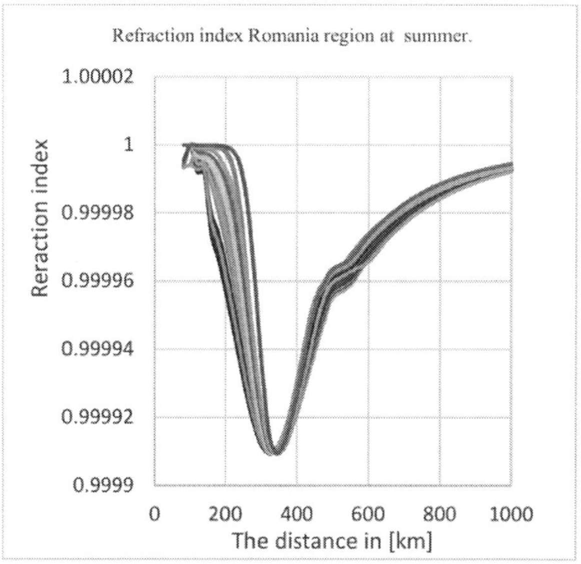

Figure 3. Refraction index Romania region at summer.

The curves in Fig.2 and Fig.3 represent all the hours in one day. These results have shown higher refraction index for Romania, compared to the Iraqi region. Higher refraction index means low perturbations in the Ionosphere region. It is definitely clear that Iraq region is a better place for reflecting higher frequency, by using Ionosphere as a reflector. The Romanian region is a better place for GPS signal, penetrating the Ionosphere with low error-distance.

TABLE III. REFRACTION INDEX ROMANIA REGION AT SUMMER.

Index	**Refraction index distance [km]**	**value**
1	350	0.999925
2	400	0.99992
3	600	0.999975
4	1000	1.000000

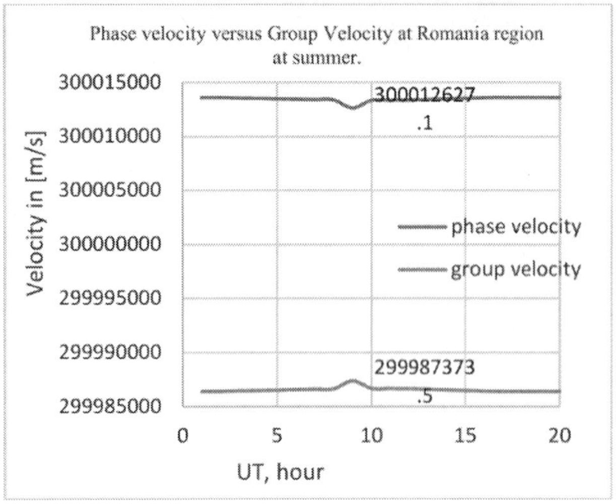

Figure 4. Phase velocity versus Group Velocity at Romania region.

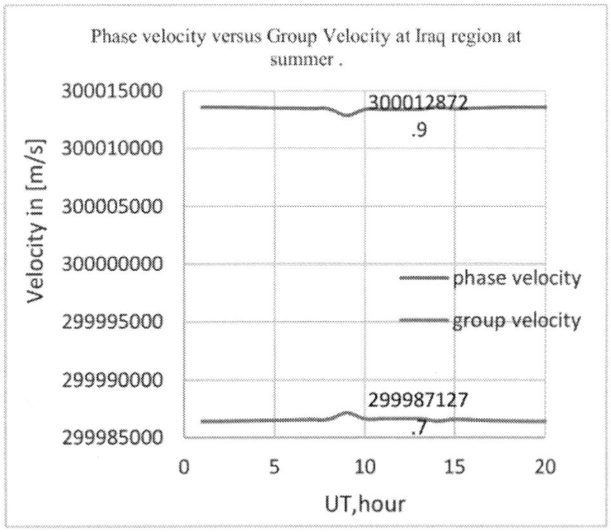

Figure 5. Phase velocity versus Group Velocity at Iraq region.

TABLE IV. COMPARISON BETWEEN ROMANIA AND IRAQ.

	Iraq		**Romania**	
1	***Phase velocity [m/s]***	***group velocity [m/s]***	***phase velocity [m/s]***	***group velocity[m/s]***
2	300012872.9	299987127.7	300012627.1	299987373.5

In this section, the refraction index is determined by simulations using a GPS signal. This refraction index shows the disturbance of Ionosphere. Higher disturbance means good reflection medium for higher frequencies. This results could be used as an estimate for the quality of the signal for long communications around the world, using reflection on Ionosphere.

B. The simulations and analyses for Iraq, Romania and Ukraine regions by using VOACAP model.

In this section, a VOACAP model is used to predict the high-frequency propagation in communications, using Ionosphere as a reflector. The quality of the Ionosphere space reflection was evaluated for two scenarios. One scenario assumed a long communication channel between Iraq and Romania, and the second scenario used a communication between Romania and Ukraine, which takes place at higher latitude. The results obtained for the reflection quality on Ionosphere were correlated with the results provided by the IRI- Plas 2017 model on refraction index and electron density.

By using online data of VOACAP model in 2018, the highest usable frequency for the communication link between Iraq and Romania was obtained. The results are presented in Fig. 6; the three curves represent the best signals with the highest SNR, maintained for at least half a day. The results demonstrate that the highest usable frequency reached up to 20 MHz, for the best signal that has the highest SNR. In Fig. 7, the highest usable frequency for the communication link between Romania and Ukraine was obtained. Romania and Ukraine have higher latitudes than Romania and Iraq. The results are shown here demonstrate that the highest frequency reached up to 7 MHz for the best signal that has the highest SNR. The comparison between Fig. 6 and Fig. 7 is shown in Fig.8, by using the mean values of the three frequencies from Fig. 6 and Fig. 7. Now, it is very clear that the Ionosphere disturbance at the space between Iraq and Romania is higher than that of Ukraine and Romania, because they have low latitudes and highest plasma frequency, as shown in Table V. Based on the previous results, it is definitely clear that low latitudes have higher disturbance than higher latitudes.

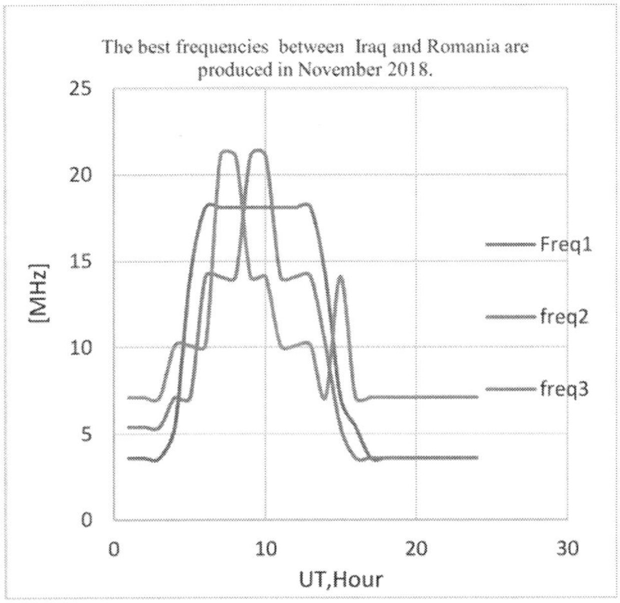

Figure 6. The best frequencies between Iraq and Romania are produced in November 2018.

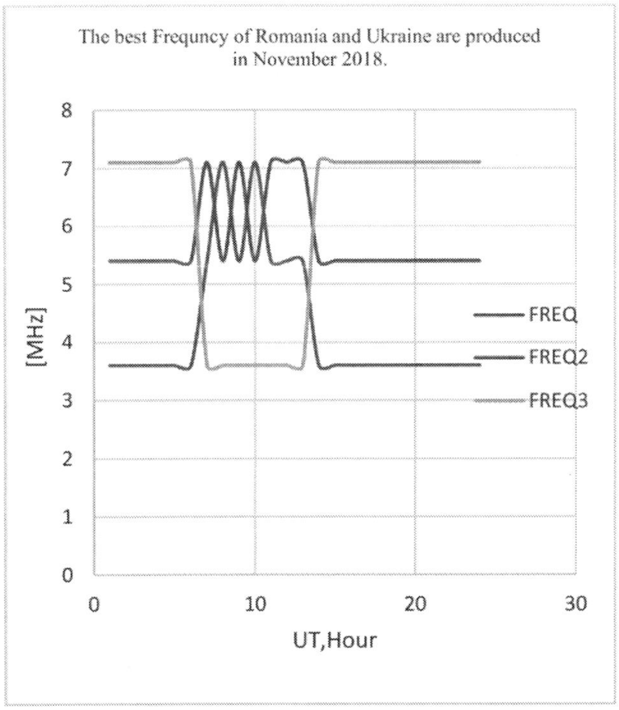

Figure 7. The best Frequency of Romania and Ukraine are produced in November 2018.

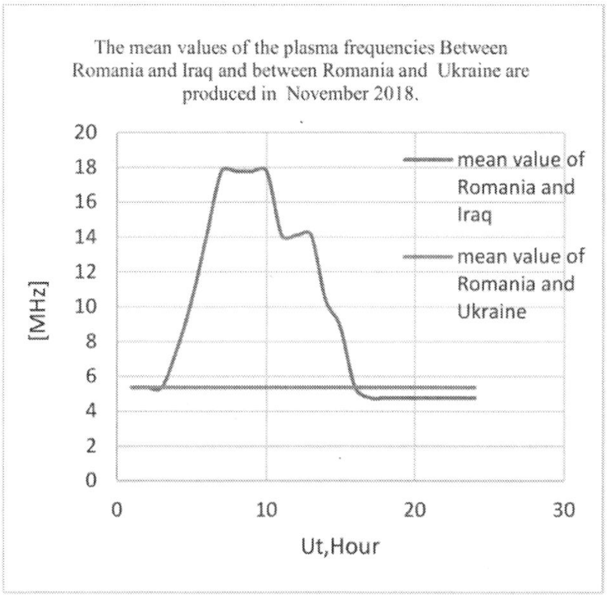

Figure 8. The mean values of the plasma frequencies Between Romania and Iraq and between Romania and Ukraine are produced in November 2018.

TABLE V. THE REFLECTED FREQUENCIES FOR LOW AND HIGH LATITUDES.

Regions	**Iraq and Romania**	**Ukraine and Romania**
time	***The mean value frequencies in [MHz]***	***The mean value frequencies in [MHz]***
10 A.M	18	5
15 P.M	10	5

VIII. CONCLUSION AND FUTURE WORK

In this paper, Iraq, Romania and Ukraine regions were investigated for the Ionosphere perturbations. The results that are based on IRI-Plas 2017 model show that Iraq has a lower refraction index than Romania in the Ionosphere. The refraction index is decreased because the electron density is higher around the equatorial region, which is closer to Iraq than Romania. As a consequence, the group velocity in Iraq region is lower compared to Romania region, as shown in Table IV. From these results, it is expected to have a higher reflection Ionosphere medium in Iraq, because Iraq is located at low latitudes compared with Romania and Ukraine. VOACAP model depends on the frequencies that are reflected directly from the Ionosphere. The results produced by VOACAP model have confirmed this conclusion, but they have also provided a better picture of the Ionosphere reflection capabilities by producing an indication of the frequency range that is usable for long distance communication. We plan to investigate the phenomenon of creating artificial Ionosphere that reflects broader bandwidth and frequencies for poor reflected frequencies region in the Ionosphere.

REFERENCES

[1] A. Gsponer, "Physics of high-intensity high-energy particle beam propagation in open air and outer-space plasmas," arXiv Prepr. physics/0409157, 2004.

[2] S.Bora, "Ionosphere and Radio Communication," Gen. Artic., 2017, Available at https://www.ias.ac.in/article/fulltext/reso/022/02/0123-0133 [retrieved March, 2019]

[3] M. K. Mardan and K. A. Hadi, "Study the Influence of Solar Activity on the Ionospheric Electron, Ion and Neutral Particle Temperatures over Iraqi Region Using Ionospheric Models," Iraqi J. Sci., vol. 59, no. 1A (2018), pp. 209–217, 2018.

[4] J. Sheffield, D. Froula, S. H. Glenzer, and N. C. Luhmann Jr, Plasma scattering of electromagnetic radiation: theory and measurement techniques, Academic press, 2010.

[5] T. Sukcharoen, F. Wu, and J. Weng, "Characteristics of ionosphere at equatorial and middle latitude zones during solar maximum," in Electrical Engineering/Electronics, Computer, Telecommunications and Information Technology (ECTI-CON), 12th International Conference on, 2015, pp. 1–6.

[6] D. S. Kotova, V. B. Ovodenko, Y. V Yasyukevichv, A. A. Mylnikova, and M. V Klimenko, "Ground-Based GNSS Data for the Ionosphere Model Correction at High-Latitudes," in 2018 2nd URSI Atlantic Radio Science Meeting (AT-RASC), 2018, pp. 1–4.

[7] Jari Perkiömäki, "VOACAP," 2018. [Online]. Available at http://www.voacap.com/ [retrieved March, 2019]

[8] A. Gsponer, "The Physics of high-intensity high-energy Particle Beam Propagation in open Air and outer-space Plasmas," Independent Scientific Research Institute Oxford, OX4 4YS, England, 2009.

[9] G. Petit and B. Luzum, "IERS conventions (2010)", 2010.

[10] K. Nagarajoo, "Improved Ionospheric Correction for Dual Frequency and Differential GPS Positioning Methods," University of Leeds, 2007.

[11] F. Arıkan. et al. (Hacettepe University), "IONOLAB" [Online]. Available at http://www.ionolab.org/ [retrieved March, 2019]

[12] M. M. Alizadeh, D. D. Wijaya, T. Hobiger, R. Weber, and H. Schuh, "Ionospheric effects on microwave signals," pp. 35–71, 2013.

[13] H. W. Bourne, "An Algorithm for Accurate Ionospheric Total Electron Content and Receiver Bias Estimation using GPS Measurements," Colorado State University, 2016.

Centralised Multihop Routing Techniques for Device-to-Device Communication

Mustafa Khaleel Hamadani
Politehnica University of Bucharest - UPB
Bucharest, Romania
E-mail: mkhaleel190@gmail.com

Al-Alwash Husam Mahdi
Politehnica University of Bucharest - UPB
Bucharest, Romania
E-mail: al.aloosh.92@gmail.com

***Abstract*—Device-to-Device (D2D) communication is a new paradigm in mobile networks that allows users in proximity to each other to communicate directly, without passing data through a central Base Station. However, due to users' mobility and their location, the users may be far away from each other and this can lead to low-performance data transmission. The multihop approach allows the source user to relay data to the destination user through hop by hop. The advantages of D2D communication can be fully exploited in a multihop communication environment given that the single-hop communication usually limits the communication scope to a specific geographic area. However, routing in multihop cellular D2D networks raises performance-related challenges, versus a traditional cellular network, if non-optimal routes decisions are made. The contribution of this paper is a short review of multihop D2D networks and then a selection is made to discuss more details on a number of centralised routing techniques. The work is still in progress and tries to identify some open research issues to be considered in the future. Therefore, this work will serve as a base model for future performance comparisons, made by simulations between multihop routing techniques.**

Keywords-multihop; routing; device-to-device; SDN; IoT; v2v; overhead.

I. INTRODUCTION

In traditional cellular communication, if two users close to each other want to communicate, the source User Equipment (UE) has to relay its message to a Base Station (BS), and the BS relays the message to the destination UE. Due to the user's mobility or physical obstruction, the communication session may suffer from varying signal quality, resulting in low data transfer. In addition, more battery life is consumed by the UEs to communicate between each other.

Device-to-Device (D2D) communication allows users in proximity to each other to exchange data directly without passing or relaying data to the BS. Moreover, this direct communication can be controlled by the BS, i.e., the BS will have responsibility for establish and authorize the D2D connection among users. Additionally, the BS can handle the Quality of Service (QoS) policies and the mobility management. D2D communication has been approved as a part of the cellular communication systems since LTE (Long-Term Evolution) Release 12 [1].

This direct communication has been offered by other technologies, such as Bluetooth, ZigBee or Wi-Fi [19], but these technologies are limited to short ranges (approximately 100 meters) [15]. In addition, interference issues exist, given the operating spectrums (The industrial, scientific and medical (*ISM*) band 2.4 GHz and 5 GHz). On the other hand, the communication range in D2D communication is about 1-2 Km. The interference issue could be handled in a centralised way due to the presence of BS [15].

However, when two UEs are not in proximity to each other, the result is a low throughput in the D2D communication session. The multihop approach allows the source UE to relay data to the destination UE through hop by hop. The multihop communication can increase the D2D communication coverage and possibly increase the throughput rate.

The advantages of multihop D2D communication can be fully realized in the public safety and commercial applications. In case of natural desasters, when the cellular infrastructural is partially unavailable or when the network is congested, the multihop approach provides an alternative solution for the mobile node by relaying the emergency messages to evacuation centers through other mobile terminals.

Many Internet of Things (IoT) applications require the transmission of data between a set of devices to a central station for processing or storage. Moreover, most IoT equipment is capable for short-range transmission due to energy constraints. Therefore, relying the information through intermediary nodes is required. The integration of cellular and multihop networks provides reliability, and flexibility, and guarantees QoS.

In multihop D2D communication, D2D devices which are out of the coverage could use the intermediary nodes to relay data to the infrastructure network or to communicate with other end-users, resulting in overall network expansion and increased network coverage.

Moreover, the multihop communication supports a number of applications, such as broadcast information (e.g., related to collisions on the roads) between vehicles, in vehicle-to-vehicle (V2V) network, or broadcast messages to specific nodes in a geographical area in the Internet of Things network.

Due to node mobility and dynamic network topology, routing in multihop D2D networks is a critical issue if wrong routing decisions are made. An efficient routing scheme needs to be designed for better performance in terms of higher network capacity and efficient energy consumption.

The rest of this paper is organised as follows. Section II gives an overview of the D2D multihop network. Section III addresses the centralised multihop routing schemes. A number of research challenges are presented in Section IV. Finally, the conclusion and future works are provided in Section V.

II. The Device-to-Device Multihop network

This section presents a short introduction to Device-to-Device communication and multihop network. The first subsection describes the D2D communication and the types of communication in the cellular network. The multihop network classifications and relay types are provided in the second subsection.

A. Device-to-Device Communication

In a traditional cellular network, a user node communicates with the BS via a single-hop path. However, despite the fact that this type of communication provides good delay characteristic, it suffers from traffic overloading, as the traffic demand grows rapidly [2]. One solution is to deploy more BSs inside a cell, but this leads to increased costs of installation and management [3]. Thus, the D2D communication can be considered as a potential candidate technology to handle the network capacity/coverage problem [4]. The 3rd Generation Partnership Project (3GPP) LTE Release 12 indicated that two devices in proximity to each other could communicate directly. This kind of communication can be seen in different network scenarios [5]: *In-coverage scenario* when both UEs are under the same network coverage, *Partial coverage scenario* - one of UEs is outside the network coverage, and the *Out of coverage scenario* when both UEs are outside the network coverage. In releases 13, 14 and 15, the UE which is out of the network coverage can use another nearby device which is within network coverage as a relay to communicate with the network. There are two types of D2D communications, either, i.e., supervised (under the control of the BS) or unsupervised (when a node is out of the coverage of the cellular network). In the supervised communication, the BS controls the communication and guarantees performance and security by complete control over the control plane and the data plane [7][8]. The control plane is responsible for the establishment of a connection, its maintenance, termination and also enforces security policies, e.g. authentication, encryption. Additional functions of the control plane include collision avoidance and mobility management. Moreover, the data plane is responsible for resource allocation based on control plane instructions. For the supervised communication, the communication can be either: *Network-based communication*, i.e., all devices are under the full control of a centralised node (BS); or *Network-assisted communication*, i.e., all devices can make decisions autonomously, but based on the measurements provided by the centralised node. Moreover, in unsupervised-communication, the devices are stand-alone and work exactly like adhoc networks. These networks do not have any constraints due to the failure of the centralised entity, e.g. the (BS). For example, in an adhoc networks, failure of any node has an insignificant effect on the overall network performance.

The only difference between adhoc routing and unsupervised D2D routing is in the usage of spectrum frequency bands. D2D nodes can use both the licensed and/or the unlicensed bands while adhoc nodes can only use unlicensed bands.

B. D2D Multihop Communication

In a multihop network, a UE communicates with another user by relaying the data hop by hop, through intermediate nodes until reaching the destination UE. Thus, the UEs can communicate in one of the four modes [6]: *Single-hop D2D communication, Multihop Device-to-Infrastructure (D2I)/Infrastructure-to-Device (I2D) communication, Multihop D2D communication*, and traditional cellular communication. In single-hop communication, two devices are in the proximity of each other and directly communicate without needing any relay. For the multihop D2I/I2D communication, the multihop route is established between the node and the network service entity, i.e., BS.

In the multihop network, the UEs communicate through an intermediate node that acts as a relay. Thus, the type of relay could be classified into: The Network Relay: The relay used by multihop D2I/I2D routing scheme, as this relay helps the UEs to communicate with the BS. This is further classified into *fixed network relay, mobile network relay*, and *Device Relay*. The fixed network relay is static and installed by the network operator. A mobile network relay can be a user node, which provides services for data forwarding between the BS and the other users.

III. Multihop Routing techniques

The multihop routing decision could have been taken by the centralised entity (BS) or *distributed*, when each node could take the route decision autonomously, while taking into account the presence of other nodes.

The multihop D2D routing schemes could be classified into *incentive-based, security-based, content-based, location-based* and *flat topology-based routing* [9]. The security-based routing is used for security concern when the content-based routing used when the frequent data has to be shared among users (e.g., video). The incentive-based routing is used when the users are encouraged to participate in relaying the data of other nodes by using some incentive.

In the location-based routing scheme, a centralised entity (location servers) has location information for all nodes. The route decision is either take by nodes using the location information (distributed routing strategy) or with a centralised approach by BS. In the flat topology-based routing case, the network nodes do not have any specific structure (e.g., cluster), nor have any location awareness mechanism.

Another classification based on *route mechanism discovery* is presented below:

- Reactive routing (on demand-driven): the information about the possible paths between end devices is obtained after a transmission request is issued in the network.

- Proactive routing (table-driven): each node always maintains a routing table containing routes for different destinations and the updates of routing tables are done regularly.

- Hybrid routing: both the reactive and proactive routings operate at the same time. Hybrid routing divides networks into local neighborhoods (known as zones).
- Adaptive routing: in this scheme, the routing mechanism switches between reactive and proactive routing depending upon network dynamics and their network zones.

Next, we review some related works for a multihop routing scheme.

In case the nodes in the network do not have any specific structure or any location awareness mechanism, then the flat topology routing protocols will be integrated into the network.

In this work, we only focus on centralised flat topology-based routing. The centralised flat topology routing schemes for multihop D2D communications are categorised into reactive and proactive routing (see Table I).

In Centralised-Based Routing schemes, a centralised entity (BS) regularly gathers neighbor nodes information from all the network nodes in order to construct and update the network topology. Serval work routing schemes have been proposed based on centralized reactive approach: *multihop cellular network* (*MCN*) [10], *cellular based source routing* (*CBSR*) [11] and A *Base-centric routing* (BCR) [12].

In the *Multihop Cellular Network* (*MCN*) routing [10], every node maintains a neighbours table based on the "HELLO" message exchange procedure. The entry of the table includes the received SNR (signal to noise ratio) of the neighbor nodes; if there is a change in the received power level, then updates will be sent to the BS. Thus, the BS has an up-to-date database about all the links in the cell.

The MCN protocol also supports the detection of a broken route. Thus, consider the following scenario when the route between two nodes A and B is (A – X – Y – B), where X and Y are intermediate nodes. Suppose that when X receives a packet from A to B, (the next hop form X is Y), X detects that the link X-Y is no longer available (e.g. timeout of the HELLO message from Y). Here, X will send a route request to the BS; then, the BS responds with a new route update to X and A (to update the cache route at A). However, this route update will result in a high routing overhead, which may severely degrade the network performance.

Another variant of the proactive centralised routing is *Cellular Based Source Routing* (*CBSR*) [11]. In this scheme, each node contains a table of its neighbor nodes and periodically exchanges HELLO packets with its neighbors. The HELLO packets contain current address and traffic load information. After receiving a HELLO message, each node updates its neighborhood table and periodically reports it to the BS. The report update contains neighbor load, link quality (between the sender node, of HELLO and its neighbor) and HELLO packet receive instant of time.

Using the information from reported neighbourhood table, the BS builds network topology based on two tables, the node table, and adjacency table. The node table stores information about each node in the cell. The adjacency table contains details about each node with its neighbours. In addition, the adjacency table includes additional information of the distance (hop count) between nodes if the hop count is 1 than the two nodes are adjacent.

If two UEs want to communicate, the source node (UE) first checks its routing table cache. If some routes are available, the source UE chooses one of the routes (if there is more than one route available) and start sending the data packet. In case there is no route information available, then the UE sends a unicast route request (RREQ) to BS, with source and the destination addresses as parameters. Then BS replies with all available routes via RREP message, or otherwise, an error route (RERR) will be returned in case of no route available.

A *Base-Centric Routing* (BCR) protocol is proposed in [12]; it is a hybrid of demand-driven and table-driven routing. The BS draws the network topology by the table driven method and can thus compute paths. The nodes use the demand-driven approach to find the route to the required destinations. These nodes send a route request to the BS, and if there is no route from BS, then the node broadcast route request like in Adhoc On-demand Distance Vector (AODV) routing protocol [16].

The designed BCR protocol is based on two ideas: the *first* is that the BS tracks the intra-cell network topology, and lists the user's nodes that reside in the cell. The *second* is that the mobile node sends a route request on demand to avoid extra overhead.

Adaptive centralised routing: In adaptive centralised routing, a central controller (usually BS) is responsible for all routing decisions.

A *Centralised Adaptive Routing* (CAR) is proposed in [6]. The algorithm switches between reactive and proactive routing based on network conditions, e.g., node density, average node mobility or traffic load [13][14].

The authors of [6] introduced six types of messages involved in building the route:

- RREQ: it is send by the node to BS requesting a route to another node.
- B-RREQ: the BS broadcast B-RREQ all node to initial neighbourhood discovery phase.
- HELLO message: the node exchange HELLO message for updating their neighborus list.
- U-RREP: after updating the neighbourhood list, the nodes broadcast the updated list to BS.
- Route reply: after the BS received the updated neighbours list from the nodes. The BS computes the route between source and distention.
- B-RREP:

In centralised proactive routing, as shown in Figure 1, each node periodically exchanges HELLO packets with each other in order to update the neighbour table, and broadcast the neighbour table (U-RREP message) to the BS. When a node wants to communicate with another node, it sends a route request (RREQ) packet to the BS. The BS either will provide a route if available (route reply message), or establishes a traditional cellular connection between them.

For the centralised reactive routing, when a node wants to communicate with another node it sent routes (RREQ message) to request to the BS as shown in Figure 2. Upon receiving a route request packet from a node, BS broadcasts the neighbour's list request (B-RREQ message) to all nodes in order to update the network topology by exchange HELLO messages between them.

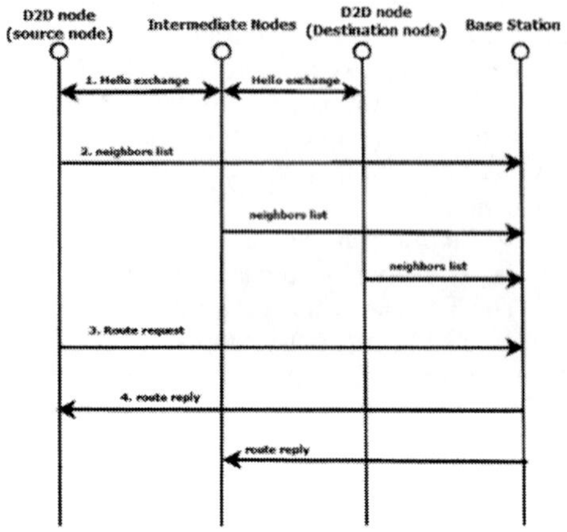

Figure 1. Centralised proactive scheme

Next, all the nodes exchange HELLO packets and then send the updated neighbour list to the BS. The BS computes the route to the destination and sends the routing message to participating nodes (step 5 in Figure 2). In order to further reduce the routing overhead, the authors proposed Node Level Decisions that allow the nodes to decide whether to participate in the route discovery or not, based on their remaining battery energy and current traffic.

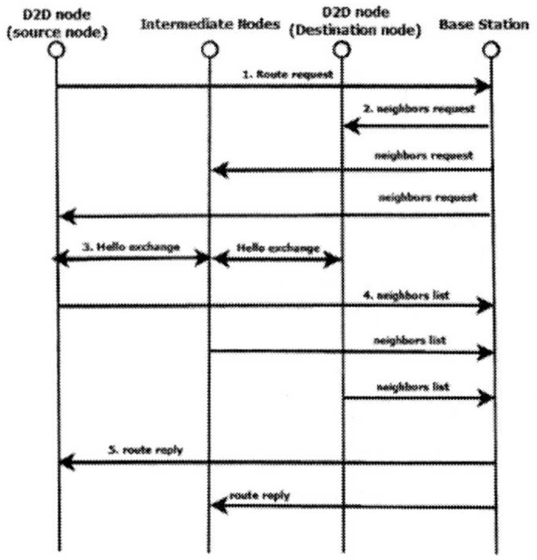

Figure 2. Centralised reactive scheme

In adaptive routing, the routing algorithm switches between the proactive and reactive scheme depending on the different network conditions (e.g., node density and traffic load). The authors proposed a threshold in order to avoid a ping pong effect from switching between the reactive and the proactive scheme (see Figure 3).

When the traffic load is above a given threshold 2, the routing switches from reactive to proactive. However, when the traffic load is below the threshold 1 the routing switches from to reactive scheme. In addition, the oscillation timer is used with the threshold value in order to avoid switching fluctuation.

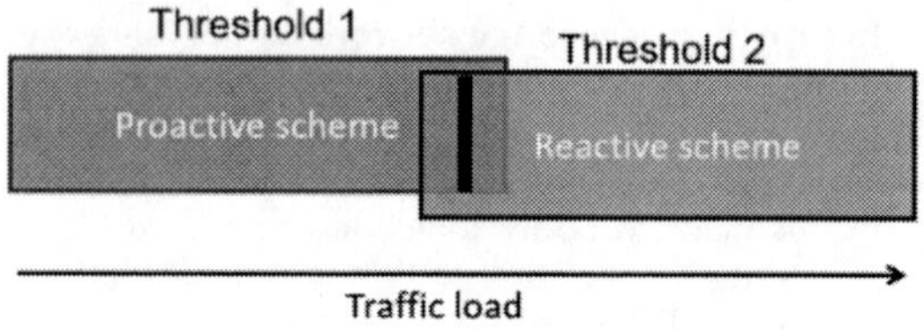

Figure 3. Threshold value

Authors introduced a number of features that could be integrated into the proposed protocol for reducing the routing overhead.

A. Node Level Decisions:

Each node autonomously decides about participation in the route discovery (i.e., neighborus discovery). The node level decision reduced the resources consumption (e.g., energy) in the route discovery phase. Serval criteria (e.g., energy and traffic load) are involved in node decisions. Authors classified the nodes based on residual energy. The nodes participate in the route discovery if residual energy is greater than 50%. Moreover, the node with residual energy less than 25% will never take part in the route discovery.

Another criterion is based on the change of the data traffic load by comparing the current load with the previous average load. When the current load is greater than 90%, then the node never participates in route discovery. However, if the current load is less than 75% and the previous average load is higher than 75%, then the node participates in the route discovery.

B. Variable route's timeout:

In order to break a route, the route expiration timer (timeout) that is defined as the minimum value of the link expiration timer among all links in the whole route is taken as the route timer. A node participates in route discovery only if the timer is greater or equal to the minimum required route timer.

C. Earlier stop message (ESTOP):

This message is broadcast by BS to inform nodes not to send any route request message due to a large number of messages received by the BS. The ESTOP message could reduce the routing overhead by limiting the number of nodes replying to a route request.

In order to provide a reliable connection and, in case the multihop route is not possible, then the BS will provide a traditional cellular link between the source and the destination node.

Both the cellular mode and multihop D2D mode could be enabled on the user device. Through cellular mode, the UE report updated neighbours list and BS draw Network topology view and provided a suitable route to UEs. This could be seen as a separation of control plane and data plane where the control plane provides the decision of the data forwarding. Moreover, the data plane route the data traffic through multihop D2D.

Based on that, the authors in [15] proposed a multihop D2D SDN network architecture and the low-overhead routing (LODR) protocol. It is known that SDN separates the control plane from the data plane; decisions on the routing of the traffic flows are taken in the control plane; then, flow tables are installed in the forwarding nodes of the data plane.

The proposed architecture assumes that each UE has an OpenFlow capability installed. In addition, the SDN controller controls the forwarding behavior of multihop D2D UE. The authors proposed five procedures to route the data traffic in the multihop D2D network. These procedures include: how to handle an unknown route, add a new UE, installing, maintaining, and updating the routing flow in the multihop D2D, etc. The results show that the proposed procedures perform better then Open Link State Routing (OLSR) [17] in terms of control overhead.

TABLE I. COMPARISON OF CENTRALIZED MULTIHOP D2D ROUTING ALGORITHMS

Routing algorithm	Routing scheme	Simulation implementation	Simulation metrics
MCN[10]	Proactive	GloMoSim	Throughput (TCP,UDP)
CBSR[11]	Proactive	NS-2	Delay, Packet delivery ratio, Routing overhead
BCR[12]	Hybrid	GloMoSim	Throughput under UDP, TCP with/without mobility
CAR[6]	Adaptive	-	No simulation evaluation
LORD[15]	Proactive	CORE	Overhead, Routing convergence time

IV. Challenges and Open Research Issues in Multihop D2D Routing

Based on the works reviewed in Section III, there are several challenges and, at the same time, open research in multihop D2D routing protocols that need to be considered and solved in the design of the future protocols. This section identifies some of the research challenges in Multihop D2D routing protocols.

A. *Reduce Routing Overhead*

In centralised multihop routing, the nodes exchange HELLO messages (periodically or on demand) with each other in order to build/update the neighbor's list. This list is sent (periodically or on demand) to the BS, which creates a global view of network topology and computes the suitable/short path between source and destination in the multihop D2D network. This exchange of messages between the nodes (i.e., BS and UEs) consumes resources. For example, the nodes regularly update their neighbor's list and send it to the BS; such a scheme leads to high-energy consumption and high delay. Thus, the control messages should be reduced.

Therefore, an open research issue is *how to route the data in multihop D2D communication while assuring a low control overhead.*

B. *Applying SDN to Multihop networks*

In the SDN approach, the control logic of network nodes is logically centralised, which programs the whole network (e.g., adjust forwarding rules on network devices based on particular policies and protocols). Applying such approach brings a number of challenges, as indicated below.

The first issue is that UEs need to discover the controller. In some studies, there is an assumption that all network devices know about the controller. In other papers, firstly, the controller broadcasts its existence to all network devices. Moreover, the network devices (UE) can communicate with the controller in one hop or in a multihop fashion. In one hop communication, network devices connected to the controller directly via a wireless link (e.g., cellular link).

While in the multihop approach, the connected UEs communicate with the controller through intermediary nodes. Thus, the shortest path between the controller and network devices (UE) is important to meet the energy constraints of mobile devices.

Minimizing the control messages exchanged between the controller and mobile devices is another issue that should be handled when applying SDN to the cellular network. The control messages are important in reducing delay and optimising the energy consumption.

The controller can be implemented as a single centralised entity or a distributed approach. Selecting an appropriate type of the control plane implementation (centralised or distributed) can affect the performance of the network. The controller manages the overall network view and consequently provides the forwarding rules (based on information collected from network nodes).

Several optimisation problems can be identified, such as: a) the amount of information to be sent to the forwarding nodes; b) how frequently should the controller setup/update flow rules, in order to avoid too much control overhead but still keeping an enough fast response to the network dynamics; c) how frequently should be updated (at the controller level) the image of the current network topology.

C. *Failure Recovery Mechanism*

In the works reviewed in Section III, a centralised entity (e.g., BS) has a network view and provides suitable routes for UEs. In case of failure of a node (e.g., BS) or no route received, a backup recovery mechanism should be introduced. The authors of [12] proposed a backup mechanism when there is no route from BS. Then the node broadcast route request via AODV routing protocol.

Therefore, *introducing a failure recovery mechanism is important to provide a reliable, stable connection between UEs.*

V. Conclusion and Future Works

In the single-hop D2D communication, the users are limited to communicate with only nodes in the proximity. However, in cases when the UEs are not in the vicinity, a UE has to relay data to a destination through a multihop route. In a centralised multihop network, an updated neighborus list is collected by the BS (periodically or on demand); then, the BS will create a global view of the network topology and will provide the suitable routes to UEs.

Several challenges for D2D centralized routing have been identified in this paper.

The control messages exchange between UEs and BS should be further minimized, aiming to meet energy constraints on UEs. In addition, in order to provide a stable connection between UEs, a backup mechanism should exist, to act in case of failure of the centralised entity or if no route is provided. Applying SDN to the multihop network is a promising approach that should be handled carefully in terms of communication between network nodes and controller and the control plane implementation.

As a future work, a simulation model and a tool (e.g., NS-3) will be developed for D2D routing, to implement the proposed centralised schemes. The simulations will provide as results a comparison of solutions, in terms of routing control overhead (in the control plane) and packet delivery ratio, network throughput and delay (in the data plane).

References

[1] X. Lin, J. Andrews, A. Ghosh, and R. Ratasuk, "An overview of 3GPP device-to-device proximity services," IEEE Commun. Mag., vol. 52, no. 4, pp. 40–48, 2014.

[2] S.-H. Kim and S.-J. Han, "Contour routing for peer-to-peer dtn delivery in cellular networks," in Communication Systems and Networks (COMSNETS), 2012 Fourth International Conference on, 2012, pp. 1–9.

[3] H. Imai, H. Okada, T. Yamazato, and M. Katayama, "The effect of a multipath hybrid routing protocol in multihop cellular networks," in Personal, Indoor and Mobile Radio Communications, 2006 IEEE 17th International Symposium on, 2006, pp. 1–5.

[4] H. Yuan, W. Guo, and S. Wang, "D2D multihop routing: Collision probability and routing strategy with limited location information," in Communication Workshop (ICCW), 2015 IEEE International Conference on, 2015, pp. 670–674.

[5] T. G. P. P. (3GPP), "LTE Device to Device (D2D) Proximity Services (ProSe) User Equipment (UE) radio transmission and reception," 2015.

[6] F. S. Shaikh, "Centralized Adaptive Routing in Multihop Cellular D2D Communications," in Computer and Communication Systems (ICCCS), 2017 2nd International Conference on, 2017, pp. 0–4.

[7] F. Malandrino, C. Casetti, and C.-F. Chiasserini, "Toward D2D-enhanced heterogeneous networks," IEEE Commun. Mag., vol. 52, no. 11, pp. 94–100, 2014.

[8] M. N. Tehrani, M. Uysal, and H. Yanikomeroglu, "Device-to-device communication in 5G cellular networks: challenges, solutions, and future directions," IEEE Commun. Mag., vol. 52, no. 5, pp. 86–92, 2014.

[9] F. S. Shaikh and R. Wismuller, "Routing in Multihop Cellular Device-to-Device (D2D) Networks: A Survey," IEEE Commun. Surv. Tutorials, no. c, pp. 1–37, 2018.

[10] R. Ananthapadmanabha, B. S. Manoj, and C. S. R. Murthy, "Multihop cellular networks: the architecture and routing protocols," 12th IEEE Int. Symp. Pers. Indoor Mob. Radio Commun. PIMRC 2001. Proc. (Cat. No.01TH8598), p. G-78-G-82.

[11] H. Li, D. Yu, and H. Chen, "New approach to multihop-cellular based multihop network," in Personal, Indoor and Mobile Radio Communications, 2003. PIMRC 2003. 14th IEEE Proceedings on, 2003, vol. 2, pp. 1629–1633.

[12] Y.-C. Hsu and Y.-D. Lin, "Base-centric routing protocol for multihop cellular networks," Glob. Telecommun. Conf. 2002. GLOBECOM '02. IEEE, vol. 1, pp. 158–162 vol.1, 2002.

[13] T. Finke, "Self-Organized Routing in Heterogeneous Mobile Ad Hoc Networks." Technische Universität Ilmenau, 2016.

[14] T. A. Ramrekha, G. P. Millar, and C. Politis, "A model for designing scalable and efficient adaptive routing approaches in emergency ad hoc communications," in Computers and Communications (ISCC), 2011 IEEE Symposium on, 2011, pp. 916–923.

[15] R. Jayadi and Y. C. Lai, "Low-overhead multihop device-to-device communications in software defined wireless networks," In *Soft Computing, Intelligent System and Information Technology (ICSIIT), 2017* (pp. 144-149). IEEE.

[16] C. Perkins, E. Belding-Royer, and S. Das, "Ad hoc on-demand distance vector (AODV) routing," IETF Net. Working Group, RFC3561, 2003.

[17] T. Clausen and P. Jacquet, Optimized Link State Routing Protocol (OLSR), RFC 3626, Oct. 2003.

[18] IEEE Std 802.15.1-2002 IEEE Std 802.15.1 IEEE Standard for Information technology- Telecommunications and informationexchange between systems- Local and metropolitan area networks- Specific requirements Part 15.1: Wireless Medium Access Control(MAC) and Physical Layer (PHY) Specifications for Wireless Personal Area Networks (WPANs).

[19] Official Homepage of the IEEE 802.11 Working Group, http://grouper.ieee.org/groups/802/11

Performance Evaluation of MultiPath TCP Congestion Control

Toshihiko Kato[1)2)], Adhikari Diwakar[1)], Ryo Yamamoto[1)], Satoshi Ohzahata[1)], and Nobuo Suzuki[2)]
1) University of Electro-Communications, Tokyo, Japan
2) Advanced Telecommunication Research Institute International, Kyoto, Japan
e-mail: kato@is.uec.ac.jp, diwakaradh@net.is.uec.ac.jp, ryo_yamamoto@is.uec.ac.jp, ohzahata@is.uec.ac.jp, nu-suzuki@atr.jp

Abstract— **In Multiptah TCP (MPTCP), the congestion control is realized by individual subflows (conventional TCP connections). However, it is required to avoid increasing congestion window too fast resulting from subflows' increasing their own congestion windows independently. So, a coupled increase scheme of congestion windows, called Linked Increase Adaptation (LIA), is adopted as a standard congestion control algorithm for subflows comprising a MPTCP connection. But this algorithm supposes that TCP connections use Additive Increase and Multiplicative Decrease (AIMD) based congestion control, and if high speed algorithms such as CUBIC TCP are used, the throughput of MPTCP connections might be decreased. This paper analyzes this issue through experiments. Specifically, this paper examines two experiments; one is to apply one of LIA, TCP Reno and CUBIC TCP to MPTCP flow, and another is to compare LIA based MPTCP flow and a single TCP flow with TCP Reno or CUBIC TCP. These experiments show that LIA is conservative compared with TCP Reno and CUBIC TCP.**

Keywords- MPTCP; Congestion Control; Linked Increase Adaptation; TCP Reno; CUBIC TCP.

I. INTRODUCTION

Recent mobile terminals are equipped with multiple interfaces. For example, most smart phones have interfaces for 4G Long Term Evolution (LTE) and WLAN. In the next generation (5G) mobile network, it is expected that mobile terminals will be equipped with more interfaces by using multiple communication paths provided multiple network operators [1].

However, the conventional Transmission Control Protocol (TCP) establishes a connection between a single IP address at either end, and so it cannot handle multiple interfaces at the same time. In order to utilize the multiple interface configuration, Multipath TCP (MPTCP) [2], which is an extension of TCP, has been introduced in several operating systems, such as Linux, Apple OS/iOS [3] and Android [4]. Conventional TCP applications can use MPTCP as if they were working over conventional TCP and are provided with multiple byte streams through different interfaces.

MPTCP is defined in three Request for Comments (RFC) documents by the Internet Engineering Task Force. RFC 6182 [5] outlines architecture guidelines. RFC 6824 [6] presents the details of extensions to support multipath operation, including the maintenance of an *MPTCP connection* and *subflows* (TCP connections associated with an MPTCP connection), and the data transfer over an MPTCP connection. RFC 6356 [7] presents a congestion control algorithm that couples the congestion control algorithms running on different subflows.

One significant point on the MPTCP congestion control is that, even in MPTCP, individual subflows perform their own control. RFC 6356 requires that an MPTCP data stream do not provide too large throughput compared with other (single) TCP data streams sharing a congested link. For this purpose, RFC 6356 defines an algorithm called Linked Increase Adaptation (LIA), which couples and suppresses the congestion window size of individual subflows. Besides, more aggressive algorithms, such as Opportunistic LIA (OLIA) [8] and Balanced Linked Adaptation (BALIA) [9], are proposed.

However, all of those algorithms are based on the TCP Reno [10]. That is, the increase of congestion window at receiving a new ACK segment is in the order of 1/(congestion window size). On the other hand, current modern operating systems uses high speed congestion control algorithms, such as CUBIC TCP [11] and Compound TCP [12]. These algorithms increase the congestion window more aggressively than TCP Reno. So, it is possible that the throughput of LIA is suppressed when it coexists with them.

Based on these considerations, we conducted two kinds of experiments. One is for comparing the performance of LIA, the standard congestion control algorithm of MPTCP, with that of the case when subflows use TCP Reno or CUBIC TCP. The other is for evaluating the performance when MPTCP with LIA and TCP Reno / CUBIC TCP share a bottleneck link. This paper describes the results of those experiments.

The rest of this paper is organized as follows. Section II explains the overview of MPTCP and the details of LIA. Here we discuss how LIA algorithm is derived. Section III describes the LIA implementation in the Linux operating system. Section IV shows the performance evaluation of LIA itself and the cases when subflows use TCP Reno or CUBIC TCP. Section V shows the performance evaluation when MPTCP with LIA and TCP with Reno/CUBIC coexist over a bottleneck link. In the end, Section V concludes this paper.

II. OVERVIEW OF MPTCP AND DETAILS OF LIA

A. *Overview of MPTCP*

As described in Figure 1, the MPTCP module is located on top of TCP. MPTCP is designed so that the conventional applications do not need to care about the existence of MPTCP. MPTCP establishes an MPTCP connection associated with two or more regular TCP connections called subflows. The management and data transfer over an MPTCP connection is done by newly introduced TCP options for MPTCP operation.

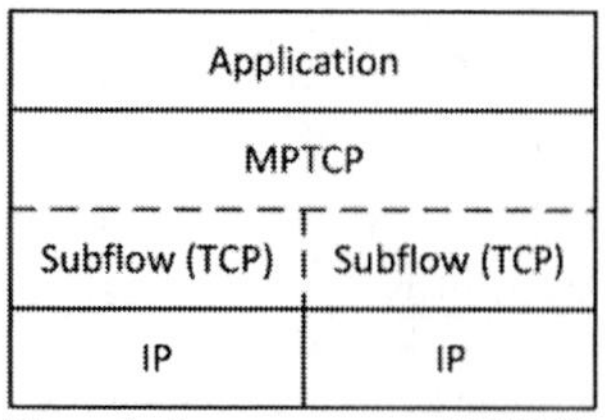

Figure 1. Layer structure of MPTCP.

When the first subflow is established, a TCP option called *MP_CAPABLE* is used within SYN, SYN+ACK, and the following ACK segments. When the following subflows are established, the *MP_JOIN* option is used so that the new TCP connections are associated with the existing MPTCP connection.

An MPTCP implementation will take one input data stream from an application, and split it into one or more subflows, with sufficient control information to allow it to be reassembled and delivered to the receiver side application reliably and in order. The MPTCP connection maintains the *data sequence number* independent of the subflow level sequence numbers. The data and ACK segments may contain a *Data Sequence Signal (DSS)* option depicted in Figure 2.

The data sequence number and data ACK is 4 or 8 byte long, depending on the flags in the option. The number is assigned on a byte-by-byte basis similarly with the TCP sequence number. The value of data sequence number is the number assigned to the first byte conveyed in that TCP segment. The data sequence number, subflow sequence number (relative value) and data-level length define the mapping between the MPTCP connection level and the subflow level. The data ACK is analogous to the behavior of the standard TCP cumulative ACK. It specifies the next data sequence number a receiver expects to receive.

B. Overview of MPTCP Congetion Control

As described above, in MPTCP, only subflows manage their congestion windows, that is, an MPTCP connection does not have its congestion window size. Under this condition, if subflows perform their congestion control independently, the throughput of MPTCP connection will be larger than single TCP connections sharing a bottleneck link. RFC 6356 decides that such a method is unfair for conventional TCP. RFC 6356 introduces the following three requirements for the congestion control for MPTCP connection.

- Goal 1 (Improve throughput): An MPTCP flow should perform at least as well as a single TCP flow would on the best of the paths available to it.
- Goal 2 (Do no harm): All MPTCP subflows on one link should not take more capacity than a single TCP flow would get on this link.
- Goal 3 (Balance congestion): An MPTCP connection should use individual subflow dependent on the congestion on the path.

In order to satisfy these three goals, RC6356 proposes an algorithm that *couples* the additive increase function of the subflows, and uses unmodified decreasing behavior in case of a packet loss. This algorithm is called LIA and summarized in the following way.

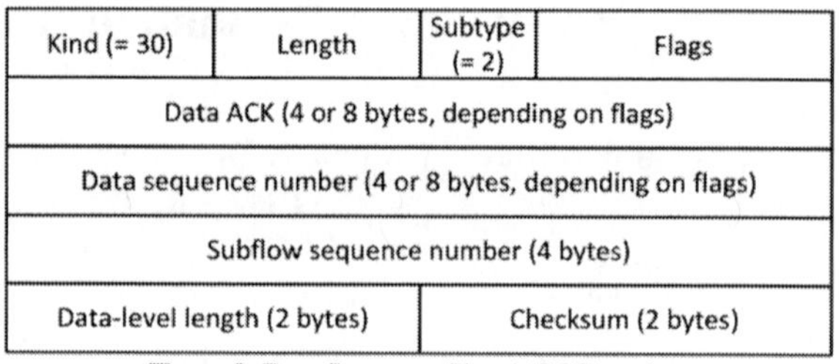

Figure 2. Data Sequence Signal (DSS) option.

Let $cwnd_i$ and $cwnd\_total$ be the congestion window size on subflow i, and the sum of the congestion window sizes of all subflows in an MPTCP connection, respectively. Here, we assume they are maintained in packets. Let rtt_i be the Round-Trip Time (RTT) on subflow i. For each ACK received on subflow i, $cwnd_i$ is increased by

$$min\left(\frac{\alpha}{cwnd\_total}, \frac{1}{cwnd_i}\right). \quad (1)$$

The first argument of min function is designed to satisfy Goal 2 requirement. Here, α is defined by

$$\alpha = cwnd\_total \cdot \frac{\max_i\left(\frac{cwnd_i}{rtt_i^2}\right)}{\left(\sum_i \frac{cwnd_i}{rtt_i}\right)^2}. \quad (2)$$

By substituting (2) to (1), we obtain the following equation.

$$min\left(\frac{\max_i\left(\frac{cwnd_i}{rtt_i^2}\right)}{\left(\sum_i \frac{cwnd_i}{rtt_i}\right)^2}, \frac{1}{cwnd_i}\right) \quad (3)$$

C. Derivation of LIA Equation

In this subsection, we give one possible derivation of (2), which is not specified in RFC 6356 explicitly. We suppose a single TCP flow corresponding an individual subflow over an MPTCP connection. Let p the packet loss rate over the bottleneck link and let $cwnd_i^{TCP}$ be the congestion window size of the supposed single TCP flow i.

We assume the balanced situation indicating that the increase and decrease of congestion window sizes are the same. That is, for subflow i on the MPTCP connection,

$$(1-p) \cdot min\left(\frac{\alpha}{cwnd\_total}, \frac{1}{cwnd_i}\right) = p \cdot \frac{1}{2} cwnd_i. \quad (4)$$

We suppose that the first argument is selected, and then

$$(1-p) \cdot \frac{\alpha}{cwnd\_total} = p \cdot \frac{1}{2} cwnd_i. \quad (4')$$

For supposed TCP flow i,

$$(1-p) \cdot \frac{1}{cwnd_i^{TCP}} = p \cdot \frac{1}{2} cwnd_i^{TCP}. \quad (5)$$

For satisfying Goals 1 and 2, we can specify

$$\sum_i \frac{cwnd_i}{rtt_i} = \max_i\left(\frac{cwnd_i^{TCP}}{rtt_i}\right). \quad (6)$$

By eliminating p using (4') and (5), we obtain

$$\alpha \cdot \left(cwnd_i^{TCP}\right)^2 = cwnd\_total \cdot cwnd_i. \quad (7)$$

By squaring both sides of (6) and substituting (7), we obtain

$$\alpha \cdot \left(\sum_i \frac{cwnd_i}{rtt_i}\right)^2 = \max_i\left(\frac{cwnd\_total \cdot cwnd_i}{rtt_i^2}\right). \quad (8)$$

This is leading to (2).

It should be noted that we assume the additive increase and multiplicative decrease (AIMD) scheme in (4) and (5). More specifically, we assume that the increase is 1/(congestion window size) for each ACK segment and the decrease parameter is 1/2, which is the specification of TCP Reno. That is, LIA supposes that MPTCP subflows and coexisting single TCP flows follow TCP Reno. In the case that the high speed congestion control is adopted, the increase per ACK segment will become larger and the decrease parameter will be small. In such a case, we need to formalize (4) and (5) in a different way.

III. LIA IMPLEMENTATION OVER LINUX

We can obtain the source program of the Linux operating system including MPTCP from the GitHub web site [13]. We examined how MPTCP are implemented in Linux.

LIA is implemented within the source file `mptcp_coupled.c`. In this file, `mptcp_ccc_recalc_alpha()` and `mptcp_ccc_cong_avoid()` are major functions. The former calculates the first argument in (1) and stores the result in variable `alpha`. The latter records the larger of 1/`alpha` and the congestion window size of the current subflow, and, when this function is called as many times as the recorded value, it increases the congestion window size by one. This procedure is considered to correspond to the specification of (3).

On the other hand, the congestion control mechanisms, strictly speaking the congestion avoidance mechanisms, are implemented as *kernel modules* in Linux. They can be compiled independently of the kernel itself, and can be loaded or removed while the operating system is running. More specifically, the pointer to the function performing congestion avoidance mechanism is stored in a kernel data structure `struct tcp_congestion_ops` within `struct inet_connection_sock` [14]. The kernel function `tcp_cong_control()` calls the function specified in this kernel data structure when it performs congestion avoidance. The pointer to the congestion avoidance function can be settled manually by using `sysctl` command setting control variable `net.ipv4.tcp_congestion_control`. The value will be set to `reno` or `cubic`.

When MPTCP LIA is used, the data structure `struct tcp_congestion_ops` points to the address of function `mptcp_ccc_cong_avoid()` described above. This means LIA is realized as one of TCP congestion avoidance mechanisms. That is, LIA is no automatically selected in MPTCP implementation, but we need to set `net.ipv4.tcp_congestion_control` to `lia` manually. (Or build the kernel to select LIA as a default congestion control algorithm.) In other word, we can use TCP Reno or CUBIC TCP in MPTCP subflows by setting the corresponding control variable.

IV. PERFORMANCE EVALUATION USING PACKET LOSSES

A. Experiment Configuration

As the first experiment, we tried to evaluate the performance of the MPTCP congestion control itself, by generating packet losses artificially. Figure 3 shows the network configuration of the experiment with packet losses inserted. A data sender is connected to 100 Mbps Ethernet and IEEE 802.11g WLAN (2.4 GHz). An 11g access point works as an access point and as an Ethernet hub. A data receiver is connected with the hub through 100 Mbps Ethernet. Both sender and receiver execute MPTCP software with stable version 0.94, which is the newest version [13]. The IP addresses assigned network interfaces of the sender and receiver are shown in Figure 3. The Ethernet interfaces belong to subnet 192.168.0.0/24, and the WLAN interface belongs to another subset 192.168.1.0/24, all of which are connected through a bridge. In the sender side, the routing table need to be specified for individual interfaces by using `ip` command. In the receiver side, a route entry to subnet 192.168.1.0/24 needs to be specified explicitly. One MPTCP connection with two subflows is established. One subflow goes through the Ethernet interface at the sender, and another goes through the WLAN interface.

The congestion control algorithm used in the sender is set to either of LIA, TCP Reno, or CUBIC TCP. We inserted packet losses with the rate of 0.1% at the Ethernet interface in the sender, and delay of 100 msec at the receiver, both by `tc` (traffic control) command with the `netem` filter. The packets sent through two interfaces at the sender are captured by using *Wireshark* [15], and the congestion window size is recorded for two subflows by using *tcpprobe* [16], both in the sender side. Data transfer is done for 10 sec by *iperf2* [17].

B. Experiment Results

Table I shows the throughput of MPTCP connection measured in two experimental runs for the cases when the congestion control algorithm of MPTCP subflows is set to each of LIA, TCP Reno, and CUBIC TCP. The throughput of LIA, the original setting in MPTCP, is lower than the other settings.

In order to investigate the detail behaviors of individual congestion control algorithms, we examined the time variation of sequence number and congestion window size of MPTCP subflows. Figures 4 through 6 show the results of the experiment runs underlined in Table I. In each algorithm, the congestion window size of a subflow via WLAN interface (WLAN subflow) increases rapidly to its maximum value. It

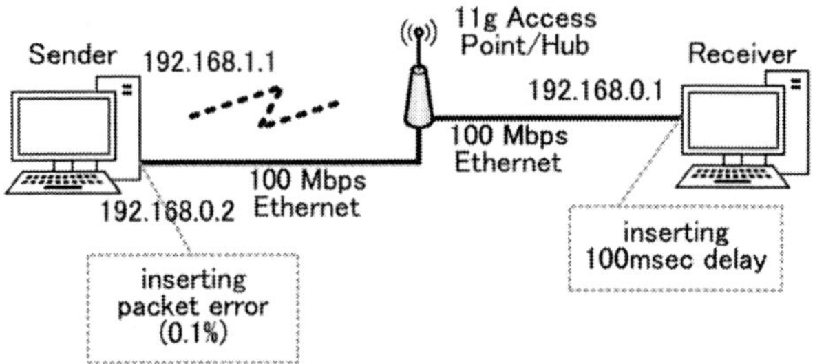

Figure 3. Network configuration by packet loss insertion.

TABLE I. THROUGHPUT WITH PACKET LOSS INSERTED (Mbps).

Algorithm	LIA	Reno	CUBIC
Throughput	<u>12.5</u>, 12.1	14.4, <u>18.8</u>	<u>23.0</u>, 16.1

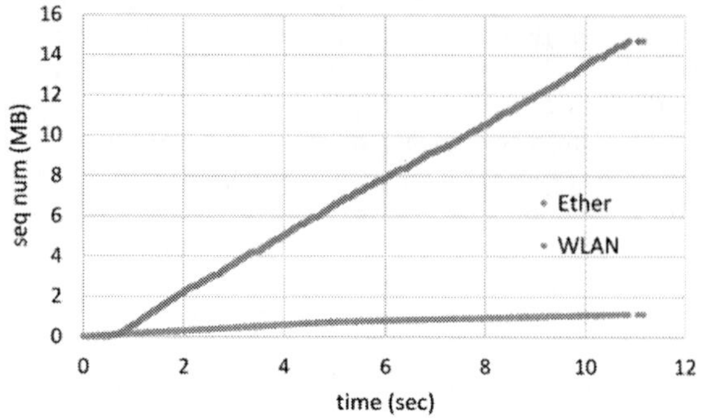

(a) sequence number vs. time

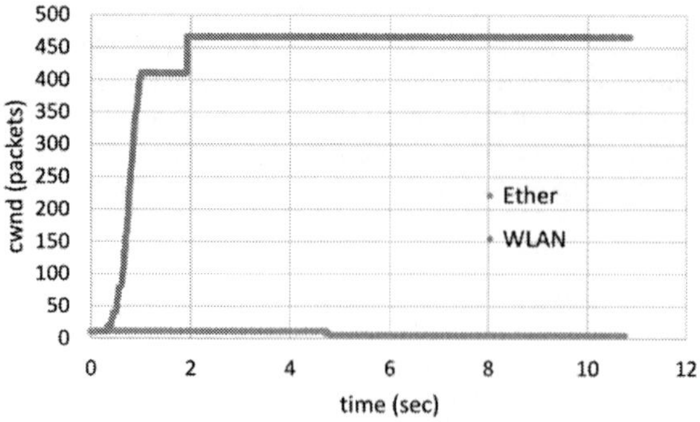

(b) congestion window size vs. time

Figure 4. Time variation of sequence number and congestion window size with packet losses inserted (LIA).

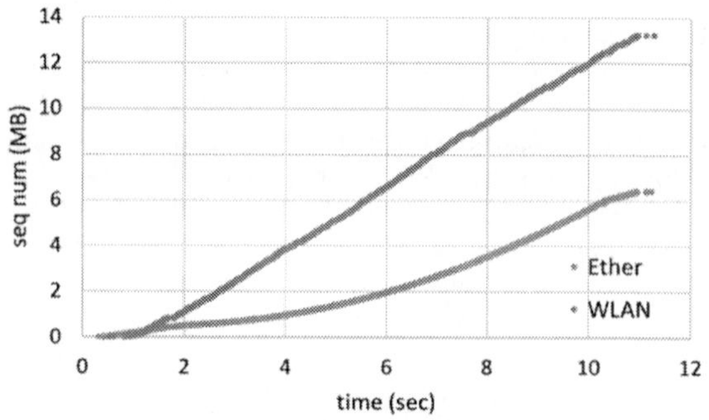

(a) sequence number vs. time

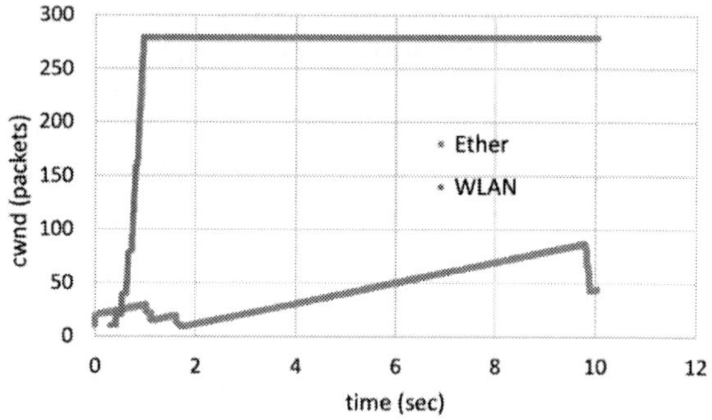

(b) congestion window size vs. time

Figure 5. Time variation of sequence number and congestion window size with packet losses inserted (TCP Reno).

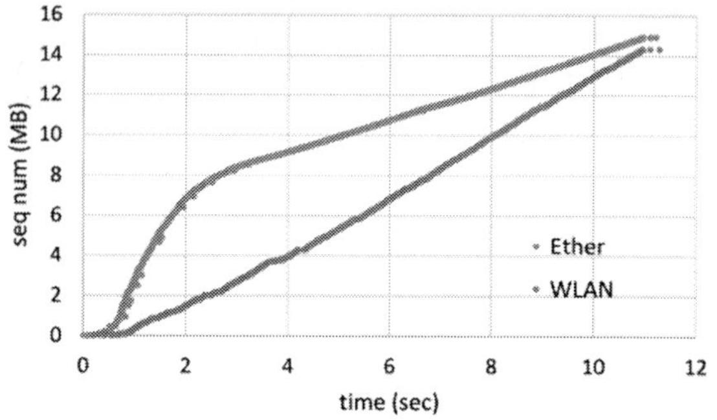

(a) sequence number vs. time

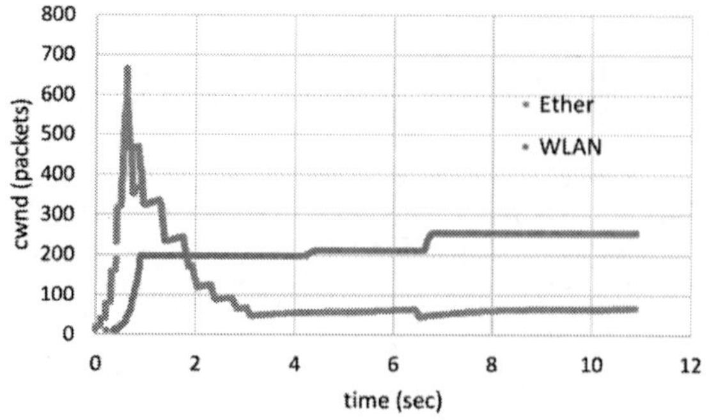

(b) congestion window size vs. time

Figure 6. Time variation of sequence number and congestion window size with packet losses inserted (CUBIC TCP).

should be noted that different maximum values are set to LIA and TCP Reno/CUBIC TCP, by the operating system. It should be also noted that there are some flat parts, before reaching the maximum value, in WLAN congestion window size in the case of CUBIC TCP. The reason for this is supposed that the data corresponding the congestion window size was not sent during one RTT, and that the rule of congestion window validation [18] was applied.

As for a subflow via Ethernet interface (Ethernet subflow), the increase of congestion window size is the smallest in LIA and the largest in CUBIC TCP. So, in the case of LIA, the increase of sequence number, that is, the bytes transmitted, is also limited. In the case that TCP Reno is used as the congestion control algorithm in MPTCP, the congestion window size over Ethernet subflow increases linearly with the elapsed time, which characterizes TCP Reno. The increase is larger than the case of LIA. In the case of CUBIC TCP, the congestion window size over Ethernet subflow increases rapidly by 0.5 sec, and after that it decreases due to several packet losses. During no packet loss period, e.g., from 3 sec to 6.5 sec, we confirmed that the congestion window size changes following a cubic function. Due to the rapid increase during the beginning, the increase of sequence number is large in this case.

For this scenario, it can be said that LIA, the original congestion control algorithm in MPTCP, may be too conservative in increasing congestion window size, compared with TCP Reno and CUBIC TCP, which are commonly used in conventional TCP communications.

V. Performance Evaluation through Actual Congestion

A. *Experiment Configuration*

As the second experiment, we tried to evaluate the performance of the MPTCP congestion control when there are actual congestion. Figure 7 shows the network configuration used in this experiment. We added a single path TCP data sender and a bridge introducing a bottleneck link in the configuration used in the first experiment. At the interface of the bridge to the data receiver, we set the limit of data link rate to 10 Mbps, by using `tc` command with the `tbf` filter. The reason for limiting the bandwidth to 10 Mbps is that the results in the previous experiment show that the MPTCP throughput is larger than 10 Mbps even if it uses LIA, and so a 10 Mbps link will become a bottleneck actually. The congestion control algorithm at the MPTCP data sender is set to LIA and that at the single path TCP data sender is set to TCP Reno or CUBIC TCP.

B. *Experiment Results*

Table II shows the average throughput of MPTCP flow and single TCP flow, for 10 sec data transfer by iperf. For each combination of LIA and TCP Reno, or LIA and CUBIC TCP, we conducted four experiment runs. When the single TCP flow uses TCP Reno, the average of four runs is 2.82 Mbps for MPTCP flow and 7.03 Mbps for single TCP flow. When CUBIC TCP is used, that is 1.58 Mbps for MPTCP flow and 8.37 Mbps for single TCP flow. In both cases, the average throughput is lower for MPTCP flow. When the single TCP flow uses CUBIC TCP, the throughput of MPTCP flow is decreased further.

In order to investigate more detailed behaviors, we examined the time variation of sequence number and congestion window size for MPTCP subflows and single TCP flow. We picked up the results indicated by gray shadow in Table II. Figure 8 shows the results when the single TCP subflow uses TCP Reno. The sequence number (transmitted

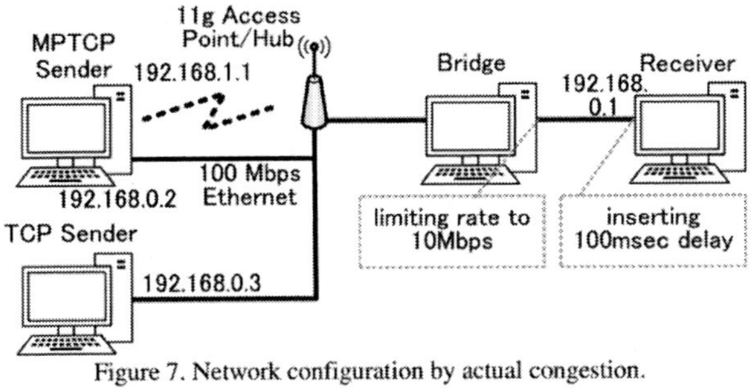

Figure 7. Network configuration by actual congestion.

TABLE II. AVERAGE THROUGHPUT WITH ACTUAL CONGESTION (Mbps).

Algorithm	LIA & Reno				LIA & CUBIC			
MPTCP	2.85	2.66	2.86	2.91	2.03	1.72	1.52	1.04
Single TCP	7.05	7.10	6.97	6.99	7.79	8.33	8.47	8.87

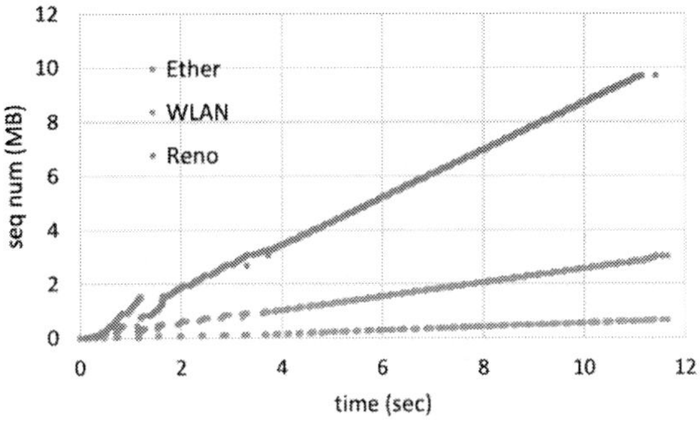

(a) sequence number vs. time

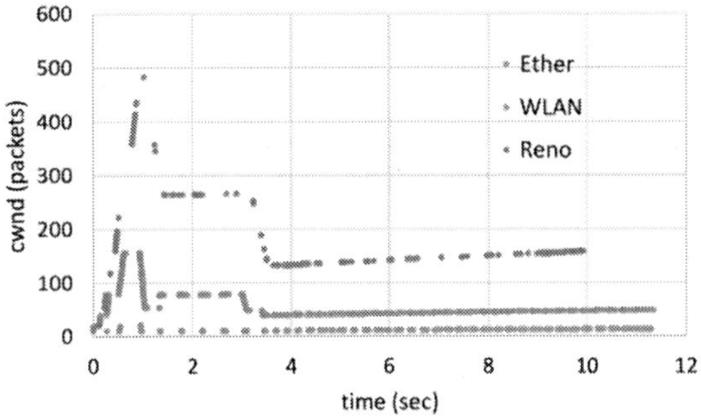

(b) congestion window size vs. time

Figure 8. Time variation of sequence number and congestion window size with actual congestion (LIA & TCP Reno).

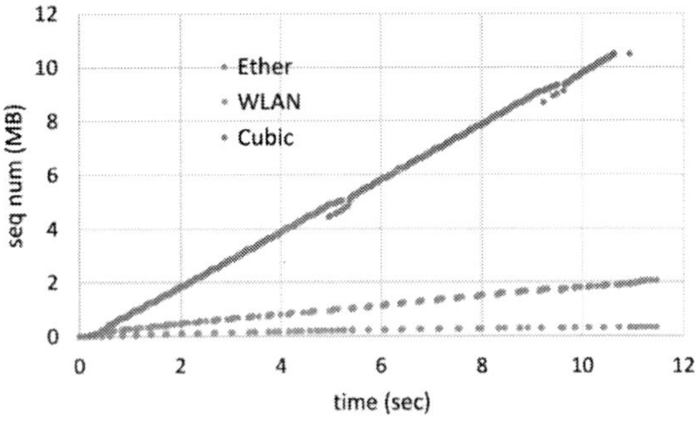

(a) sequence number vs. time

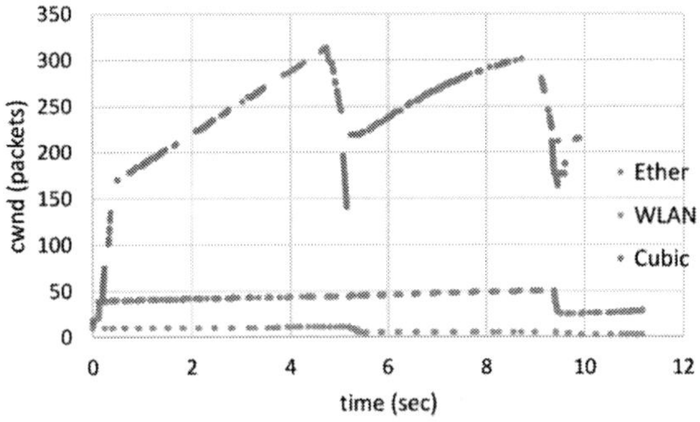

(b) congestion window size vs. time

Figure 9. Time variation of sequence number and congestion window size with actual congestion (LIA & CUBIC TCP).

bytes) increases fastest in the single TCP flow, next in the Ethernet subflow and most slowly in the WLAN subflow. As for the time variation of congestion window size, the graph of the single TCP flow and that of the Ethernet subflow are in a similar shape, but the value itself is larger for the single TCP flow. The increase of congestion window size of WLAN subflow is suppressed largely.

Figure 9 shows the results when the single TCP subflow uses CUBIC TCP. In this case, the increase of sequence number is much larger for the single TCP flow. The time variation of congestion window size is also much larger for the single TCP flow. The congestion window size of the MPTCP subflows does not increase but is almost flat along the time. This is similar with the results shown in Figure 4, and this decreases the throughput of MPTCP flow.

From those two results, it can be said that the increase of congestion window in MPTCP subflows using LIA is restricted when they share a congested link with other single TCP flows. The congestion window in LIA is suppressed even when MPTCP subflow shares a bottleneck link with TCP Reno. If LIA coexists with CUBIC TCP, the congestion window is suppressed largely.

VI. Conclusions

This paper described the experimental analysis of the standard congestion control algorithm for MPTCP, Linked Increase Adaptation. As the first experiment, we used a network configuration with Ethernet subflow and WLAN subflow, among which packet losses are inserted in Ethernet subflow. We set the congestion control algorithm for subflows to LIA, TCP Reno, and CUBIC TCP. As a result, the throughput of LIA was smallest. As the second experiment, we used a network configuration using a bridge node introducing a bottleneck link. We also used a node for a single TCP flow. In this configuration, we executed one MPTCP flow using LIA and one single TCP flow with TCP Reno or CUBIC TCP. In this experiment, we obtained a result that MPTCP with LIA is suppressed largely by the single TCP flow with Reno or CUBIC. These results come from the fact that the LIA, the standard congestion control algorithm for MPTCP, is conservative in order to maintain the "Do no harm" principle that requires an MPTCP flow not to use too much network resource compared with single TCP flows. It may be expected to introduce more aggressive congestion control algorithms comparative with high speed congestion control algorithms like CUBIC TPC.

Acknowledgment

This research was performed under the research contract of "Research and Development on control schemes for utilizations of multiple mobile communication networks," for the Ministry of Internal Affairs and Communications, Japan.

References

[1] NGNM Alliance, "NGMN 5G White Paper," https://www.ngmn.org/fileadmin/ngmn/content/downloads/Technical/2015/NGMN_5G_White_Paper_V1_0.pdf, Feb. 2015, [retrieved: Jan. 2019].

[2] C. Paasch and O. Bonaventure, "Multipath TCP," Communications of the ACM, vol. 57, no. 4, pp. 51-57, Apr. 2014.

[3] AppleInsider Staff, "Apple found to be using advanced Multipath TCP networking in iOS 7," http://appleinsider.com/articles/13/09/20/apple-found-to-be-using-advanced-multipath-tcp-networking-in-ios-7, [retrieved: Jan. 2019].

[4] icteam, "MultiPath TCP – Linux Kernel implementation, Users:: Android," https://multipath-tcp.org/pmwiki.php/Users/Android, [retrieved: Jan. 2019].

[5] A. Ford, C.Raiciu, M. Handley, S. Barre, and J. Iyengar, "Architectural Guidelines for Multipath TCP Development," IETF RFC 6182, Mar. 2011.

[6] A. Ford, C. Raiciu, M. Handley, and O. Bonaventure, "TCP Extensions for Multipath Operation with Multiple Addresses," IETF RFC 6824, Jan. 2013.

[7] C. Raiciu, M. Handley, and D. Wischik, "Coupled Congestion Control for Multipath Transport Protocols," IETF RFC 6356, Oct. 2011.

[8] R. Khalili, N. Gast, M. Popovic, and J. Boudec, "MPTCP Is Not Pareto-Optimal: Performance Issues and a Possible Solution," IEEE/ACM Trans. Networking, vol. 21, no. 5, pp. 1651-1665, Oct. 2013.

[9] Q. Peng, A. Valid, J. Hwang, and S. Low, "Multipath TCP: Analysis, Design and Implementation," IEEE/ACM Trans. Networking, vol. 24, no. 1, pp. 596-609, Feb. 2016.

[10] S. Floyd, T. Henderson, and A. Gurtov, "The NewReno Modification to TCP's Fast Recovery Algorithm," IETF RFC 3728, Apr. 2004.

[11] S. Ha, I. Rhee, and L. Xu, "CUBIC: A New TCP-Friendly High-Speed TCP Variant," ACM SIGOPS Operating Systems Review, vol. 42, no. 5, pp. 64-74, Jul. 2008.

[12] K. Tan, J. Song, Q. Zhang, and M. Sridharan, "A Compound TCP Approach for High-speed and Long Distance Networks," Proc. IEEE INFOCOM 2006, pp. 1-12. Apr. 2006.

[13] GitHub, "Linux Kernel implementation of MultiPath TCP," https://multipath-tcp.org, [retrieved: Jan. 2019].

[14] A. Jaakkola, "Implementation of Transmission Control Protocol in Linux," https://wiki.aalto.fi /download/attachments/70789052/linux-tcp-review.pdf, [retrieved: Jan. 2019].

[15] "Wireshark," https://www.wireshark.org/, [retrieved: Dec. 2018].

[16] Linux Foundation Wiki, "Trace: tcpprobe," The Linux Foundation, https://wiki.linuxfoundation.org/networking/tcpprobe, [retrieved: Jan. 2019].

[17] ESnet, "iperf2/iperf3," https://fasterdata.es.net/performance-testing/network-troubleshooting-tools/iperf/, [retrieved: Jan. 2019].

[18] M. Handley, J. Padhye, and S. Floyd, "TCP Congestion Window Validation," IETF, RFC 2861, Jun. 2000.

Vehicular to Grid Technologies– A Survey on Architectures and Solutions

Al-Alwash Husam Mahdi
University Politehnica of Bucharest - UPB
Bucharest, Romania
Email: al.aloosh.92@gmail.com

Mustafa Khaleel Hamadani
University Politehnica of Bucharest - UPB
Bucharest, Romania
mkhaleel190@gmail.com

***Abstract*—Nowadays, the novel Vehicle to Grid (V2G) technology is becoming of high interest in the domain of Electric Vehicles (EVs). In the context of many EVs connected to the power grid, the V2G technology has as its primary objective to control and assure a necessary balance between the consumption of the energy by some EVs and possible energy delivery into the power grid by other EVs. The V2G applications potentially help to increase the supply grid performance, concerning system stability, efficiency, and reliability. Given the novelty of V2G networking, this paper exposes a short survey on the V2G technology, focusing on identifying the challenges and open research issues for our future work. Also, some solutions and not yet solved problems in V2G are discussed. The approach of using a Software Defined Network (SDN) type of control is briefly introduced. The advantages of SDN-Based Smart Grid (SG) are identified, as well as some challenges, especially related to the centralised concept of the SDN.**

Keywords-V2G; Electric Vehicles; SDN-Based Smart Grid; Software Defined-V2G.

I. INTRODUCTION

The Vehicle to Grid (V2G) technology has recently received increased interest from researchers because of its advantages for both the environment and for power systems. From the environmental perspective, Electric Vehicles (EVs) are nature-friendly because of their reduced pollution when compared with conventional vehicles (fuel and gasoline). From the power system perspective, by exploiting the battery of the EV, it can act as power storage that can be used based on demand. The Smart Grid (SG) is a comprehensive innovation proposed for managing and monitoring the traditional power grid. The SG introduces a bidirectional communication (two-way) between service companies, and consumers and has sensors over the transmission lines that why it is called "Smart Grid". Therefore, the main objective of the V2G technology is to provide available distributed power to serve the EVs connected to the SG.

Figure 1 illustrates the bidirectional connection between EVs and the SG. The power can flow in two directions: from the power generator, over the SG to reach EVs or back, from the EVs to the SG. Usually, the EVs are supposed to have appropriate resources in order to benefit from the advantages the V2G technology has to offer [1]. Software, processing power, and power electronics devices should be included in the design of EVs. The EVs can be attached to Distributed Networks (DNs) [2], to deliver power to a grid at peak hours of load and thus enhance the overall system efficiency and reliability. Moreover, the EVs must have three essential elements:

- A connection to the SG for power flow.
- Physical and logical communication connections to the grid operator, used for control purposes.
- Onboard metering capabilities and controls of the EVs.

The power grid arranges the vehicles in a group called an aggregator. Also, it coordinates the charging and discharging processing in order to provide reliable operation.

SDN offers flexible control by separating the control plane from the data plane. The control plane has programmable controllers and logical centralisation. Controllers can have access to the entire network information, so it is easy to configure the network and deploy new protocols. Switches in the data plane provide only simple data forwarding function, thus matching packets can be processed rapidly to adjust the growing traffic.

As a novel technology, the V2G is facing challenges, and therefore, several open research issues exist. This work identifies several open problems, some of which have solutions and some are still unresolved.

The structure of this paper is the following: Section II describes some relevant work in the field. Section III presents the features of SDN control integration into the SG. In Section IV, we address EVs charging issues in the SG and we outline the usage of SDN as a control solution in the V2G environment. In Section V, we describe a general SDN-Based V2G framework. Section VI identifies some open research challenges. The conclusion is summarised in Section VII.

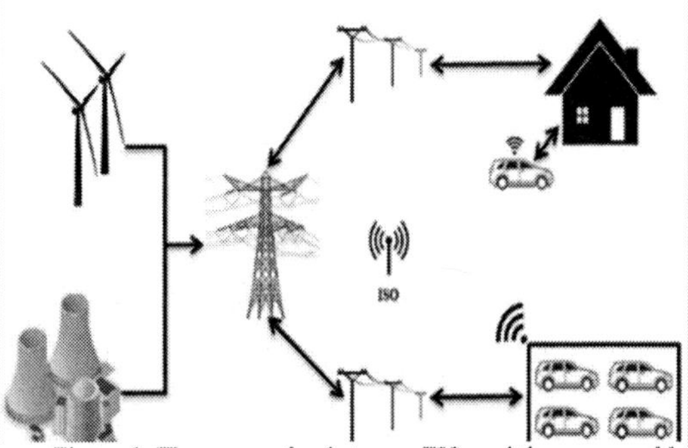

Figure 1. The connection between EVs and the power grid.

II. Summary Of Related Work

Wang et al. [3] introduce a novel architecture of distributed energy management for the integration of V2G networks with EV aggregator, aiming to achieve energy balancing between the grid side and the EVs side. The paper analyses theoretically what are the constraints of charging, incorporated in the form of *Willingness To Pay* (WTP) and proposes a distributed framework to coordinate the system behaviour during charging and discharging.

According to SDN features as mentioned above, SDN can solve two problems of V2G. First, V2G have the problem of complex network configuration and management due to the dynamic of V2G. Second, unbalanced the energy distribution in V2G, so the importance of communication data is different. The SDN can accelerate forwarding time and achieve traffic control.

Zhang et al. [4] proposed for V2G communication model, software-defined V2G (SD-V2G), aiming to apply SDN in V2G. This proposal deals with the dynamic communication and security for the V2G system. Also, a security communication mechanism (SCM) is proposed to ensure non-repudiation, confidentiality, integrity, and authentication.

Sun et al. [5] proposed a software-defined charging network architecture for hybrid EVs having three architectural planes: physical, control and application plane. Some more details are provided in Section IV.

Li et al. [6] exploit the multicast communication to collect information on the battery status and *State of Charge* (SOC) from EVs. They propose a battery status sensing by a software-defined multicast (BSS-SDM) scheme, where the battery status of each EV is identified during SOC transitions and maintained by a centralised controller. Additionally, a battery-status-based multicast scheduling algorithm is proposed to implement the V2G regulation optimisation. The work presented simulation results that verified the effectiveness of the proposed schemes. The BSS-SDM is shown to be more adaptive than to achieve optimal costs of the V2G regulation delay time in IEC 61850 advanced for V2G. Li et al. [6] also propose the coordination of EVs during charging/discharging sessions.

Integration benefits of the SDN with the SG in terms of improving the system operations are proposed by Chen et al. [7].They introduce a ‘‘two-tier SDN based framework’’. The results have shown that it is easier to upgrade and configure the SG. However, there are other open issues (e.g., request balance between tiers) required to be solved.

Rehmani et al. [8] presented a comprehensive survey on the SDN-controlled SG, including a taxonomy of the advantages and the architectures. Also, this work identifies some challenges, open research issues, and future directions.

Considering the recent developments in Fog computing, technology, Tao et al. [9] proposed a new hybrid computing model for V2G networks, to integrate Fog and Cloud for 5G-Enabled V2G networks, (called Foud).

III. Major Advantages of Software Defined Networking In Smart Grids Context

The SDN technology can successfully be used to manage in a centralised way the communication entities in the SG system and also to improve the efficiency, scalability, and resiliency. By deploying the SDN in SG technology, one can reduce the system cost and management complexity, making easier the system upgrades. In particular, this solution is appropriate to satisfy the demands of charging operation.

The SDN controller can offer (Rehmani et al. [8]):

- *Programmability:* this feature is an added value that SDN brings to SG. For instance, appropriate decisions (dynamically changeable) can be taken, in situations when a specific link should be used, based on differences in SG communication traffic. However, an open research issue is related to the fact that different SG components might use different protocols and are based on different standards. Therefore, the SDN controller should be able to handle diverse communication technologies. This issue can be solved by taking benefit from the abstraction capability of the SDN architecture (data plane is abstracted at the control plane level). This separation can also be exploited in SG, in terms of management and communication support.
- *SDN independence on vendor specific data plane solutions:* SG can implement and run diverse applications, networking technologies, and protocols.
- *Powerful traffic management*: SDN controller can naturally identify data flows, i.e., it can install appropriate flow tables in the forwarding nodes. The traffic flows are treated accordingly to their particular requirements; this allows the SG to meet some specific *Quality of Service* (QoS) requirements (in terms of reliability, delay, and throughput).

The SG operates on different types of traffic. The SDN controller can simultaneously identify the traffic types, and set priorities to the traffic flow by dynamically programming the SDN switches. However, there is an open issue on horizontal scalability, in terms of the number of devices in the vehicular network that can be managed by a single SDN controller.

IV. V2G Charging/Discharging Solutions

A. Charging Coordination

A critical issue faced by V2G technology is how to coordinate a large number of EVs via the aggregator to perform charging or discharging actions, in order to offer an efficient service. This problem is a challenging one because it is hard for the aggregator to directly control the charging/discharging activities of each EV individually. Moreover, the privacy of the EVs owners should be met (some of them would not want to disclose their personal activities).

To solve this problem, Wang et al. [3] defined for an EV a parameter named WTP (Fan et al. [10]). They formulated the V2G adjuvant services and applied methods of the contract theory (Laffont et al. [11]). A framework has been developed for distributed coordination of the EVs activities (charging/ discharging). The aggregator can coordinate the EVs and also can increase EVs revenue. One main objective is to reach a balance between power supplier and consumer. Some numerical results of their framework show that this solution can make a higher income to the aggregator.

From our point of view, the work in [3] can further continue in our future work by simulating the model and make a comparison between practical and theoretical results. Also, the location awareness of the EVs by the SG is required to apply in this model. Therefore, the SG will be able to send a request to the EVs based on demand.

B. Multicast

In multicast communication, the information is sent to multiple receivers (e.g. users) in the network. In term of SG, multicasting has been used to distribute time-critical information such as control instructions or measurement data from the Phasor Measurement Units (PMUs). Generally, one PMU is deployed on a substation. Where, PMUs are responsible for monitoring the level of voltage and phasor angle of the transmission lines. Then, this information is collected by different PMUs and sent to a Phasor Data Concentrator (PDC). Then, this collected measurement data forwarded by the PDC to the control centre of the service [8].

In wide area monitoring systems, the PMUs measure information of current and voltage current and this measured information is multicasted to the control centre for immediate actions. Also, multicast can be used to inform a large number of consumers to turn-off their appliances at peak time, in order to manage and control the power level in the SG. In the substation, the multicast communication can distribute an emergency alert across substation Local Area Networks (LANs). In SDN-Based SG, multicast has been applied to V2G networks, PMUs, and substation communication.

The EVs can be considered as moving power storage which may support to supply power to entities where is energy is required. In a functional of V2G network, several sensors are installed at *Charging Stations* (CSs) as well on the EVs itself. These sensors help the EVs owners to monitor the charging situations of their vehicles. Consequently, by sharing this information of sensing to the V2G network, the global power grid can be stabilised. For example, the SG can schedule the charging/discharging at EVs, based on the power grid demand. This makes necessary that the V2G knows the battery status of EVs and their SOC. Through multicasting, the V2G can instruct the EVs and implement the regulations relating SOC.

Li et al. [6] proposed a battery status sensing by a software-defined multicast (BSS-SDM) scheme, the EVs access to the SG system for charging or discharging operation, controlled by the SD-V2G controller. During the power transition, the SD-V2G controller directly communicates via *Southbound Interface* (SBI) with data plane. The data plane is distributed devices and contains different devices: routers, Road Side Units (RSUs), smart meters, EVs, smart sensors, etc.).

The central SD-V2G controller includes functions of monitoring and controlling the EVs sensors. SD It supports the V2G multicast in order to support EVs mobility, as well to provide a capability for dynamic configuration. The simulation results show that the BSS-SDM scheme could reduce the average delay time of the V2G operation.

C. Type of Charging

Management of the regulation charging is required for the SG (especially when the number of EVs is high), in order to avoid unregulated charging that could lead to grid overload and even provoke SG breakdown. A solution to this problem is to design EVs to support the SG aiming to achieve a balance for the SG (Wang et al. [12]). Another problem is how to balance between the charging demand and the capability of service while a large number of EVs are onboard.

There are two types of charging; wired and wireless charging technologies. These two technologies have advantages of increasing the efficiency of charging and provide a bidirectional power transition. Wang et al. [13] introduced a Demand-Side Management (DSM) scheme for the wireless charging, showing that in this way the process of wireless charging can be easier and economical. Integrating both of wired and wireless charging technology into the SG required an extensive communication network to implement the DSM scheme for the EVs keeping the stability of the grid in the real time.

By investigating the advantages of SDN, Sun et al. [5] proposed a framework of Software-defined Green (SD-G), which provides both wired and wireless charging and efficient charging management. The objective is to evaluate the SD-Based EVs charging network. The architecture of SD-G framework contains three planes: physical, control, and application plane. The EVs and SG networks have both elements in the physical plane while the control plane is responsible for control, of the data and power flow. The centre of intelligent decision is served by the application plane. The EV owner will get specific information about the SG to practice the charging decision.

The simulations performed by Sun et al. [5] attempted a comparison between two cases: with SDN and without SDN control. The result shows that the demand setting time and the cost of SG operation for nodes can also be controlled.

V. A General SDN-Based V2G Framework

The increasing number of EVs or Plug-in Electric Vehicles (PEVs) and Internet of Thing (IoT) devices, and their interaction with the SG need further study to improve the efficiency, reliability, and stability of the system operation. The integration of EVs and SG has a feature of increasing the power storage through V2G technology and corporate the SG with *Renewable Energy Source-*

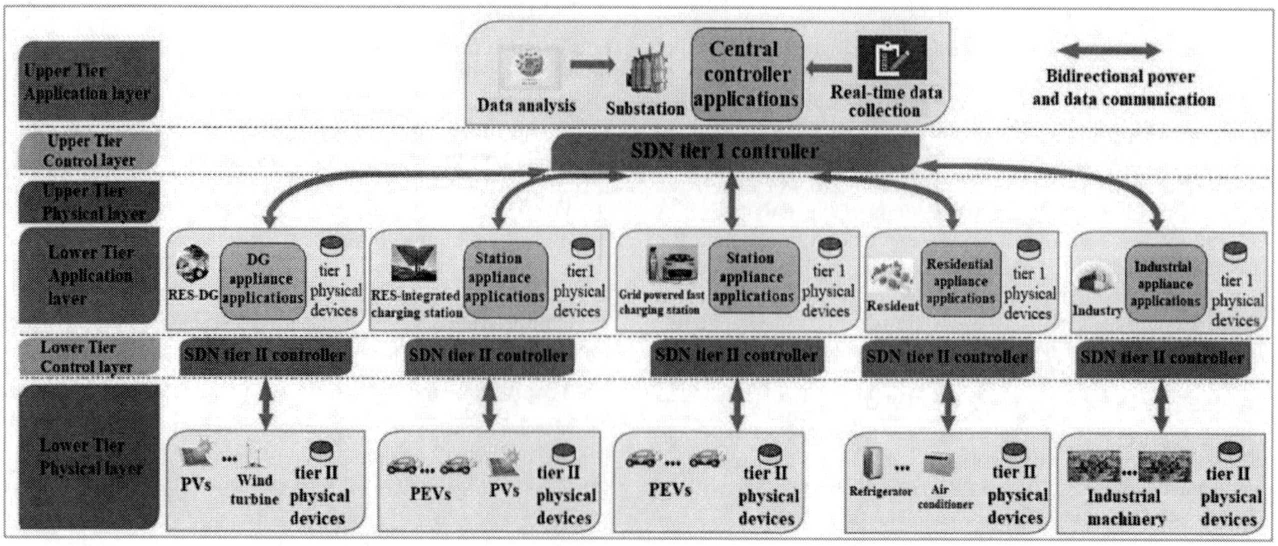

Figure 2.The SDN Framework for the distribution system in the PEV integrated SG [7].

Distributed Generations (RES-DGs). Moreover, with the integration of EVs with RES-DG into the power system, SG faces the challenges of increasing large numbers of EVs and IoT, which will affect the system scalability. Also, the connection of EV, RES-DG, IoT, sensors, etc. to the network require a hard/effort to configure the devices and maintain a convenient cost at the same time.

To address the challenges mentioned above, many contributions proposed general solutions, to cover any gaps and satisfy the consumers. The approach adopted in [7] (see Figure 2) comprises a two-tier SDN based framework for the integration of EV with SG, aiming to provide a scalable and stable system. The distribution system power flow has two tiers. First, the power flows from sub-stations to primary feeders to provide power for large-size commercial and industrial loads. Then, the power flows from primary feeders to secondary feeders to supply the small-size resident loads.

Consequently, the SDN framework also has two tiers. The tier-1 controller is located in the substation to have a global system view, while the tier-2 controller is managed by every aggregator in primary feeders to perform the power and data operations. SDN controllers on each tier collect the information frequently. This information is analysed by the application layer to achieve optimal operation then, the application layer sends new instructions to the devices in the physical layer to update their commands.

A case study [7] based on PEVs and RES-DGs can contribute to identifying the requirement of applying SDN

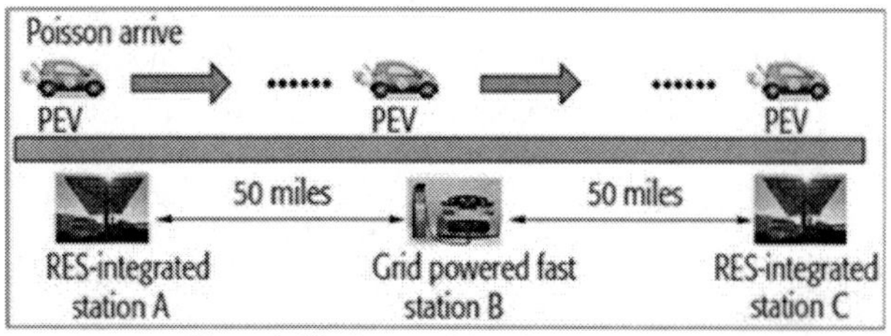

Figure 3. The layout of fast charging stations [7].

into the SG. Three fast charging stations (A B and C) are deployed along a highway and distance between each one is 50 miles, (figure 3). The stations A and C get power generated from solar radiation, while B is a powered by the It has been supposed that PEVs arrive at each station following a Poisson process through hourly variant arrival rates. The charging stations send requests to the passing PEVs for power supplement.

The first case considers 15 per cent of PEVs entering the station, following a uniform distribution. In this hypothesis, most PEV resources are wasted. The arrival rate of PEV in the stations (A and C) are increases, while the grid powered station (B) does not require any PEV, because the grid powered station is stable and consistent source for the V2G services. Note that the cloudy station would require more PEVs than the sunny station.

The second case applies the SDN lower-tier operation. The passing PEVs can be fully used to help the stations to complete their V2G services. The SDN coordinated performance is improved, while the PEV arrival rate increases. The cloudy station requires far more PEVs than the other two stations. The SDN-based system can analyse the service requests depending on weather conditions; it is able to direct more PEVs to the most needed station to help the V2G service.

VI. Open Research Issue And Challenges

Given that V2G is a new technology, many frameworks have been proposed; however, some of them have not yet been implemented, given many open issues. In this section, we identify the challenges of the V2G technology from the communication side in order to guide for our future work investigations.

A. Wired and Wireless Charging

In practice, many different charging standards have been adopted (in single wireless or wired charging technology). A unified charging standard would be necessary to be studied and defined. Wireless EVs charging may have two significant behaviours; static and dynamic charging. By applying the dynamic charging in the road, one can reduce the traffic in the SG. If both of wireless/wired charging are supported by EVs/SG, a selection decision is required to get optimal charging operations.

B. Synchronising Between Tiers

The aggregators in primary-feeders [7] obtain and implement the instructions from the upper-tier. On the other hand, they obtain requests from the physical devices in the lower-tier, and provide suitable responses. Unsynchronised data transmission of instructions from upper-tier and the lower-tier requests may cause a lack of consistency at the controllers in lower-tier. In some situation, the analysis process at controllers in the lower-tier possibly will meet different operation circumstances so that the controller will be confused. The problem of balancing and evaluating process between the instructions in upper-tier and requests in the lower-tier, will be study and simulate in our future work. Additionally, we will apply a simulation for the charging and discharging decision and control process using the tools of OMNET++.

C. SDN-Based V2G and Energy Internet (EI)

A novel concept has been proposed recently called Energy Internet (EI), aiming to connect numbers of SG devices for the purpose of management of the power flows. Similar to traditional internet, the EI has routers and the idea is to find the optimal routs and/or paths. That approach will achieve high efficiency in the power distribution. Also, EI has Local Area Networks (LAN), called (e-LAN) in the Energy Internet standard. The power routers are responsible for power flows management between various SG devices and, in this regard, Wang et al. [14] proposed different algorithms of energy routing. Chelmis et al. [15], Zhang et al. [16], and Hou et al. [17] presented some results about the integrating EI and SDN; this novel concept still requires hard efforts in order to achieve an efficient and reliable system operation of SDN-Based Energy internet. For instance, it is hard for a single power router to have the information of the entire network status at a short time. Therefore, the real global smart control is not achieved yet.

D. Integrating Fog and Cloud (Foud) For 5G-Enabled V2G Networks

To deal with the high mobility of EV, the computing resources provided by mobile computing devices are integrated with the provisional Fog dynamically. So, the performance of the V2G applications and services in Foud computing is affected by the mobility of EVs. Efficient *resource management* can be implemented by dynamically integrating the mobile computing resources with provisional fog, and integrating cloud computing with temporary fog (Foud), which is constitute a significant open issue needs to study further. Also, integrating between Foud and two-tiers framework could be a useful solution to reduce the large data in the SDN controller.

E. Failures Detection

A central SDN controller may face failure issues, such as breakdown, resource limitation by a malicious switch, and so on, that is could be causing a loss of SDN controller service. Therefore, solution for this problem is required. Also, fast failure detection and recovery using the OpenFlow should be analysed; in the situation of communication link failure, the packets should be routed to additional rout with/without asking the SDN controller.

VII. CONCLUSION

The novel V2G technology is still facing many problems and challenges, especially from the communication perspective. The SDN is a powerful solution to have a global view on the network. It can also solve problems management and control for V2G service. The EVs represent an available power storage distribution to the grid based on the demand, integrating the SDN in the SG; one can control the EVs onboard and coordinate their charging status. In this paper, we have discussed some open research issues concerning the integrations of SDN in SG. Multicasting and scheme of SDN-Based V2G will be considered in our future work. Finally, we have identified and discussed some challenges, open research issues, and future research directions related to SDN-based V2G.

REFERENCES

[1] W. Kempton and J. Tomić, "Vehicle-to-grid power fundamentals: Calculating capacity and net revenue," *J. Power Sources*, vol. 144, no. 1, pp. 268–279, 2005.

[2] S. Habib, M. Kamran, and U. Rashid, "Impact analysis of vehicle-to-grid technology and charging strategies of electric vehicles on distribution networks - A review," *J. Power Sources*, vol. 277, pp. 205–214, 2015.

[3] K. Wang *et al.*, "Distributed Energy Management for Vehicle-To-Grid Networks," *IEEE Netw.*, vol. 31, no. 2, pp. 22–28, 2017.

[4] S. Zhang, Q. Li, J. Wu, J. Li, and G. Li, "A security mechanism for software-defined networking based communications in vehicle-to-grid," *2016 4th IEEE Int. Conf. Smart Energy Grid Eng. SEGE 2016*, pp. 386–391, 2016.

[5] Y. Sun, X. Hu, X. Liu, X. He, and K. Wang, "A Software-Defined Green Framework for Hybrid EV-Charging Networks," *IEEE Commun. Mag.*, vol. 55, no. 11, pp. 62–69, 2017.

[6] G. Li, J. Wu, J. Li, T. Ye, and R. Morello, "Battery status sensing software-defined multicast for v2g regulation in smart grid," *IEEE Sens. J.*, vol. 17, no. 23, pp. 7838–7848, 2017.

[7] N. Chen, M. Wang, N. Zhang, X. S. Shen, and D. Zhao, "SDN-Based Framework for the PEV Integrated Smart Grid," *IEEE Netw.*, vol. 31, no. 2, pp. 14–21, 2017.

[8] M. H. Rehmani, A. Davy, B. Jennings, and C. Assi, "Software Defined Networks based Smart Grid Communication: A Comprehensive Survey," pp. 1–26, 2018.

[9] M. Tao, K. Ota, and M. Dong, "Foud: Integrating Fog and Cloud for 5G-Enabled V2G Networks," *IEEE Netw.*, vol. 31, no. 2, pp. 8–13, 2017.

[10] Z. Fan, "A Distributed Demand Response Algorithm and Its Application to PHEV Charging in Smart Grids," *IEEE Trans. Smart Grid*, vol. 3, no. 3, pp. 1280–1290, Sep. 2012.

[11] J. Laffont and D. Martimort, *The theory of incentives: the principal-agent model*, Princeton University press, 2009.

[12] K. Wang *et al.*, "A Survey on Energy Internet: Architecture, Approach, and Emerging Technologies," *IEEE Syst. J.*, vol. 12, no. 3, pp. 2403–2416, Sep. 2018.

[13] T. V. Theodoropoulos, I. G. Damousis, and A. J. Amditis, "Demand-

Side Management ICT for Dynamic Wireless EV Charging," *IEEE Trans. Ind. Electron.*, vol. 63, no. 10, pp. 6623–6630, Oct. 2016.

[14] R. Wang, J. Wu, Z. Qian, Z. Lin, and X. He, "A Graph Theory Based Energy Routing Algorithm in Energy Local Area Network," *IEEE Trans. Ind. Informatics*, vol. 13, no. 6, pp. 3275–3285, Dec. 2017.

[15] C. Chelmis, K. Rajgopal, and V. K. Prasanna, "Software defined connected prosumer communities," in *2016 IEEE 3rd World Forum on Internet of Things (WF-IoT)*, 2016, pp. 684–685.

[16] Q. Zhang, H. Wang, and Y. Song, "Efficiency evaluation algorithm of SDN for energy internet," in *2017 7th IEEE International Conference on Electronics Information and Emergency Communication (ICEIEC)*, 2017, pp. 292–295.

[17] W. Hou *et al.*, "Cooperative Mechanism for Energy Transportation and Storage in Internet of Energy.," *IEEE Access, 2017, vol. 5, pp. 1363-1375.*

The Strategic Role of Inter-Container Communications in RAN Deployment Scenarios

Carlo Vitucci
Ericsson AB
Stockholm, Sweden
Email: carlo.vitucci@ericsson.com

Luca Abeni, Tommaso Cucinotta and Mauro Marinoni
Scuola Superiore Sant'Anna
Pisa, Italy
Email: {name.surname}@santannapisa.com

***Abstract*—This paper elaborates on the importance of having efficient inter-container communications at the edge of the network in Software Defined Network – Network Function Virtualization (SDN-NFV) architectures, when deploying services close to the end-user, due to the broad range of bandwidth and latency requirements as coming from novel scenarios in the 5th telecommunication generation (5G). This results in a proposed service deployment framework that is exploited within the Virtualized Radio Access Network (V-RAN) split architecture, a scenario where the crucial role of efficient communications becomes evident. After a short comparison among common technologies available today for efficient inter-containers communications, this paper identifies primary areas of improvement for future research.**

***Keywords*–5G; V-RAN; Edge computing; Server at the edge; Service deployment; Inter-containers communication channel.**

I. Introduction

Nowadays, the 5th telecommunication generation (5G) is at its first deliveries, with trials running everywhere in the world. Telecommunication operators and manufacturers have a clear understanding of the 5G architecture and its benefits [1]. Indeed, 5G brings significant innovations, with a new architecture based on a mindset shift from connection-centric to service-centric [2]. There are different 5G solutions offered by telecommunication operators or infrastructure providers, and all of them agree on the vision of 5G enabling a new era where vertical services can be deployed end-to-end in the network. In such a view, the role of the edge of the network, and especially the Radio Access Network (RAN), is strategic. In the 5G architecture, there is a strong need to deploy a wide range of vertical services with low-latency requirements, in order to increase the Quality of Experience (QoE) for the end-user. This means flexible deployment across the physical infrastructure, as achievable by embracing the Software Defined Network – Network Function Virtualization (SDN-NFV) paradigm, and optimized communications at all levels, where traditional Virtual Machines (VMs) have decidedly been superseded by containers thanks to their reduced overheads.

Optimizing end-to-end vertical services in 5G can take advantage of SDN-NFV, so that having a multitude of nodes, e.g., data-center, core network or RAN nodes, managed by a (logically) centralized controller, allows for achieving high flexibility in the network architecture, enabling an optimum deployment of services. However, this also introduces a number of challenges, because the characteristics, requirements and acceptable latencies can be quite heterogeneous for the various nodes, where distance from the RAN plays a crucial role [3] [4] [5]. Novel Virtualized RAN (V-RAN) solutions may also tackle the important foreseen explosion of power consumption, especially in urban environments with high population density [6]. The new architecture for 5G in the RAN domain could be not mature enough to allow seamless deployments. For this reason, the most important operators worldwide established the O-RAN alliance [7] to drive the technology evolution, attracting all the technology providers too.

The rest of this paper is organized as follows: Section II presents the background about service deployment, while Section III proposes an overview on the related 5G issues and Section IV focuses on PoP transparency. In Section V key inter-container communication solutions are compared. The paper is concluded with some final remarks and an overview of future works in Sections VI and VII, respectively.

II. Background on Service Deployment

It the SDN-NFV architecture, as described by European Telecommunications Standards Institute (ETSI) [8], the two concepts work together to provide, manage and control the underlying common end to end infrastructure (topology view) where to deploy, secure and supervise any type of vertical service (service view), as shown in Figure 1.

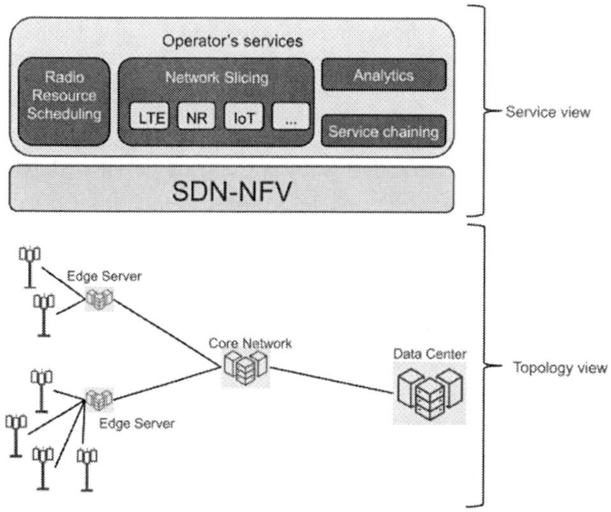

Figure 1. Example of a SDN-NFV architecture views.

The service view shows how the SDN-NFV Management and Orchestration (MANO) framework deploys different vertical services. These are composed into service-chains, "common bricks" that let new services be deployed quicker. Moreover, establishing and supervising communication channels between two or more services is needed to provide security and protect sensitive data from malicious access. A Virtualized Network Function (VNF) deployment is the responsibility of the MANO framework, where any infrastructure resource is assigned to a service through network slice assignments. Indeed, network slicing is an End-to-End network characterization of a service deployment and is based on resource allocation and control. Any available resource in any node shall be manageable via resource slices. Then, slice definition is actually the assignment of a different network, computing, storage, and radio resources to a vertical service, from access to data center node (see Figure 2).

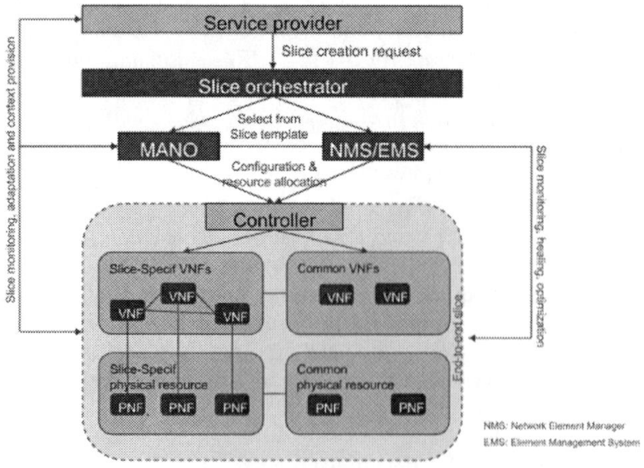

Figure 2. End-to-End slice allocation and control, from [9].

Radio Resources are critical for the RAN, so while bringing the SDN-NFV paradigm into the RAN, constraining placement locations through the Point of Presence (PoP) [10] assignment is mandatory for latency control. This paper is not concerned about how slices are assigned, but it focuses on the need for a *slice definition that includes the function-to-function communication requirements* as a crucial resource to manage. It is critical to consider appropriately the various options that are available to accelerate said communications both in hardware and in software, among services deployed throughout the various servers within the edge infrastructure. For example, the computing allocation in edge servers, and so the definition itself of computing slicing, may be based on radio access service characteristics like bandwidth, latency, and deadline [11]. Network slicing in multiple domains is a foundational building block in the SDN-NFV architecture [12].

Therefore, an effective service framework needs to handle [13] service deployment along with resource allocation and control, coupled with proper network slice definition and management (see Figure 3). To this purpose, it is essential to frame the slice definition in the context of the VNF file descriptors [10]. This makes a service framework usable in the context of service deployment and for the RAN.

III. 5G, SDN-NFV and V-RAN

The RAN evolution needed to meet the 5G expectations is entirely driven by the new challenging requirements [5]:

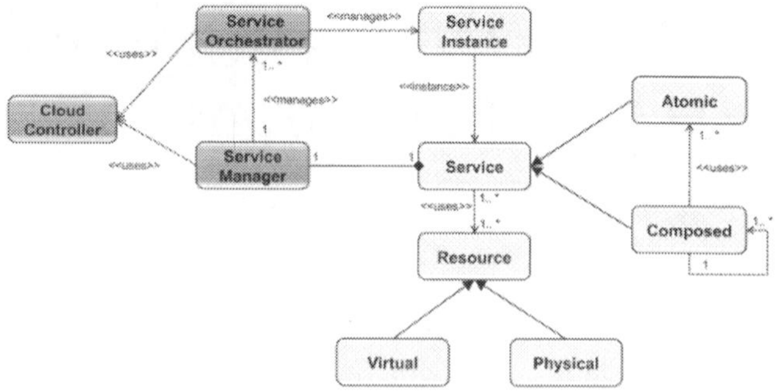

Figure 3. The service deployment framework, from [13].

latency constraints, radio bandwidth and available resources (computing, storage, and connectivity). This is a bare consequence of the primary 5G goal: support a wide range of services, from Internet of Things (IoT) to Machine-Type Communication (MTC) or Machine-to-Machine (M2M), that look promising also in the perspective of expanding operators' opportunities. In such a scenario, RAN architectures need to evolve, embracing more and more reconfigurable radio platforms, flexibility in resource management via a fully compliant SDN-NFV framework (towards V-RAN), and the use of commercial off-the-shelf hardware when possible, to reduce the cost of the infrastructure [14]. In this context, the RAN internal protocol-layer functional decomposition is widely accepted today and brings to have a wide range of deployment options to explore. Possible solutions involve the RAN functions spread throughout the Radio Unit (RU), Distributed Unit (DU) or Centralized Unit (CU) in the 5G case, as exemplified in Figure 4, or throughout the Remote Radio Head (RRH) and Baseband Unit (BBU) in the 4G case. The

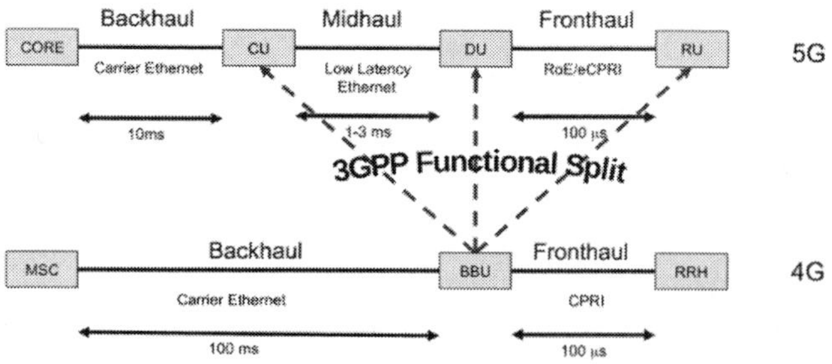

Figure 4. Function view of maximum delays in 5G with respect to 4G.

RAN functional split point can be chosen as a compromise between higher flexibility and higher complexity, in a range that moves from the so-called "Distributed RAN" to the so-called "Centralized RAN" [15]. A specific terminology has been defined [16] to describe the RAN functional split options:

- LLS: Low layer Split; defines the connection and interface between Radio and central units. It is based on CPRI, eCPRI or RoE;
- HLS; High Layer Split; defines the splitting of the internal protocol stack in a typical base-station between distributed and centralized units. Depending on splitting option implemented, interface can be F1, F1-C and F1-U or E1;

- RU: Radio Unit. Contains all RAN functions placed below the LLS interface;
- DU: Distributed Unit. Contains all RAN functions places between LLS and HLS interfaces;
- CU: Centralized Unit. Contains all RAN function above HLS interface and terminates inter-RAN (X2, Xn) interfaces.

Figure 5 shows the 5G splitting architecture concept and the max latency value (based on IEEE 1914.3 [17]), where a proper configuration can be chosen according to the available latency budget for the service [18]. It is worth to note that, in

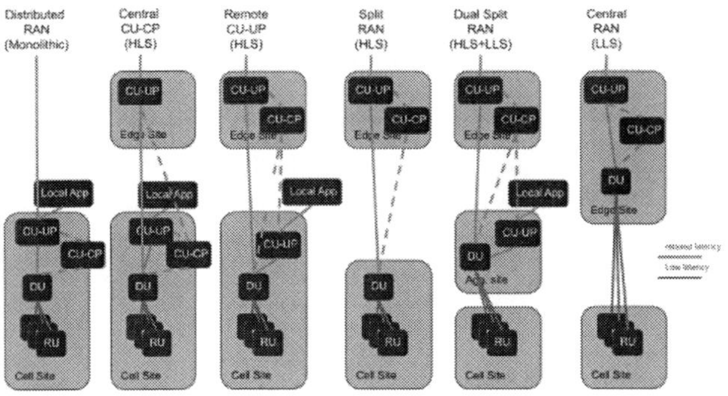

Figure 5. Functional placement scenarios.

the resulting architecture, different functions are not required to be placed at different physical locations. Indeed, where the RU, DU, CU-CP (Control Plane) and CU-UP (User Plane) may be placed depends on:

- the operators' requirements;
- the transport network topology;
- the physical site constraints;
- the latency and capacity infrastructure limitations.

In other words, theoretically, Radio Service Providers should design their split architecture to guarantee all suggested deployment options, unless this needs a too costly orchestration software complexity.

IV. PoP Transparency

The different placement scenarios can also be seen as a modular migration path from 4G to 5G or, in other words, a smooth method for the introduction of 5G. Technical pros and cons of the RAN functional split are well known and have already been described in literature [5] [19]. Deployments are normally based on OS-level virtualization (i.e., containers) in order to support optimized resource usage [11]: the cost of virtualization is minimized while at the same time the compute slice can be managed at a fine-grain resolution level, allowing a higher degree of flexibility in matching aggressive end-to-end deadline constraints. However, a service deployment approach to 5G architecture implementations implies that, for example, the blue boxes in Figure 5 can be containers managed according to the full flexibility of a service deployment framework. This flexibility in placement throughout the available PoPs in the physical infrastructure needs to be done *transparently* from the applications' viewpoint, and the mapping between the logical topology of containers and their interconnections, on top of the physical infrastructure and PoPs, needs to happen exploiting the descriptive capabilities of MANO VNF descriptors (see Figure 6).

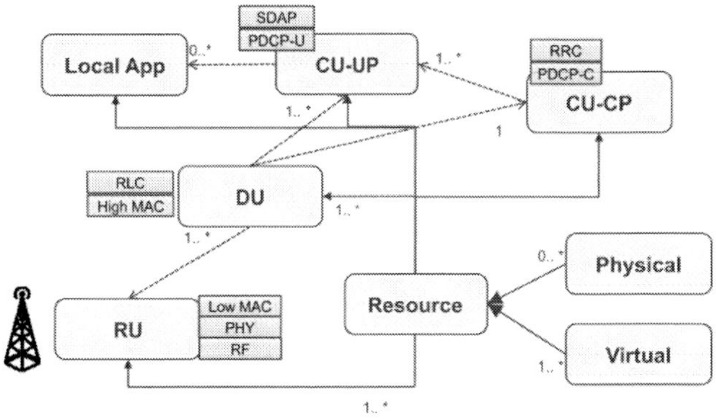

Figure 6. Service chain for functional placement scenarios.

With this new service-oriented mindset, containers need to use communication primitives that:

- are virtualized, so as to be slice definable;
- are always providing the same virtual port to a container, independently of where containers are housed in the infrastructure (see Figure 7);
- are designed in a performance-oriented way, i.e., inter-container communications exhibit the lowest possible latency, fully using special hardware acceleration and software/OS/kernel features to let that be possible.

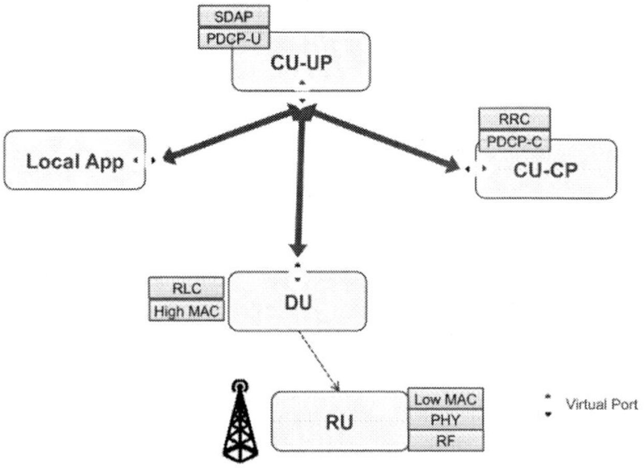

Figure 7. The Virtual Port concept representation.

It is thus crucial to optimize inter-container communications. From a general point of view, this is a key enabler for a RAN solution supporting all possible deployment scenarios.

V. Inter-Container Communication Performance

Network connections between containers and external nodes have traditionally been implemented by using virtual ethernet pairs and software bridges / virtual switches. When a virtual ethernet pair is created, the kernel creates two software Network Interface Controllers (NICs) (there is no physical NIC attached to them) connected point-to-point (packets sent to one of the two interfaces are received by the other, and vice-versa). To allow a containerized application to communicate with the external world, one of the two interfaces is inserted in the container namespace, while the other one is attached to a software bridge or a virtual switch (such as openvswitch or similar). This means that, in order to exchange data between applications executing in two containers running on the same physical machine, the following data-path is used:

- The first application sends a network packet using send(), sendto(), write() or similar on the virtual ethernet visible in its namespace.
- The packet is copied from the application address space to the kernel space.
- The kernel networking code moves the packet to the software bridge or virtual switch, that forwards it to the other application.
- The second application receives the packet using recv(), recvfrom(), read() or similar on the virtual ethernet visible in its namespace.
- The packet is then copied from kernel space to the address space of the second application.

As it can be seen, this implies the invocation of at least two system calls, various switches from user-space to kernel space, at least two data copies, different scheduling decisions, and so on. As a result, the networking performance could be penalized. This can be a substantial limitation in supporting the desired 5G functional split, that could be reduced exploiting different communication technologies.

For example, for communications between containers located on the same physical node, it would be possible to map a shared memory region in the address spaces of the two containerized applications and use it for exchanging data. This can be done in a transparent way by using the Intel Data Plane Development Kit (DPDK) framework [20].

DPDK provides a set of libraries originally designed to use a NIC in user space, without passing through the kernel every time a packet is sent or received. Moreover, DPDK allows for sending/receiving packets without relying on hardware interrupts generated by the NIC. This is done by mapping in the application memory the NIC buffer ring and control registers, and directly accessing them at the application level (polling on the NIC registers instead of waiting for interrupts). These techniques allow for a dramatic decrease in the overheads, increasing the achieved throughput and decreasing the latency. DPDK also provides support for virtual NICs, that can be useful for inter-container communications. In particular, it provides drivers for virtio and vhost-user.

Virtio [21] [22] is a para-virtualization standard, also defining virtual NICs based on virtual queues of received and transmitted packets, that can be shared between guest and host. Virtio network devices are generally implemented by hypervisors such as qemu/kvm, that can rely on external services such as vhost [23] to move packets between guest and host, or between different guests on the same host.

The vhost functionalities can be implemented either in kernel space or in user-space. In the former case, the vhost-net kernel module is used, that creates a kernel thread to move packets. In the latter case, a user-space process is responsible [24] for implementing the vhost functionalities, mapping the shared buffers in guest memory. In this approach, known as vhost-user, the user-space process implementing the vhost functionalities uses a UNIX domain socket for low-bandwidth signalling.

DPDK provides a virtio driver that is able to connect to virtio-net virtual interfaces, and a vhost-user driver that can be used by user-space processes (for example, virtual switches) to implement the vhost-user functionalities connecting different VMs. But the vhost-user driver can also be used to implement the virtual interfaces a virtio driver can directly connect to. Hence, a DPDK-based virtual switch running in the host can create virtio-net interfaces which DPDK-based applications running in the containers can connect to. Figure 8 shows the inter-container communication support provided by the presented approaches.

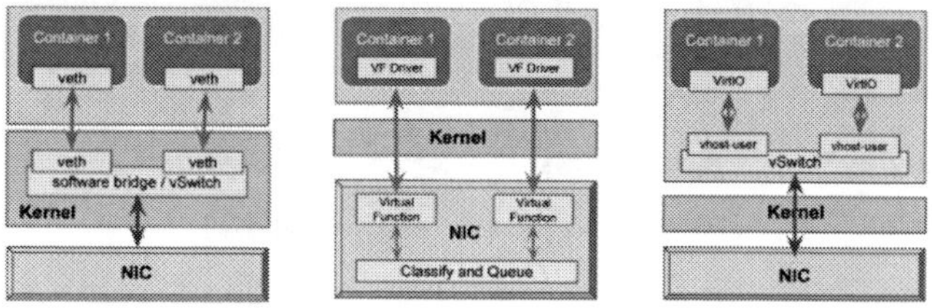

(a) (b) (c)

Figure 8. Inter-container virtual switching: (a) software-only solution; (b) using SR-IOV support; (c) using DPDK with vhost in user mode.

In order to evaluate the impact of the overhead introduced by the packet transmission mechanism (and the advantages of using different software architectures), we performed some experiments on an Intel(R) Xeon(R) CPU E5-2640 at 2.40GHz.

The first experiment is designed to measure the overhead caused by the system calls needed to send packets through virtual Ethernet pairs. It is based on two applications sending and receiving small User Datagram Protocol (UDP) packets, located on the same physical machine: the first application (running in an lxc container) sends packets at the maximum possible rate, and the second application (running in a different container) measures the received packet rate. Even without using a software bridge or switch (inserting one of the two virtual Ethernets in the first container and the other one in the second container), the maximum achievable packet rate is about 310000 packets per second (pps). Considering a payload of 64 bytes, this results in a throughput of less than 160 Mbps.

To evaluate the advantages of using the DPDK virtio and vhost-user drivers (running in user space), we performed a second experiment using two lxc-based containers and the "testpmd" DPDK application:

- an instance of testpmd running in the host provides two virtio interfaces (one per container) using vhost-net, and forwards packets between them, acting as a bridge;
- an instance of testpmd in the first container produces packets and sends them on the first virtio interface;
- an instance of testpmd in the second container receives packets from the second virtio interface.

Using this setup, it has been measured that the applications can transmit about 12800000 pps (considering 64-bytes packets, this is about 6.5Gbps). Note that the "testpmd" application connecting the two containers is not a real switch, but a DPDK application that is used only to test the drivers' performance.

Vector Packet Processing (VPP) [25] is a technology used in the virtual switch provided by the Fast Data Project (FD.io) [26]. In a standard switch, each packet is received, processed, and forwarded before receiving the next packet from the NIC queue, and this way of serving packets can have bad effects on cache locality (and on the forwarding performance). Hence, VPP receives, processes, and forwards packets in batches, resulting more cache friendly and achieving a higher networking performance.

We performed a third experiment using VPP (which can be used as a real bridge, switch, or router) instead of testpmd to connect the two containers. This experiment, performed with the goal of evaluating the performance of a complete switching solution (and not only the performance of the userspace drivers) revealed that the packet rate drops to about 6400000pps (3.27Gbps). Such a lower performance is due to the real switch logic that is present in VPP and not in testpmd.

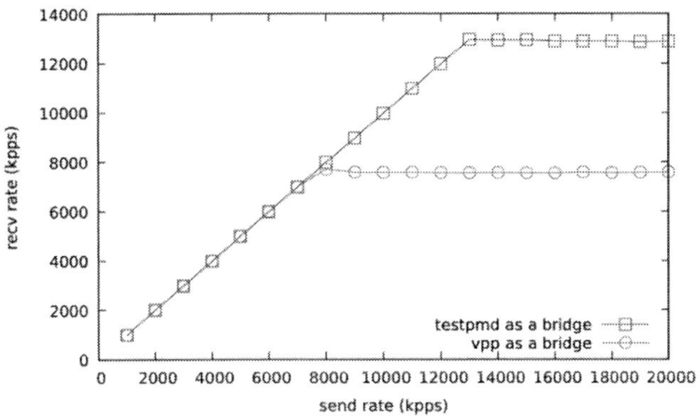

Figure 9. Throughput of testpmd and VPP (in kilo packets per second) as a function of the input packet rate.

To better characterize the performance of the DPDK polling drivers (evaluated using the "testpmd" application as a bridge) and of a DPDK-based switch (we used VPP in this case), we repeated the previous experiments changing the rate at which the 64-byte packets are generated. Figure 9 shows the packet rate (in kpps) that "testpmd" and VPP are able to forward as a function of the input packet rate. While testpmd manages to handle 13 million packets per second, VPP sustains only 8 million pps, due to its higher functional complexity.

VI. Conclusions

SDN-NFV enables unprecedented flexibility and ease of maintenance for service chains deployments, but the achievable end-to-end performance is greatly affected by what mechanisms are used for the underlying communications among micro services, regardless of these being hosted as traditional Virtual Machines or containers. Solutions based on containers are becoming the de-facto standard for efficient usage of resources, and inter-container communications can bootstrap an effective Radio Access Technology (RAT) software architecture for 5G. This becomes even more important for critical latency-sensitive RAT services, that cannot be hosted anywhere, being constrained to be located not too far from their needed radio elements. In this context, it is also possible to leverage the specification of the PoP through VNF file descriptors, so as to achieve a RAT service chain configuration corresponding to the needed trade-off between distributed and centralized RAN solutions. However, as shown elsewhere [27] and remarked in this paper, the performance of container-to-container communications has a great potential to affect the finally achievable End-to-End performance, also depending on the hardware accelerations and software optimizations that are available in the underlying infrastructure. Therefore, inter-container communication is a key element to realize 5G implementations fully exploiting the potential of SDN-NFV architectures, where the work presented in this paper, including the general overview of the involved technological hardware and software solutions, along with the experimental comparison among a few of them, is just a starting point for a more structured in-depth study, needed to design effective and efficient solutions that become enablement factors for future 5G scenarios.

VII. Future Work

Concerning directions for future work on the topic, additional experimentation evaluating the impact of different software and hardware architectures on the performance of inter-container communications is needed. For example, the use of SR-IOV capable NICs has the advantage of off-loading CPU packet-processing workload to the NIC [28], but in the case of communications among entities on the same physical node this might be easier to handle in software, avoiding unnecessary bus cycles. This has to be evaluated also in light of the fact that high-performance software-based switching solutions within hypervisors and operating systems is already going towards dropping the support of the full set of features of a switch, in favour of more static (but faster) solutions like macvlan/macvtap [29] or Virtual Ethernet Bridge (VEB) [30] [31]. Indeed, static solutions such as macvtap have been shown [32] to perform better in high-packet rate scenarios than more dynamic and flexible solutions like full-featured virtual switching. Further trade-off points between performance and flexibility might become possible in presence of specific hardware features, like full SR-IOV support. It is also interesting to perform additional experimental results, and compare them with benchmarks already appeared in literature [33] [34]. In this context, the optimality of the solution has to face additional possible constraints, like the ones behind the Virtual Ethernet Port Aggregator (VEPA) [31] and its use with switches supporting the hairpin-mode. This forces packets to reach the external adjacent switch even in case of local communications, due to the need for exposing all traffic, including the internal one, to the networking monitoring and management layer in a uniform way, however the performance is expected to lower in this case. Also, in the context of high-performance packet processing for NFV, approaches that are gaining popularity are the kernel-bypass ones [35] [36], that do not rely on traditional TCP/IP networking support by the operating system or hypervisor, whilst direct access to the hardware NIC is preferred (either its physical or virtual functions if SR-IOV is in place), on top of which custom and optimized user-space networking stacks are built. Having the possibility to control such features from a high level, such as through VNF MANO descriptors, is all but straightforward [37], so additional work is needed along such direction.

REFERENCES

[1] "Open Network Survey Report," NetGate, White Paper, February 2018. [Online]. Available: https://www.netgate.com/resources/whitepapers/open-networking-survey-report.html

[2] "5G White Paper," NGMN Alliance, White Paper, February 2015. [Online]. Available: https://www.ngmn.org/fileadmin/ngmn/content/images/news/ngmn_news/NGMN_5G_White_Paper_V1_0.pdf

[3] "IMT vision – framework and overall objectives of the future of IMT for 2020 and beyond – International Telecommunication Union," ITU-R, Standard Recommendation I.2083-0, September 2015.

[4] Delivering an Integrated, Secure, and Radio-Aware 5G Transport Network. [Online]. Available: https://www.juniper.net/assets/us/en/local/pdf/solutionbriefs/3510647-en.pdf [retrieved: September, 2018]

[5] C. Vitucci and A. Larsson, "Flexible 5G Edge Server for Multi Industry Service Network," International Journal on Advances in Networks and Services, vol. 10, no. 3-4, 2017, pp. 55—65.

[6] "View on 5G Architecture – version 2.0," 5GPPP Architecture Working Group, Standard, December 2017. [Online]. Available: https://5g-ppp.eu/wp-content/uploads/2018/01/5G-PPP-5G-Architecture-White-Paper-Jan-2018-v2.0.pdf

[7] "Building the Next Generation RAN," O-RAN Alliance, White Paper, October 2018. [Online]. Available: https://static1.squarespace.com/static/5ad774cce74940d7115044b0/t/5bc79b371905f4197055e8c6/1539808057078/O-RAN+WP+FInal+181017.pdf

[8] "Network Functions Virtualisation (NFV); Use Cases," ETSI, Standard ETSI GS NFV 001, v.1.1.1, October 2013. [Online]. Available: https://www.etsi.org/deliver/etsi_gs/nfv/001_099/001/01.01.01_60/gs_nfv001v010101p.pdf

[9] A. Kaloxylos, "A Survey and an Analysis of Network Slicing in 5G Networks," IEEE Communications Standards Magazine, vol. 2, no. 1, March 2018, pp. 60–65.

[10] "Network Function Virtualisation (NFV); Management and Orchestration," ETSI, Standard ETSI GS NFV-MAN 001, v.1.1.1, December 2014. [Online]. Available: https://www.etsi.org/deliver/etsi_gs/NFV-MAN/001_099/001/01.01.01_60/gs_NFV-MAN001v010101p.pdf

[11] M. Marinoni, T. Cucinotta, L. Abeni, and C. Vitucci, "Allocation and Control of Computing Resources for Real-Time Virtual Network Functions," in Proc. of the international Symposium on Advances in Software Defined Networking and Network Function Virtualization (SoftNetworking 2018), April 2018, pp. 52–57.

[12] "5G End-to-End architecture Framework," NGMN Alliance, Standard 180226 NGMN E2EArchFramework V2.0.0, February 2018. [Online]. Available: https://www.ngmn.org/fileadmin/ngmn/content/downloads/Technical/2018/180226_NGMN_RANFSX_D1_V20_Final.pdf

[13] "D2.5 Final Overall Architecture Definition, Release 2," April 2015. [Online]. Available: https://cordis.europa.eu/docs/projects/cnect/9/318109/080/deliverables/001-318109MCND25renditionDownload.pdf

[14] C. Vitucci and A. Larsson, "SEED, A Server Platform for the Edge of the Network," in ICN 2017: The sixteenth Conference on Networks, April 2017, pp. 118–123.

[15] "Study on new radio access technology: Radio access architecture and interfaces," 3GPP, Standard 38.801, TR V14.0.0, March 2017. [Online]. Available: https://portal.3gpp.org/desktopmodules/Specifications/SpecificationDetails.aspx?specificationId=3056

[16] "MGMN Overview on 5G RAN Functional Decomposition," NGMN Alliance, Standard 180226 NGMN RANFSX D1 V20 Final, February 2018. [Online]. Available: https://www.ngmn.org/fileadmin/ngmn/content/downloads/Technical/2018/180226_NGMN_RANFSX_D1_V20_Final.pdf

[17] "IEEE Standard for Radio over Ethernet Encapsulations and Mappings," IEEE, Standard IEEE 1914.3-2, October 2018. [Online]. Available: https://standards.ieee.org/standard/1914_3-2018.html

[18] H. Gupta, D. Manicone, F. Giannone, K. Kondepu, A. Franklin, P. Castoldi, and L. Valcarenghi, "How much is fronthaul latency budget impacted by RAN virtualisation ?" in Proc. of the IEEE Conference on Network Function Virtualization and Software Defined Networks (NFV-SDN 2017), November 2017, pp. 315–320.

[19] J. Harrison and M. Do. Mobile Network Architecture for 5G Era - New C-RAN Architecture and distributed 5G Core. Netmanias. [Online]. Available: http://www.netmanias.com/en/post/blog/8153/5g-c-ranfronthaul-kt-korea-sdn-nfv-sk-telecom/mobile-networkarchitecture-for-5g-era-new-c-ran-architecture-and-distributed-5g-core (2015)

[20] Intel Corporation. Data Plane Development Kit (DPDK). [Online]. Available: http://www.dpdk.org [retrieved: 14 February, 2019]

[21] R. Russell, "VIRTIO: Towards a De-facto Standard for Virtual I/O Devices," ACM SIGOPS Operating Systems Review, vol. 42, no. 5, 2008, pp. 95–103.

[22] R. Russell, M. Tsirkin, C. Huck, and P. Moll, "Virtual I/O Device (VRTIO) Version 1.0," OASIS Specification Committee, Standard, 2015. [Online]. Available: http://docs.oasis-open.org/virtio/virtio/v1.0/csd01/virtio-v1.0-csd01.html

[23] M. S. Tsirkin, "vhost-net and virtio-net: Need for Speed," in Proc. of the KVM Forum, May 2010.

[24] M. Paolino, N. Nikolaev, J. Fanguede, and D. Raho, "SnabbSwitch user space virtual switch benchmark and performance optimization for NFV," in Proc. of the IEEE Conference on Network Function Virtualization and Software Defined Network (NFV-SDN 2015), November 2015, pp. 86–92.

[25] D. Barach, L. Linguaglossa, D. Marion, P. Pfister, S. Pontarelli, and D. Rossi, "High-Speed Software Data Plane via Vectorized Packet Processing," IEEE Communications Magazine, vol. 56, no. 12, 2018, pp. 97–103.

[26] LF Projects, LLC. Fast Data Project (FD.io). [Online]. Available: http://www.fd.io [retrieved: 14 February, 2019]

[27] T. Cucinotta, L. Abeni, M. Marinoni, and C. Vitucci, "The Importance of Being OS-aware - In Performance Aspects of Cloud Computing Research," in Proc. of the 8th International Conference on Cloud Computing and Services Science, CLOSER 2018, March 2018, pp. 626–633.

[28] P. Kutch and B. Johnson, "SR-IOV for NFV Solutions," Technical Brief, February 2017. [Online]. Available: https://www.intel.com/content/dam/www/public/us/en/documents/technology-briefs/sr-iov-nfv-tech-brief.pdf

[29] H. Liu. Introduction to Linux interfaces for virtual networking. [Online]. Available: https://developers.redhat.com/blog/2018/10/22/introduction-to-linux-interfaces-for-virtual-networking/ [retrieved: October, 2018]

[30] R. Jain and S. Paul, "Network virtualization and software defined networking for cloud computing: a survey," IEEE Communications Magazine, vol. 51, no. 11, November 2013, pp. 24–31.

[31] "Virtual Networking Management White Paper – Version 1.0.0," Distributed Management Task Force (DMTF), Standard DSP2025, February 2012. [Online]. Available: https://www.dmtf.org/sites/default/files/standards/documents/DSP2025_1.0.0.pdf

[32] L. Abeni, C. Kiraly, N. Li, and A. Bianco, "On the performance of KVM-based virtual routers," Computer Communications, vol. 70, 2015, pp. 40–53.

[33] J. Anderson, H. Hu, U. Agarwal, C. Lowery, H. Li, and A. Apon, "Performance considerations of network functions virtualization using containers," in Proc. of the International Conference on Computing, Networking and Communications (ICNC 2016), February 2016, pp. 1–7.

[34] J. Jose, M. Li, X. Lu, K. Kandalla, M. Arnold, and D. Panda, "SR-IOV Support for Virtualization on InfiniBand Clusters: Early Experience," in Proc. of the 13th IEEE/ACM International Symposium on Cluster, Cloud, and Grid Computing, CCGrid 2013, May 2013, pp. 385–392.

[35] K. Mahabaleshwarkar, N. Mundada, A. Chavan, and A. Panage, "TCP/IP protocol accelaration," in Proc. of the International Conference on Computer Communication and Informatics, January 2012, pp. 1–4.

[36] J. Tan, C. Liang, H. Xie, Q. Xu, J. Hu, H. Zhu, and Y. Liu, "VIRTIO-USER: A New Versatile Channel for Kernel-Bypass Networks," in Proc. of the Workshop on Kernel-Bypass Networks, ser. KBNets '17. New York, NY, USA: ACM, August 2017, pp. 13–18.

[37] X. Luo, F. Ren, and T. Zhang, "High Performance Userspace Networking for Containerized Microservices," in Proc. of the 16th International Conference on Service-Oriented Computing (ICSOC 2018), November 2018, pp. 57–72.

IaaS Environment Creation Experiments with OpenStack

Silviu – Gabriel Topoloi, Eugen Borcoci
Department of Telecommunications
University POLITEHNICA of Bucharest
Bucharest, Romania
Emails: silviutopoloi@gmail.com, eugen.borcoci@elcom.pub.ro

Abstract—**OpenStack is an open cloud computing software platform that allows the users to create Infrastructure as a Service (IaaS) cloud environments suited for all types of deployments and environments (prod, pre-prod, test, dev, etc.). The platform is backed-up by a large and active community that continuously improves it, thus making it a serious competitor in today's cloud market. This paper presents a complete experimental work for IaaS environment creation with OpenStack as an alternative to others presented in the public literature. It can provide the baseline for future integration of different modules, e.g., between OpenStack and OpenDaylight (Open Source Software Defined Networking Platform), where OpenDaylight is used to create networking services, together with the default module provided by OpenStack (called Neutron). Developers, researchers, academic members and user communities can use the information in this paper as a practical guide to create their own cloud environments, allowing integration of their own work in many possible contexts: cloud, Software Defined Networking (SDN), Network Function Virtualization (NFV), Data Centers, and so on.**

Keywords - OpenStack; cloud; Software Defined Networking; Network Function Virtualization ; Infrastructure as a Service.

I. Introduction

OpenStack is a set of software tools for building and managing cloud computing platforms for public and private clouds. It is backed by some of the biggest companies in software development and hosting (AT&T, Ericsson, Huawei, Intel, Rackspace, Redhat, Suse, Tencent Cloud), as well as thousands of individual community members. OpenStack is managed by the OpenStack Foundation, a non-profit organization that oversees both development and community-building around the project [1].

OpenStack supports users to deploy Virtual Machines (VM) and other instances that handle different tasks for managing a cloud environment on the fly. It is horizontally scalable, i.e., it can concurrently serve more or fewer users on the fly by just spinning up more instances. For example, a mobile application that needs to communicate with a remote server can divide the communication work across many different instances, all communicating with one another but scaling quickly and easily as the application gains more users [1].

OpenStack is an open source software giving open access to the source code, to make any changes or modifications needed, and freely sharing these changes back out with the community at large. Consequently, it has the benefit of thousands of developers all over the world cooperating to make the product stronger, more robust and more secure [1] - [3].

As mentioned in the abstract, this paper presents a complete, pragmatic work for IaaS environment creation with OpenStack. Note that, currently, it is hard for users to find a complete view on how OpenStack should be deployed without bottlenecks in a carefully defined environment.

Different OpenStack deployment scenarios [4][5][7][8] are available on the Internet; however, after several attempts to have OpenStack installed following those steps only, the developer discovers that some additional steps and problem solving solutions are missing. In this paper, we try to fill this gap by presenting in one place a complete installation of OpenStack using Devstack, as well as the configurations problems, along with their solutions, thus guiding the developer during the process.

The structure of the paper is as follows: Sections I and II present a high level view on OpenStack and what can and has been achieved with this platform until now. Section III describes the architecture and services. Section IV elaborates a step by step OpenStack IaaS deployment. Section V presents some hints for the deployment to end users and developers.

II. OpenStack as a Solution Enabler and Related Work

OpenStack is a key enabler in the adoption of cloud technology, while following Public, Private, or Hybrid models [2].

OpenStack, as is, can be adopted by any user who wants to start exploring the cloud world or by any developer who wants to have a free cloud environment, built up in minutes, to test the applications that he/she develops. The platform has a wide variety of usage scenarios.

Big industry players like Oracle and Huawei offer OpenStack also for Enterprise usage. For example, Huawei OpenStack-based platform is called Flexible Engine, while Oracle's is named Oracle OpenStack. Naturally, an enterprise platform is more elaborated and reliable than a free one, especially for the support it provides and the available structure of the information needed for different implementations. However, a significant price has to be paid if wanting an enterprise solution.

Many companies have already adopted OpenStack. According to iDatalabs [9] there are around 6,856 companies that use OpenStack; the reason is the openness and wide variety of usage scenarios.

The work that has been done until now can be marked in several fields, like: security, monitoring, cloud Service Orchestration, Networking (SDN, NFV), cloud IaaS and so on. Several references can provide further details [10]-[13].

However, given the large spread of published work related to OpenStack, it is difficult to find a thorough nutshell document presenting the development steps. This article tries to do it. In our knowledge, the practical hints and ideas provided in Section V cannot be found all in one place. Here, the practical hints are based on a real experience gathered when the user/developer actually interacts and works with OpenStack.

Therefore, this document can provide a good and helpful guide to all people wanting to use OpenStack as a development, test or production cloud Platform. It can be considered as a good and practical contribution to what has been done until now.

III. OPENSTACK ARCHITECTURE AND SERVICES

A. *OpenStack Architecture*

This section shortly presents the OpenStack architecture and services (see Figure 1, [2]).

B. *OpenStack Services*

The above architecture presents the OpenStack Services and how they communicate. Further, the paper will speak shortly about each presented service.

OpenStack embraces a modular architecture (Figure 2) to provide a set of core services that facilitate scalability and elasticity as core design tenets [2].

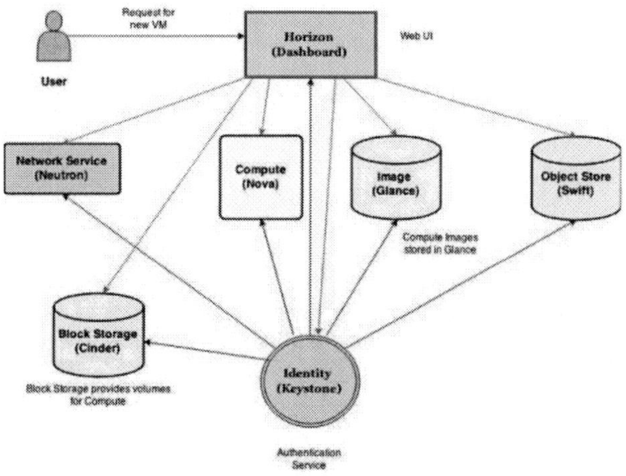

Figure 1. Loosely coupled architecture of OpenStack [6]

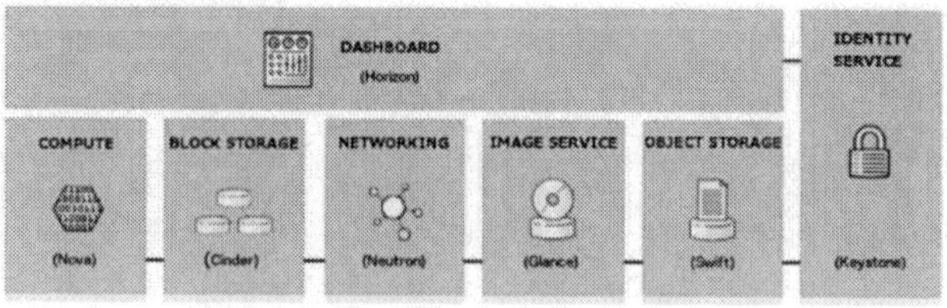

Figure 2. OpenStack modular architecture [2]

The OpenStack services are:

a. *Compute (Nova)* provides services to support the management of VM instances at scale, instances that host multi-tiered applications, dev or test environments, "Big Data" crunching Hadoop clusters, or high-performance computing [2].
b. *Object Storage (Swift)* provides support for storing and retrieving arbitrary data in the cloud [2].
c. *Block Storage (Cinder)* provides persistent block storage for Compute instances [2].
d. *Networking (neutron, previously called quantum)* provides various networking services to cloud users (tenants), such as IP address management, Domain Name Server (DNS), Dynamic Host Configuration protocol (DHCP), load balancing, and security groups (network access rules, like firewall policies) [2].
e. *Dashboard (Horizon)* provides a web-based interface for both cloud administrators and cloud tenants [2].
f. *Identity (Keystone)* is a shared service that provides authentication and authorization services throughout the entire cloud infrastructure. The Identity service has pluggable support for multiple forms of authentication [2].
g. *Image (Glance)* provides disk-image management services, including image discovery, registration, and delivery services to the Compute service, as needed [2].

Messaging is used for internal communication between OpenStack services. By default, message queues are used, based on the Advanced Messaging Queuing Protocol (AMQP). Like most OpenStack services, AMQP supports pluggable components. Today, the implementation back end could be RabbitMQ, Qpid, or ZeroMQ [2].

C. *Data Protection & Security*

The OpenStack Identity Service (Keystone) takes care of both the user's and customer's data, because the authentication uses a combination of domains, projects (tenants), users and roles. By creating tenants, logical customer (and their respective data) segregation is possible. This means that each customer has access to his/her own data and no other data. Therefore, customer data is secured.

For example, in public clouds, logical segregation is very important, because each customer is deployed in the same public cloud; however, it is logically separated from the rest of the customers with the help of tenants.

With OpenStack, private clouds can also be created for customers that do not want a logical segregation, but a physical one. Thus, if a customer opts for a private cloud, the customer can have access to a dedicated OpenStack environment that is deployed on a dedicated server, where no other customer has access to. Of course, this implies higher costs, but the data is physically separated. Either way, OpenStack assures that the customer's data is fully protected and secure.

At a user level, all the access is controlled and logged. Also, the access is segregated based on users and roles. Therefore, a user cannot see or access the data and elements for another user. Also, in this way, customer data is protected and access to it is fully controlled.

IV. Creation of an IaaS Environment in OpenStack

A. *Role of the Environment*

The environment that is going to be created has the role of providing a basic cloud platform for experiments in different areas like: SDN, NFV, application development, integration with other cloud platforms and more.

OpenStack services used for the platform implementation are: *Keystone, Horizon, Nova, Cinder, Neutron* and *Glance.* With the help of these services, the user will be able to create the necessary IaaS environment, meaning, Compute instances with Networking and Storage that are ready for the user's purposes.

B. *The Implemented Architecture*

The implemented architecture (Figure 3) shows the OpenStack services, as components used to implement the OpenStack cloud IaaS Environment and its capabilities. The capabilities are presented in Figure 3, with dotted-lines emphasizing future integration and work that can be done based on the created environment:

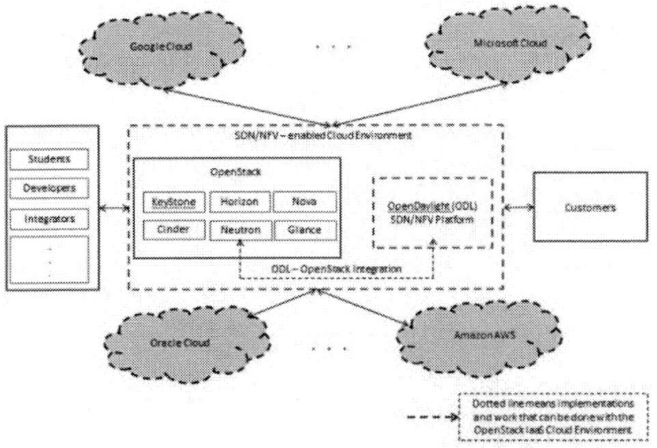

Figure 3. The implemented architecture

- Integrations with different platforms, like OpenDaylight;
- Integrations with different cloud providers;
- Providing cloud services to users and customers.

C. *Implementation steps*

The section will show the steps to be followed to install OpenStack and use this framework to create the cloud IaaS Environment that can be further used, as mentioned earlier, for example, as a Production environment for Application development and more.

After the creation of the IaaS Environment, the following tests can be performed:

- Ping the Compute instances from the external network (Internet Service Provider network in this case). This will be done from the Ubuntu machine;
- Connect to the Compute instances, using SSH, from the external network. This will be done from the Ubuntu machine;
- Test the connection between the Compute instances;
- Test if the Compute instances have access to the Internet. This will be tested by issuing a ping command to "google.com", from the Compute instances.

D. *The System Resources*

To support the implementation, a virtual machine image, Ubuntu 16.04.4, has been used, installed on a local machine. The hardware resources are:

Physical Host

Processor: Intel Core i5-8350U CPU @ 1.70 GHz (8 Virtual CPUs)

RAM Memory: 16 GB, HDD: 256 SSD

Ubuntu Virtual Box Image

Processor: 1 Virtual CPU, Memory: 4 GB

HDD: Starting from 10 GB and Dynamic Growing

The installation has been done locally, for testing purposes, on a powerful machine, but it can be scaled up easily to a datacenter environment capable of providing cloud services.

DevStack [14] has been used to automatically deploy OpenStack.

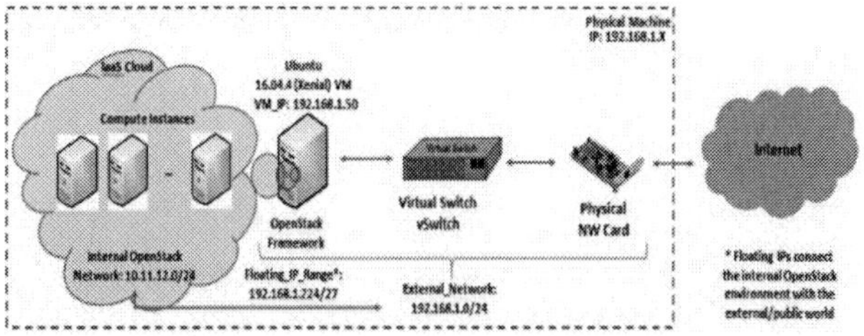

Figure 4. OpenStack deployment components

E. *Installation of OpenStack Framework*

1) Download and install Oracle Virtual Box;

a) Download and deploy Ubuntu 16.04.4 (Xenial) virtual box image;

b) Setup the Network to bridged mode;

c) Access the machine and install OpenStack Framework:

- First, run the following commands to pre-configure the Ubuntu environment: sudo apt-get update, sudo apt-get upgrade, sudo apt-get install openssh-server, sudo apt-get install git;
- Assign static ip to the network interface:
  sudo nano /etc/network/interfaces
  ```
  # interfaces(5) file used by ifup(8) and ifdown(8)
  auto lo
  iface lo inet loopback

  auto enp0s3
  iface enp0s3 inet static
    address 192.168.1.50
    netmask 255.255.255.0
    network 192.168.1.0
    gateway 192.168.1.1
    dns-nameservers 192.168.1.1
  ```
- Create "stack" user that will be used for OpenStack installation:
  sudo useradd -s /bin/bash -d /opt/stack -m stack
- Assign password to stack: sudo passwd stack;
- Add "stack" user to sudo group:
  sudo usermod -aG sudo stack
- Make sure it has sudo privileges:
  echo "stack ALL=(ALL) NOPASSWD: ALL" | sudo tee /etc/sudoers.d/stack
  Output should be:
  stack ALL=(ALL) NOPASSWD: ALL
- Login as stack: sudo su – stack;
- Download Openstack DevStack:
  git clone https://github.com/openstack-dev/devstack.git -b stable/pike devstack/
- Create local.conf file. This file will be used in the installation of OpenStack. The parameters that are setup here will be used to pre-configure the environment so that the user makes sure that the environment is fully working and accessible.
  ```
  cat > local.conf <<EOF
  [[local|localrc]]
  FLOATING_RANGE=192.168.1.224/27
  FIXED_RANGE=10.11.12.0/24
  FIXED_NETWORK_SIZE=256
  FLAT_INTERFACE=enp0s3
  ADMIN_PASSWORD=secret
  DATABASE_PASSWORD=$ADMIN_PASSWO
  RD
  RABBIT_PASSWORD=$ADMIN_PASSWORD
  SERVICE_PASSWORD=$ADMIN_PASSWORD
  RECLONE=yes
  ```

Note: The Fixed Range Subnet represents the subnet that will be used for the internal OpenStack Network.

- Open and edit the file stack.sh as follows:

  Comment the below lines:
  # Start Services # =============== # Dstat # ----- # A better kind of sysstat, with the top process per time slice #start_dstat # Etcd # ----- # etcd is a distributed key value store that provides a reliable way to store data across a cluster of machines #if is_service_enabled etcd3; then # start_etcd3 #fi

  Save the above file.

- Run ./stack.sh and wait for the script to finish.
  Note that it will take some time!
  Final output should contain following elements:

  This is your host IP address: 192.168.1.50
  This is your host IPv6 address: ::1
  Horizon is now available at
  http://192.168.1.50/dashboard
  Keystone is serving at http://192.168.1.50/identity/
  The default users are: admin and demo
  The password: secret

A fully working OpenStack environment is now available for deploying cloud environments.

F. *Creating an IaaS environment in OpenStack*

a) Login to the OpenStack Dashboard (192.168.1.50/dashboard) using the following credentials: user: admin & pass: secret. The User will be logged as admin, using the Project (workspace) admin.

b) First, create an internal network using the subnet specified in the local.conf file: 10.11.12.0/24.

Access Project -> Network -> Create Network and name the Network "internal".

c) Assign a subnet to the internal network using the following specifications:

Subnet name: subnet

Network address: 10.11.12.0/24

Gateway IP: 10.11.12.1

Enable DHCP

Allocation Pools: 10.11.12.2,10.11.12.10

DNS: 192.168.1.1

d) The external network, called public, is automatically created by the OpenStack stack.sh script, with the subnet specified in the local.conf file. The subnet is: 192.168.1.224/27.

e) Create a Router that will route the traffic in the internal network and will make the connection with the public network, thus the Compute instances will be able to communicate with the outside world.

Note: For the device to be able to route the traffic as mentioned before, the Router will have a Gateway interface with an IP automatically setup from the public network and an interface connected in the internal network, with an IP corresponding to the Gateway IP of the internal network (10.11.12.1).

Access Project -> Network -> Router -> Create Router

Router name: router_public

Enable Admin State: Thicked

External Network: public

Note: The Gateway is automatically created and has an IP assigned from the public network. In this case, the IP is 192.168.1.227. Still, remains to be created the Interface to the internal network, to route the internal traffic.

Access Project -> Network -> Routers -> router_public -> Add Interface

Note: Here you can see the Gateway that has been created automatically at the creation of the Router.

Parameters for the Interface to the internal network:

Subnet: Select the internal network.

IP Address: 10.11.12.1 (If the Gateway IP of the internal network is already in use, please assign another IP address).

f) Create the Floating IPs that will be assigned to the Compute instances. The Floating IPs will be used to connect the instances to the Outside world.

Access Project -> Network -> Floating IPs -> Allocate IP To Project. The IP will be allocated from the pool mentioned in the local.conf file: 192.168.1.224/27.

After clicking the Allocate IP button, a Floating IP will be automatically allocated.

g) Create the Compute instance.

Access Project -> Compute -> Images -> Launch

In the Details section:

- Instance Name: compute_2
- Availability zone: nova
- Count: 1

Note: To make sure that on Create New Volume Tab, the button No is selected. So, the volume assigned from the selected Flavor can be used. Otherwise, the image might not be created.

In the Flavor Section, select *m1.tiny* (any type of image can be selected based on the power provided by the host machine).

In the Network Section, select the internal network.

After the above steps, Launch Instance button is clicked to create the Instance.

In order to see the created Compute instance, access Project -> Compute -> Instances.

h) Assign Floating IP to be able to connect the created instance to the outside world (public network).

Access Project -> Compute -> Instances. And from the Create Snapshot dropdown list, select Associate Floating IP.

IP Address: Select the Floating IP Address that was allocated at Step 11.

The Port to be associated is represented by the internal network IP address, which is assigned to the compute_2 instance that was created at Step 12.

After these steps, click the button called Associate.

Note: Now, the Floating IP is associated to the Compute instance and the link with the public network is done.

The process is complete. A working and public network connected Compute instance has been created.

In order for the environment to be complete, create another Compute Instance following the same steps.

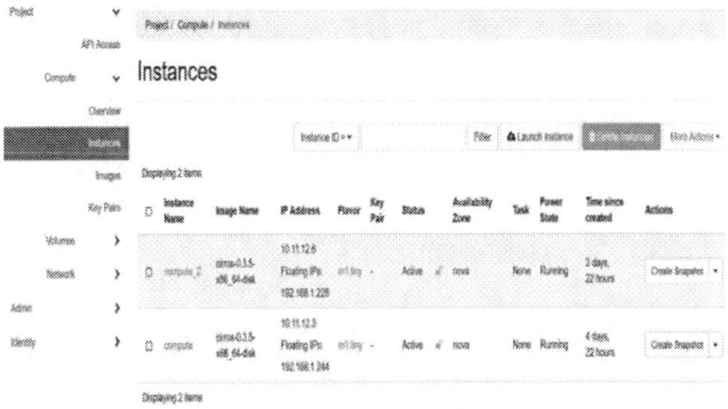

Figure 5. Compute instances

i) Allow Internet Control Message Protocol (ICMP) and Secure Shell (SSH) Ingress traffic to be able to do PING and SSH from the Ubuntu machine towards the OpenStack Compute instances.

Access Project -> Network -> Security Groups -> Manage Rules -> Add Rule.

In the Add Rule Window, for the Rule section, select All ICMP and leave the rest of the sections default. Then, click Add.

Note: To proceed in the same manner for SSH.

G. Testing the IaaS environment

Compute Instance One:

Name: compute

Internal IP: 10.11.12.3
Floating IP: 192.168.1.244

Compute Instance Two:

Name: compute_2
Internal IP: 10.11.12.6
Floating IP: 192.168.1.228

a) Ping the Compute instances from the external network (ISP network in this case). This will be done from the Ubuntu Machine;

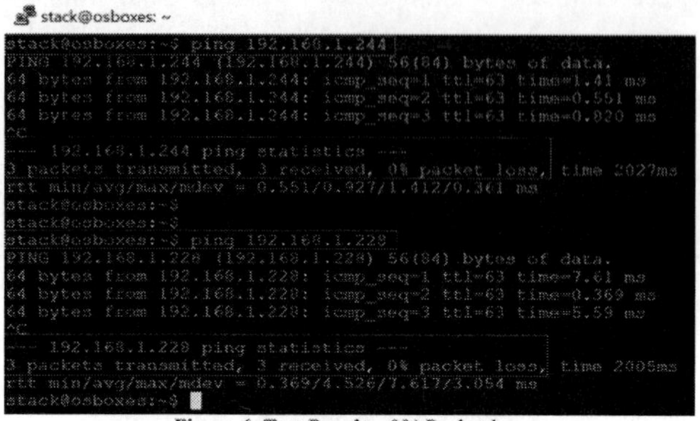

Figure 6. Test Result – 0% Packet loss

b) Connect to the Compute instances, using SSH, from the external network (this will be done from the Ubuntu Machine).

Use the following commands:
ssh cirros@192.168.1.244 (password is "cubswin:)")
ssh cirros@192.168.1.228 (password is "cubswin:)")

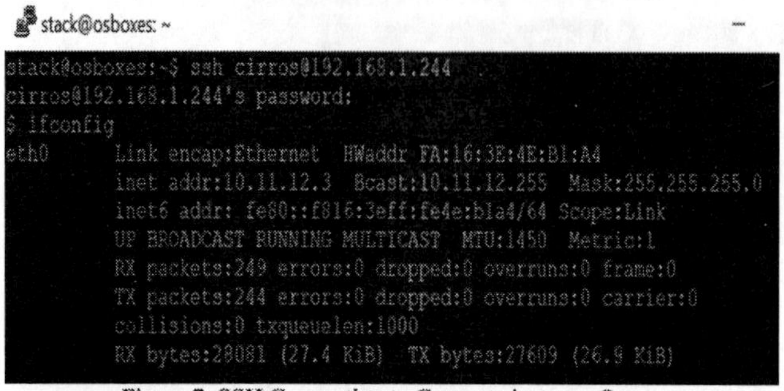

Figure 7. SSH Connection to Compute instance One

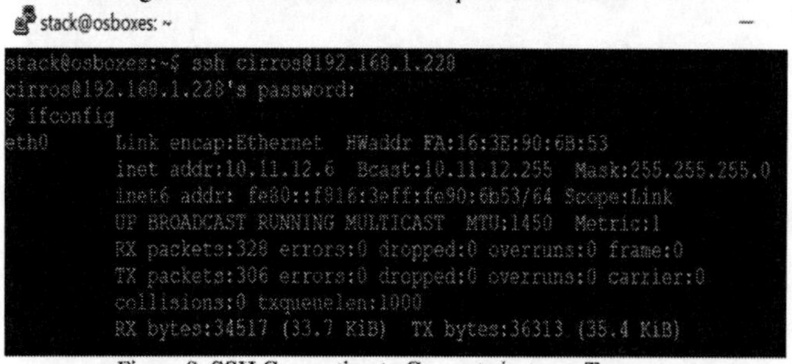

Figure 8. SSH Connection to Compute instance Two

c) Test the connection between the Compute instances and the connection to the Internet.

Remain connected (using the last SSH Connection) on Compute instance One and ping Compute instance Two on the internal IP and then google.com.
Repeat the process being connected on Compute instance Two and ping Compute instance One.

Figure 9. Internal connection and Internet connection from the first Compute instance

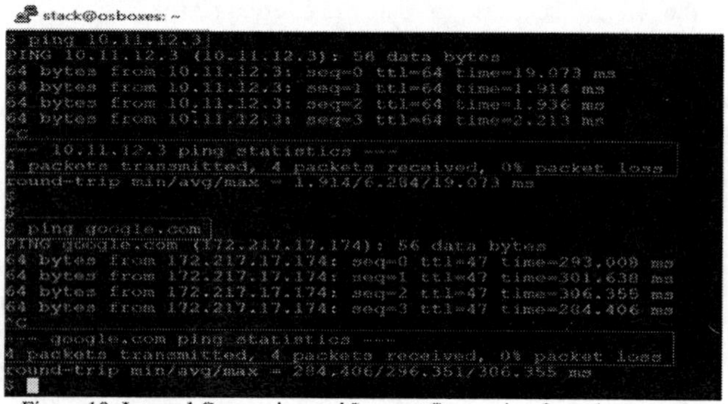

Figure 10. Internal Connection and Internet Connection from the second Compute instance

All the tests have been successful. The Infrastructure as a Service environment can be used without hesitations for any type of deployment and application development.

V. PRACTICAL HINTS FOR DEVELOPMENT

This section suggests some practical hints that the user needs to take into consideration when deploying OpenStack.

The following hints should be considered in the development process:

a. When DevStack is used to install and configure OpenStack, one should assure that Ubuntu 16.04.4 is used as Operating System (OS). Even though DevStack supports a wide range of OSs, it is recommended to use the aforementioned OS, because it will run the smoothest and it is the most tested one. This does not mean that it cannot be installed on other OSs, but it might take a little bit more time, due to possible bottlenecks that were not tested before and need a little bit of troubleshooting from the user's part. Like any other software,

OpenStack needs to be tested on each OS and its versions.

b. When installing OpenStack, one should setup a static IP to the host. This IP is going to be embedded throughout the installation, in various locations. This means, that if the user changes the host's IP address, the user will not be able to access anymore the OpenStack Dashboard and its services and it will be very difficult to change the IP due to its wide spreading in the OpenStack environment. Most likely OpenStack will not work anymore and the installation needs to be done from the start.

c. When creating a Compute instance, in the Source section, one should select "No" as answer for the option "Create New Volume". This needs to be done to avoid an error when creating the Volume for the instance. For example, if the user selects YES and also adds a value of 2 GB to the new Volume, but the selected Flavor offers the possibility for only a 1GB Volume, then an error is issued and the Volume cannot be created, due to the fact that it is a contradiction between what the Flavor can offer and the user's selection from the Source section. Better said, OpenStack tries to create something bigger than it can be offered by the selected Flavor.

VI. CONCLUSION

Based on the work done during installation and configuration of the OpenStack IaaS environment, several conclusions can be drawn.

Taking advantage of OpenStack, the deployment developed in this paper can be easily replicated to another machine/server or it can be scaled to an entire Data Center, with clustering, load balancing and enhanced Disaster Recovery (DR) features, capable of providing cloud services to customers. The enhanced DR capabilities are provided with the help of SDN and NFV functions that offer the possibility to create Availability Zones and Regions, to extend Data Protection in case of a Disaster.

The implementation presented here proved that the users can actually access OpenStack resources and code to improve it or change it according to their needs and then share the results with the entire community for verification and further utilization.

The OpenStack-based system developed here can be a useful choice for users that want to start experiencing the cloud world. It can also be used for academia labs and small enterprises that want to get a competitive and at the same time affordable cloud platform.

Further developments are possible, based on this platform, in SDN and NFV combined environment, e.g. in 5G slicing management control and data planes, etc.

REFERENCES

[1] What is OpenStack?. [Online]. Available from: https://opensource.com/resources/what-is-openstack 2019.02.15

[2] Introduction to OpenStack. [Online]. Available from: https://docs.openstack.org/ 2019.02.15

[3] Introduction to OpenStack. [Online]. Available from: https://docs.oracle.com/cd/E64747_01/E64749/html/osusg-openstack-what.html# 2019.02.15

[4] How to install OpenStack on your local machine using Devstack. [Online]. Available from: https://www.mirantis.com/blog/how-to-install-openstack-on-your-local-machine-using-devstack/ 2019.02.15

[5] All-In-One Single Machine. [Online]. Available from:https://docs.openstack.org/devstack/latest/guides/single-machine.html 2019.02.15

[6] Loosely coupled architecture of OpenStack. [Online]. Available from: https://www.researchgate.net/figure/Loosely-coupled-architecture-of-OpenStack_fig1_305297793 2019.02.15

[7] How to Install Single Node OpenStack on CentOS 7. [Online]. Available from: https://www.alibabacloud.com/blog/how-to-install-single-node-openstack-on-centos-7_594048 2019.02.18

[8] How to install OpenStack on Ubuntu Server with DevStack. [Online]. Available from: https://www.techrepublic.com/article/how-to-install-openstack-on-ubuntu-server-with-devstack/ 2019.02.18

[9] Companies using OpenStack. [Online]. Available from: https://idatalabs.com/tech/products/openstack 2019.02.18

[10] N. Saranya and S. Nivedha, "Implementing authentication in an Openstack environment-survey" 2016 International Conference on Computer Communication and Informatics (ICCCI) Jan. 2016, pp 1-7, DOI: 10.1109/ICCCI.2016.7479966

[11] E. Luchian, P. Docolin and V. Dobrota, "Advanced monitoring of the OpenStack NFV infrastructure: A Nagios approach using SNMP" 2016 12th IEEE International Symposium on Electronics and Telecommunications (ISETC) Oct. 2016, pp 51-54, DOI: 10.1109/ISETC.2016.7781055

[12] P. Jain, A. Datt, A. Goel and S.C. Gupta, "cloud service orchestration based architecture of OpenStack Nova and Swift" 2016 International Conference on Advances in Computing, Communications and Informatics (ICACCI) Sept. 2016, pp 21-24, DOI: 10.1109/ICACCI.2016.7732425

[13] R. Cohen, K. Barabash and L. Schour, "Distributed Overlay Virtual Ethernet (DOVE) integration with Openstack" 2013 IFIP/IEEE International Symposium on Integrated Network Management (IM 2013) May 2013, pp 1088 – 1089, INSPEC Accession Number: 13684410

[14] DevStack. [Online]. Available from: https://docs.openstack.org/devstack/latest/ 2019.02.20

Lepida: a Passive WDM Fiber Access Technology Example in Europe

Andrea Odorizzi*, Denis Ferraretti† and Gianluca Mazzini‡
LepidaScpA
Via della Liberazione, 15 - 40128 Bologna, Italy
Email: *andrea.odorizzi@lepida.it, †denis.ferraretti@lepida.it, ‡g.mazzini@ieee.org

***Abstract*—Likely unique in Europe, due to its own peculiar service delivery paradigm Lepida, the network of the public government organizations of the region Emilia-Romagna, in the north of Italy, chooses a passive Wavelength Division Multiplexing (WDM) fiber access technology. Passive WDM deeply exploits the frequency domain in order to multiplex multiple signals in the same optical fiber. In particular, a full Coarse WDM (CWDM) approach, deployed in a pre-existent network, can increase reliability, bandwidth, security and configuration cleanliness in a pay-as-you-grow way. In this paper, we present benefits, costs, pros and cons, and how we achieve them, of an interesting concrete implementation of WDM fiber access technology in a wide and complex territory.**

Keywords–Passive WDM; CWDM.

I. Lepida Network Introduction

Lepida Network (Lepida for simplicity in the following) is the fiber optic network that reaches almost all the public administration offices in the Emilia-Romagna (Italy) regional territory; one of its design constraints is that Customer Premise Equipment (CPE) uplinks should be GigaEthernet (GE) links or 10GE links. A second design constraint is the CPE capabilities: they have to be simple and cheap switching devices.

LepidaScpA [1], the entity that currently owns Lepida Network, is an in-house providing company established by a Regional Law (11/2004, "Regional Development of the Information Society") to represent the operational instrument in the service of its shareholders (Public Administrations, Public Entities, Universities). Currently, it counts 436 shareholders, all Public Administrations and Public Entities. LepidaScpA is involved in the governance of the regional Information and Communications Technology (ICT) plan and has been given responsibility for planning, development and management of the ICT infrastructures and for development and supply of ICT services for the Public Administrations.

Lepida has been originated by a public investment in which public organizations contributed to build multiple networks cooperating with different network operators, retaining a fraction of fiber in each fiber cable. After that, from 2010, a single network has been obtained by combining all the local infrastructures; because of the original design each backbone cable of the unified network Lepida consists of at most of 24 fibers. Moreover, in 2010, in order to cut the Total Cost of Operation (TCO), the Points of Presence (POPs) number has been minimized and typical inter POP distances are since close to 80km.

As seen in Figure 1, the 12 fiber optic pairs in each section, i.e., a network segment between Lepida POPs, have to be used both to interconnect POPs and to connect the end-users to POPs. As the need of a network growth appeared, the impact of the increase in the number of users was essentially twofold:

- counterintuitive fiber optic pair routes design, i.e., users positioned in the same backbone cable (*Users 3* and *4*) could be connected to a different couple of POPs;
- transit on CPEs in order to connect new users, i.e., some CPEs, in Figure 1 *Users a, b, c, d,* e and *f*, have been configured as if they were a POP.

We point out that, if the first point "just" leads to a greater effort to the Network Operations structures, the second one will be deeply investigated. First of all, the latter leads to a more complicated network topology and, in order to achieve better uptime, to build CPE meshes, i.e., *User a* relies on *POP a* and *User b* in order to reach *POP c* instead of being connected to *POP a* only. This interdependence leads to a more complicated troubleshooting effort and to upgrade most of the equipment of the mesh on the basis of a single user needs, e.g., if *User b* needs a 10 Gigabits bandwidth, *Users a, c* and *d* should also be upgraded.

In this paper, we present how LepidaScpA faced the above presented issues, implementing a passive Wavelength Division Multiplexing (WDM) fiber access technology in its network, over a wide and complex territory. Benefits, costs, pros and cons, and comparison between different technology approaches are also discussed.

The rest of the paper is organized as follows: Section II briefly presents the previously used technology and then it introduces the passive WDM solution; Section III describes the events that lead LepidaScpA to choose a full passive WDM access approach; Section IV briefly illustrates the used solution in order to track passive WDM uses; Section V describes and compares passive WDM costs between different solutions; Section VI concludes the paper.

II. PON vs Passive WDM

A Passive Optical Network (PON) [2] is a fiber access technology used to provide fiber to the end-user. PON implements a point-to-multipoint architecture, in which unpowered fiber optic splitters/combiners are used to enable a single optical fiber to serve multiple end-points. PON consists of an Optical Line Terminal (OLT) at the service provider's POP (hub) and a number of Optical Network Units (ONUs) or Optical Network Terminals (ONTs), near end-users. Typically, downstream signals are broadcast to all premises sharing multiple fibers. Upstream signals are combined using a multiple access protocol, usually Time Division Multiple Access (TDMA). Downstream signals are combined by OLT and transmitted at the same wavelength. When the signal reaches a splitter, it does not strip off the individual signal but instead splits the signal. This results is a duplication of the same signal with reduced power. At this point, the split signal is sent into

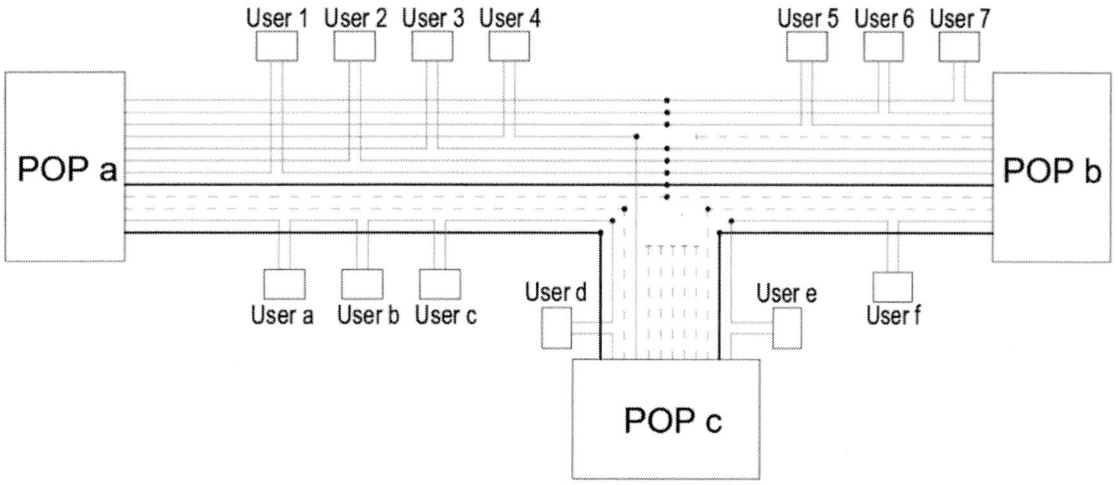

Figure 1. An arrangement of a group of 12 fiber optic pairs in a network segment between Lepida POPs.

ONU/ONT and it pulls off the data that is meant for that user based on addressing. In the upstream, all the subscribers go through the ONU or ONT and get put together again, though not necessarily sequentially, and sent upstream on another wavelength.

Passive WDM [3] deeply exploits the frequency domain in order to multiplex multiple signals in the same optical fiber. There is no need of point to multi-point media access control or to define different roles such as OLT and ONTs: each signal is *assigned* to a wavelength, also named "Color", at the device port. This means that the switch or router that originates the signal will utilize a WDM transceiver instead of a standard 1310nm or 1550nm one. Moreover, it also means that signals are combined, multiplexed, but do not interact. In Passive WDM technology there are two main kinds of multiplexer: simple multiplexer (MUX) and Optical Add and Drop Multiplexer (OADM). The first one picks the Colors from single Color fiber pairs (of fiber patches) and multiplexes them into a single fiber pair. The second one adds and drops a selected subset of Colors to and from dedicated fiber pairs and allows all the others to pass.

III. Full passive WDM access approach

In this section, we focus on the events that lead to choosing, in the Lepida network, a passive WDM solution as the main fiber access technology.

The first attempts of passive WDM multiplexing were done at the beginning of 2013. The goal was to free fiber pairs in a fiber cable and the key idea was to exploit WDM (both Coarse and Dense WDM) instead of buying new dark fibers or building new infrastructures.

Subsequently, we started replacing some active devices with passive WDM ones in order to reduce some housing costs. In the previous SDH-like [4] network topology (Figure 2.a) the backhaul devices were located in other Internet Service Provider (ISP) sites. The updated network topology became an hub-and-spoke one: passive WDM devices are fully transparent and all the end-user are logically connected to the main Lepida POP site by means of a Color, i.e., a single GE WDM signal (Figure 2.b).

The focal point was the awareness of a new capability: introducing passive WDM equipment, the physical topology and the "colored topology" can be splitted. The passive WDM quickly became a design weapon that has been used to overcome the exhaustion of optical fibers or simply to redesign the access network.

Due to the introduction of passive WDM, the paths of the Colors stretch to longer distances compared to the ones of the links in the outdated network topologies. The availability of cheap WDM transceivers whose power budget can span up to 41 dB allows us to overcome the distance constraints. A flexibility improvement leads to a network redundancy improvement like in Figure 2.c . If we compare Figures 3 and 1, we see that passive WDM is exploited in order to free 6 fiber pairs and to remove a POP site (*POP C*).

Until the end of 2015, passive WDM devices have been installed close to the active devices (see Figure 3). The capability to route WDM signals directly inside the fiber optic splice closure leads to a Color path optimization like in Figure 4; moreover, by means of the integration between passive WDM device and fiber splice closure each signal in fiber pair can be added (and dropped) into another fiber pair without any kind of cabinet or power supply.

The end of 2016 was the end of the experimentation phase. A massive transition to passive WDM fiber access technology was rolled out after a 4-year test, more than two hundred passive WDM devices installed and about five hundred CWDM transceiver plugged in existing equipment. The transition has been split into two steps:

1) the standard transceivers have been and will be replaced by WDM ones taking advantage of the POP devices upgrade planned between 2017 and 2019 without any fiber optics rerouting;
2) deploying a passive CWDM solution, FIST-FCASA2 [6], that can be smartly managed within the Fiber Infrastructure System Technology (FIST) fiber splice

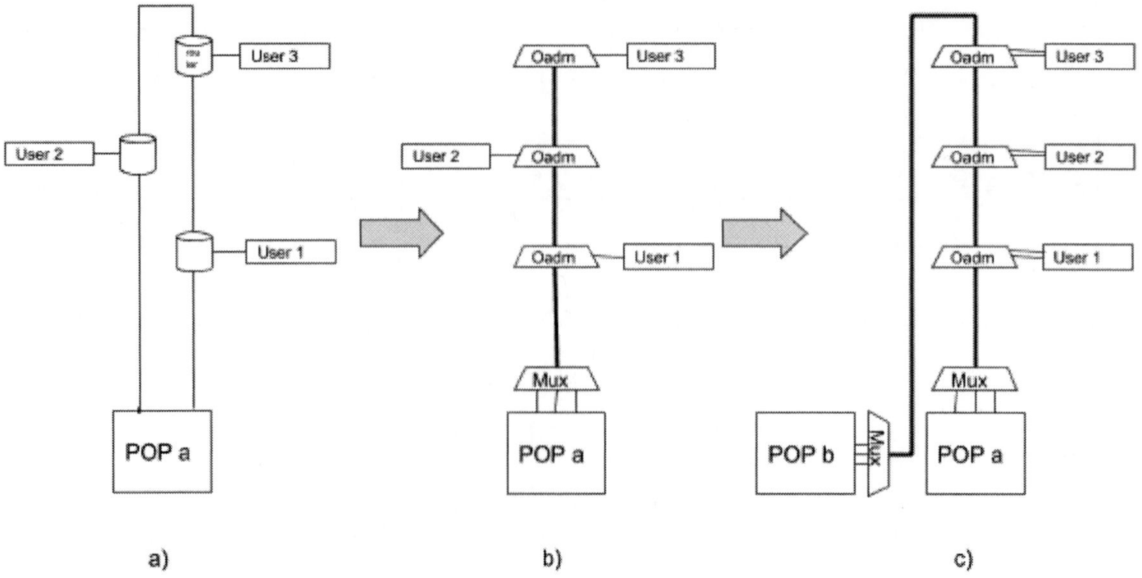

Figure 2. Evolution of implemented multiplexing solutions.

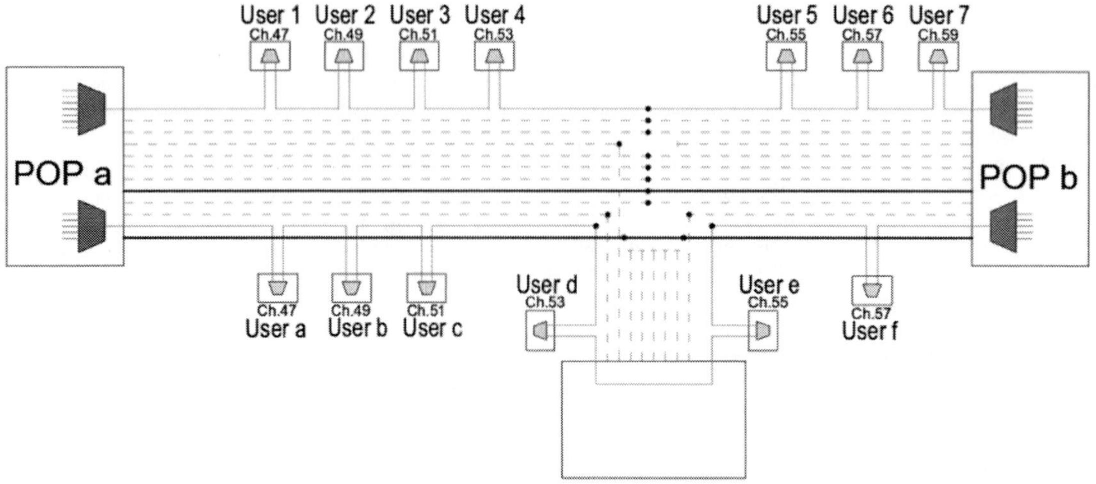

Figure 3. An arrangement of a group of 12 fiber optic pairs in a network segment between Lepida POPs exploiting CWDM Multiplexing devices.

closures, i.e. the most common fiber splice closure in Lepida.

In order to shrink the supply chain, a framework agreement with CommScope [5], the owner of the FIST brand, has been done.

A representative figure: the 6-month forecast of June 2017 indicates a need for more than 3 hundred (about 10% of the number of Lepida users) of FIST-FCASA2 devices. Each FIST-FCASA2 should have added and dropped a single CWDM Color toward a Lepida end-user. The aim is to connect each end-user to a couple of POPs by means of a single Color like in Figure 4.

What are the advantages of this full passive WDM approach? Those pursued by Lepida are the following:

- In each section between two POPs, the maximum number of end-users directly connected to two POPs are constrained by the amount of the available fiber pairs. The end-user maximum number is the product of the available fiber pairs and the number of Colors admitted by the chosen passive technology, e.g., passive CWDM solutions fix the gain to 8 or 18 compared to the solution without WDM.
- Switching from a dedicated fiber pairs approach to a dedicated WDM Colors approach frees fiber pairs that can be rented or exploited in order to connect new users.
- Each user can be connected directly to POP without any aggregation equipment: a) Each user can be in-

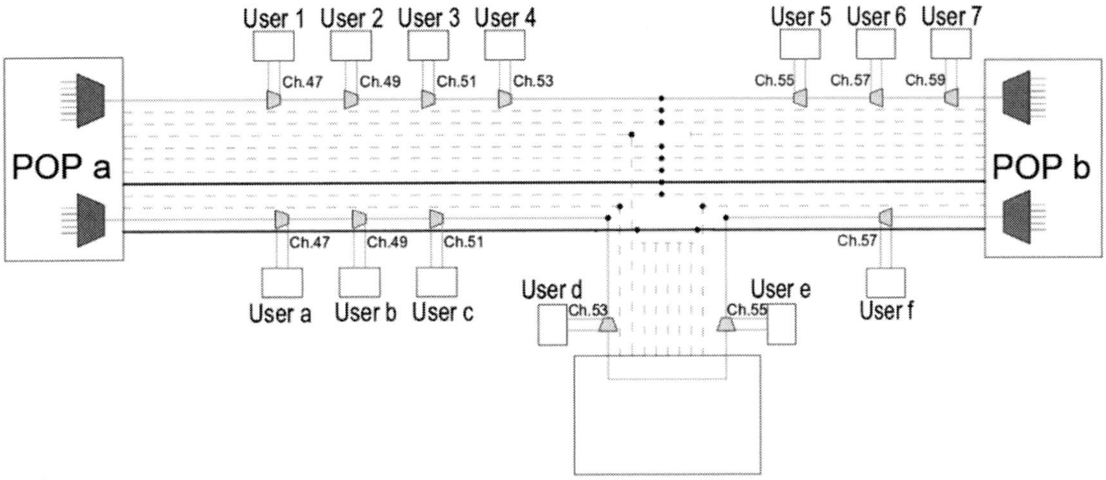

Figure 4. An arrangement of a group of 12 fiber optic pairs in a network segment between Lepida POPs exploiting CWDM Multiplexing devices inside the fiber optic splice closure.

dependently upgraded from 1GE links to 10GE links b) Aggregation network devices can be avoided (nor maintained or upgraded).

- The same regular "colored" network topology (and also the same set of configuration rule between CPE and POPs) can be achieved in distinct fiber optic network topologies.

IV. Passive WDM Colors tracking and troubleshooting

Each Color spans over multiple fiber links and has its own path. Working in a network environment without the Colors, a signal loss can be related to different failures: an electrical failure, a device failure or a fiber cut. On the other hand, working in a network environment that exploits the Color paths, a fiber cut can be located by overlapping the path of the Colors involved in the failure event. Vice versa, single active equipment failure can suggest an electrical or device failure. At the end, the color path diversity can help to improve the troubleshooting process.

Colors are essentially a new degree of information about the network and have to be mapped on top of a traditional fiber network documentation. Maintaining all the information related to the Color paths require a new asset management layer. This new layer should also aid the correlation between the Color path diversity and the failure events.

In order to operate and to maintain a such complex network architecture, in a business environment, it is crucial to provide reliable and complete information about network topologies, free/used fibers and Color paths. LepidaScpA implemented a resource manager software, provided with a web-based interface and a relational database.

This resource managers software adds to the main Lepida geo-database, that stores all the network asset data, all the Color-related information. This Colors tracking function, available through web URL endpoints, provides a simple web interface that the network manager can use to check the paths

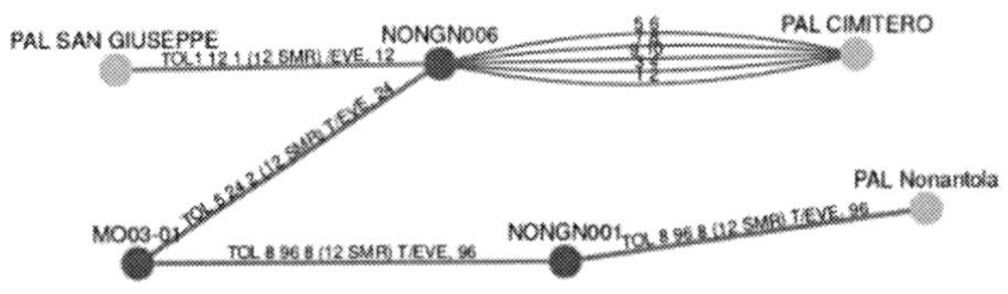

Figure 5. Resource Manager: selection of a fiber pair.

of the failure affected Colors (Figure 5) and network designer can use to manage name and path for each selected Color (Figure 6).

V. Passive WDM equipment costs

An application on such a large scale of Passive WDM is not so common in Europe and finding a partner that can deliver a complete solution has not been easy.

CommScope proposes a CWDM FIST-FCASA2 Solution in EMEA but It is not able to share detailed information on its end customers; It only declares, referring to applications such as mobile backhauling and point-to-point interconnection, that widespread use of this technology can be found only in the Far East (Korea or Malaysia).

Nevertheless, the transition to a passive WDM approach can be achieved step-by-step in a pay-as-you-grow model and without large investments.

Which is the right passive WDM technology? It depends only on the number of users. CWDM ones range between 8 and 16 end-users, DWDM ones range between 40 and 96. CWDM solutions are cheaper than the DWDM ones but, today, all the solutions settle down, if exploited to reach the maximum number of users, to 300 € per user (see Figure 7).

Lepida users are not so dense, hence we started by choosing a CWDM solution in order to reduce the initial economic

Figure 6. Resource Manager: Color assignment to a fiber pair.

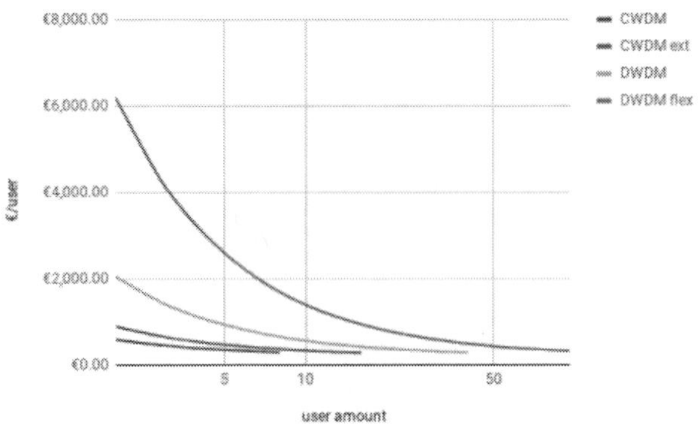

Figure 7. Cost per user comparison between WDM solutions.

effort; the main obstacle to starting the transition to the passive CWDM solution was to find a product that could be integrated inside a fiber optics splice closure.

Thanks to the frame agreement with CommScope, FIST-FCASA2 device series have been re-introduced in the Italian market and now it is the easiest-to-install and highest reliable solution.

VI. Conclusion

Both PON and Passive WDM are broadband access technology for optical networks.

PON and its evolution (G, XG, etc.) have the advantage of a huge deployment that has lead to product maturity and to shrink the equipment cost. Nevertheless, OLT and ONT introduce power budget constraints, i.e., a short distance between OLT and ONT. PON is designed to match a small point-to-multipoint environment with a huge number of end-users with shared bandwidth and shared computational resources.

Passive WDM addresses point-to-point systems that can be managed or upgraded independently. A passive WDM solution can decouple the fiber pair routes and the Color routes over the same network. Moreover, Colors with very high power can be exploited in order to span between a very long distance. The result is that Passive CWDM can be exploited in a pre-existent network in order to increase reliability, bandwidth or configuration cleanliness in a pay-as-you-grow approach. Passive WDM Color routing can also achieve greater security: using a dedicated channel per each subscriber is often considered to be safer than sharing resources. At last, passive WDM can aid fault handling.

What is the best technology? No one. They target different applications: XG-PON is envisioned for residential applications while Passive WDM is investigated for business or bandwidth intensive backhaul. Passive WDM is quite unused in Europe but has found in Lepida the perfect match as described in this contribution.

References

[1] Lepida ScpA company website [Online]. Available from: http://www.lepida.it, 2019.01.11.

[2] A. Banerjee et al. , "Wavelength-division-multiplexed passive optical network (WDM-PON) technologies for broadband access: a review", *Journal of Optical Networking* Vol. 4, Issue 11, 2005, pp. 737-758.

[3] Passive DWDM vs Active DWDM, Fs.com website [Online]. Available from: https://community.fs.com/blog/passive-dwdm-vs-active-dwdm.html, 2019.01.11.

[4] ITU-T, "Architecture of transport networks based on the synchronous digital hierarchy (SDH)", International Telecommunication Union, Recommendation No. G.803, Geneva, March, 2000.

[5] COMMSCOPE company website [Online]. Available from: https://www.commscope.com, 2019.01.11.

[6] FIST-FCASA2 datasheet [Online]. Available from: https://www.commscope.com/Docs/FIST-FCASA2-Field-Installable-CWDM-322644EU.pdf, 2019.01.11.

Soft MUD

Implementing Manufacturer Usage Descriptions on OpenFlow SDN Switches

Mudumbai Ranganathan, Doug Montgomery, Omar El Mimouni
Advanced Networking Technologies Division
National Institute of Standards and Technology
Gaithersburg, Maryland, USA
E-mails: {mranga, dougm, omarilias.elmimouni}@nist.gov

Abstract -- **A Manufacturer Usage Description (MUD) is a generalized network Access Control List that allows manufacturers to declare intended communication patterns for devices. Such devices are restricted to only communicate in the manner intended by the manufacturer, thus reducing their potential to launch Distributed Denial of Service attacks. We present a scalable implementation of the MUD standard on OpenFlow-enabled Software Defined Networking switches.**

Keywords- IOT; MUD; Network Access Control.

I. INTRODUCTION

Internet of Things (IoT) devices (henceforth called "devices") are special purpose devices that have dedicated functions. Such devices typically have communication requirements that are known to the device manufacturer. For example, printer might have the following requirement: Allow access for the printer (LPT) port, local access on port 80 (HTTP) and deny all other access. Thus, anyone can print to the printer, but local access would be required for the management interface which runs on port 80 as a web server. All other access would be in violation of the intended use of the device. The idea behind the Manufacturer Usage Description (MUD) [1] is to declare the intended communication pattern to the network infrastructure using a generalized network Access Control List (ACL) which is specified by the manufacturer, the integrator or the deployer of the device. These are realized as network access controls, by which the device can be constrained to the intended communication patterns.

MUD provides an effective defense against malicious agents taking control of the device and subsequently using it to launch attacks against the network infrastructure. It can also prevent compromised devices from attacking other devices on the network. Thus, MUD substantially reduces the threat surface on a device to those communications intended by the manufacturer.

Because the manufacturer cannot know deployment parameters of devices such as device IP addresses and IP addresses of device controllers, MUD defines class abstractions, using which, the MUD ACLs are defined. For example, the manufacturer may state an intent that devices can only communicate with other devices on the local network, or may state an intent that devices may only communicate with other devices made by the same manufacturer, or that devices may communicate with other devices made by a specific manufacturer on a defined port, or that devices may communicate with specific internet hosts or combinations of the behaviors above. To enable such generality, ACLs are defined with placeholders known as *classes*. These place holders are associated with Media Access Control (MAC) or IP addresses when the ACL is deployed on the switch.

In brief, the system works as follows: A device is associated with a MUD URL. The MUD URL is a locator for the MUD ACL file. The MUD server fetches the MUD file for the device from the manufacturer site, verifies its signature and installs network access controls using whatever mechanism the network switches and firewalls provide. There are several mechanisms that may be available for enforcing access control; for example, iptables could be used or the switch may already support an implementation of network ACLs.

In this paper, we describe a scalable design and implementation of the MUD standard on OpenFlow 1.5 [2] capable Software Defined Network (SDN) switches. An OpenFlow switch supports flow rules that are logically arranged in one or more flow tables in the data plane. The switch connects to one or more controllers that can install flow rules in the switch either reactively, when a packet is seen at the controller, or proactively when the switch connects to the controller. Flow rules have a MATCH part and an ACTION part. The MATCH part can match on different parts of the IP and TCP headers. The ACTION part forwards or drops the packet or sends it to the next table. As packets hit flow rules, metadata can be associated with the packet to provide a limited amount of state as packet processing proceeds from one table to the next. More details are found in [2].

In related work, Hamza et al. [3] consider how MUD may be used with real-world devices to build an Intrusion Detection System (IDS). They present a simulation based on captured trace data. Details on how to organize flow tables to implement MUD are not presented in their work. The focus of our work is different; in our work, we describe how to implement MUD and demonstrate that it can be done in a scalable fashion.

The rest of this paper is organized as follows: In Section II, we outline our design; Section III provides an analysis of our design; Section IV describes our implementation; Section V presents emulation results followed by Section VI which gives measurement on a commercially available home/small business router.

Note that certain commercial equipment, instruments, or materials are identified in this paper to foster understanding. Such identification does not imply recommendation or endorsement by the National Institute of Standards and Technology, nor does it imply that the materials or equipment identified are necessarily the best available for the purpose.

II. DESIGN SKETCH

MUD Access Control Entries (ACEs) can be divided into two categories – those that define intent for communication between a device and a named host, and those that define intent for communication between a device and other classes of devices. The former kind presents no scalability challenges and can be easily implemented using MAC and destination IP address match rules. The main challenge with MUD arises when implementing ACEs that define intent for communication between classes of devices or between the device and hosts on the local network.

Figure 1 shows an example "same-manufacturer" ACE. This indicates the intent that the device may communicate with other devices made by the same manufacturer.

```
{
  "name": "myman0-todev",
   "matches": {
        "ietf-mud:mud": {
          "same-manufacturer": [
            null
          ]
        }
      },
      "actions": {
        "forwarding": "accept"
      }
}
```

Figure 1. Example of a "same-manufacturer" ACE.

Similarly, an ACE can be set up that indicates that the device may communicate with other devices on the local network on a specific port. Such ACEs present scalability problems when naively implemented. For example, if the Same Manufacturer ACE were implemented as MAC to MAC flow rules, there can be $O(N^2)$ rules in the flow table (where N is the number of devices belonging to the manufacturer that are associated with the switch). This is unfeasible as an implementation strategy because switches may be limited in ternary content-addressable memory. Similarly, an explosion of rules will result if the Local Networks ACE were implemented in a single table using MAC address to destination IP match flow rules. We seek a solution that is memory scalable and operator friendly. We make the following assumptions:

- Device Identification: Devices are identified using their MAC addresses on the local network and are dynamically associated with MUD URLs at run-time.
- Flexibility: MAC addresses of devices that will be managed at a switch are not known to the network administrator a priori.
- Network Administration: The network administrator configures information about the network - such as the range of local addresses and the controller classes for the Domain Name System (DNS), Network Time Protocol (NTP) and Dynamic Host Configuration Protocol (DHCP) and device controller.

To achieve scalability and flexibility, ACEs are implemented using SDN flow rules in three flow tables. The source and destination MAC address are classified in the first two flow tables and metadata is associated with the packet. The third table implements the MUD ACEs with rules that stated in terms of the packet classification metadata that is assigned in the first two tables.

The flow pipeline is as shown in Figure 2, with the packet being finally sent to a table that implements L2Switch flow rules which is provided by another application.

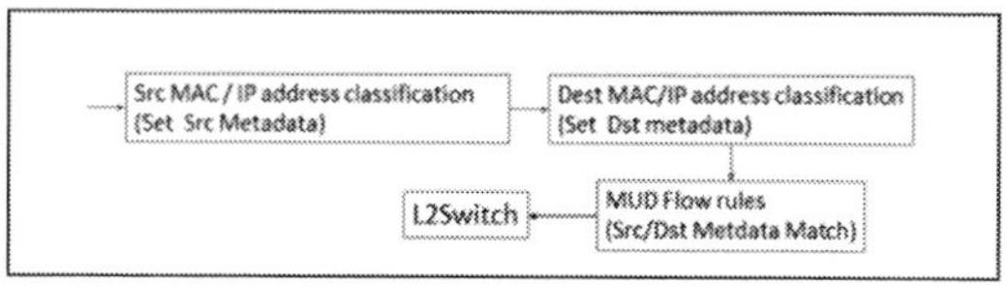

Figure 2. Flow Pipeline structure

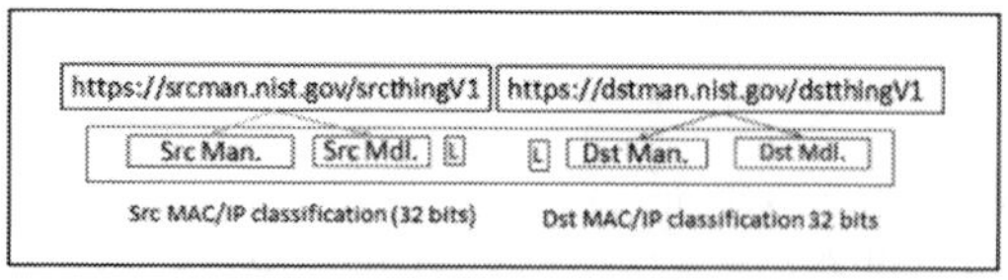

Figure 3. Source and destination metadata assignment.

The OpenFlow metadata field consists of 64 bits. We organize this as two 32-bit segments. Each 32-bit segment encodes a triple <*manufacturer, model, local-networks flag (L)* > as shown in Figure 3. The manufacturer and model are determined from the MUD URL and the local-network flag is determined from Source / Destination IP address and network configuration.

The packet classification metadata rules are reactively inserted when packets arrive at the switch as follows: When the switch connects to the controller, the source and destination classification tables are initialized with low priority rules that unconditionally send IP packets up to the controller. This generates a *PacketIn* event at the controller which then inserts Source (or destination) MAC match rules that assign metadata to the packet and forward to the next table at a higher priority. Subsequent packets that match on the same MAC will have metadata associated with it and be forwarded to the next table without controller intervention. The next stage is to do the same for the destination MAC match rule.

The controller maintains a table associating MAC address with a MUD URI. This mapping is learned dynamically during DHCP processing, i.e., when the device sends out its own MUD URL when requesting an address (using the newly defined DHCP options 161) or it can be configured by the administrator for the device if DHCP support has not been implemented on the device. Each manufacturer (i.e., the "authority" portion of the MUD URL) and model (i.e., the entire MUD URL) is assigned a unique integer, which is placed in the metadata as shown in Figure 3. The controller also has knowledge of what constitutes a "local network" (typically the local subnet) which is assigned a bit in the metadata. If a MAC address does not have a MUD URL associated with it (e.g., a laptop) then it is assigned an implementation reserved metadata classification of UNCLASSIFIED that cannot be assigned to any real MUD URL.The next table implements the MUD ACEs. Note that at this stage of the pipeline, metadata has already been associated with the packet. MUD rules are implemented as ACCEPT rules. That is, if the metadata assigned to a packet matches the match part of the mud rule, it is sent to the next table.

Default unconditional high priority rules are initially inserted that allow interaction of the device with the reserved ports for DHCP and NTP. These are inserted into the MUD rule table on switch connect with the controller. The DHCP match rule has a "send to controller" Action part so that the controller may extract the MUD URL from the DHCP request if it exists. This enables the controller to associate a MUD URL with the source MAC address based on the DHCP request.

After the MUD URL is associated with the device, the MUD profile is retrieved by the SDN controller and flow rules that implement the MUD ACEs are inserted into the MUD table in the following order:

- High priority source (or destination) metadata and TCP Syn. flag match drop action rule to enforce TCP connection directionality. MUD ACEs can specify which end of a TCP connection is the initiator. For such MUD ACEs, we insert rules that drop packets where the connection is initiated from the wrong direction.
- Lower priority Rules that match on source metadata and destination IP addresses for access to specific named hosts or classes of hosts (e.g. Controller or my-controller) as specified by the MUD ACEs.
- Rules that match on source IP address and destination metadata for inbound packets to the IOT device as specified by the MUD ACEs.
- Rules that match on source and destination metadata for allowing access to manufacturer or model or local network classes as specified by the MUD ACEs.
- Lower priority Drop rule for packets that match on Source Model metadata but do not match on one of the rules above.
- Lower priority Drop rule for packets that match on Destination Model metadata but do not match on one of the higher priority rules above.
- Lower priority default UNCLASSIFIED packet pass through rule. The default MUD behavior allows all packets that are metadata tagged as UNCLASSIFIED to pass through the pipeline.

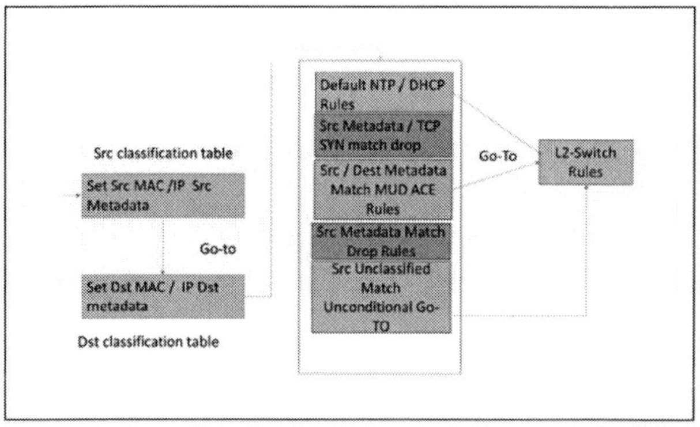

Figure 4. Detailed Flow Pipeline structure. The first two tables are classification tables which assign metadata. The third table is the MUD rules table. Drop rules are color coded Red.

III. ANALYSIS

The scheme we have described above is dynamic and memory scalable with O(N) rules for N distinct MAC addresses at switch. By dividing the rules into packet classification rules and MUD rules which are dependent on the metadata assigned on the first two tables, MUD rules can be installed independently of packet classification. The devices may appear at the switch prior to the MUD rules being installed or vice versa. This allows for dynamic configuration i.e. the MUD ACL table can be changed dynamically at run time without needing to re-configure the rules in the first two tables that classify the packets and vice versa. The packets may be initially marked as UNCLASSIFIED and later when they are associated with a MUD profile (using the DHCP or other mechanism outlined in the MUD specification), the appropriate metadata is assigned to them.

Because the MUD ACEs are expected to be relatively static and few, the flows in the MUD rule table have hard timeouts to match the cache timeout in the MUD file. This can be in the order of days. The packet classification flow rules have short (configurable) idle timeouts. This limits the size of the table and allows for dynamic adjustment of the table when MAC addresses appear and disappear at the switch. The shorter the idle timeout for the classification rules, the less time it takes for reconfiguration and the less time it takes to purge the table from unreferenced entries. However, the shorter the timeout, the more overhead by way of communication with the controller due to the increased number of *PacketIn* events at the controller. We present experimental results in section V.

Our scheme, as described thus far, requires that a packet must be processed at the controller and a rule installed before packet processing may proceed. The initial rule in the MAC address classification stage that is installed when the switch connects, sends the packet to the controller but not to the next table. Thus, a packet may not proceed in the pipeline before it can be classified. This may be necessary if strict ACL-dictated behavior is required but there are some resultant performance consequences i.e., a disconnected or failed controller causes a switch failure because no packets from a newly arriving device can get through prior to the classification rule being installed.

To address this problem, we loosen up the interpretation of the ACE specification. We define a "relaxed" mode of operation where packets can proceed in the pipeline while classification flow rules are being installed. This may result in a few packets being allowed to proceed, in violation of the MUD ACEs with the condition that the system will become eventually compliant to the MUD ACEs.

To implement this behavior, the initial rule installed in the packet classification table with infinite timeout, allows the packet to proceed through the pipeline and delivers the packet to the controller simultaneously. If the controller is offline or fails during rule installation, the packet is sent to the next table with the initial rule and there is no disruption. When the controller comes online again, it will get a packet notification and install the appropriate rule – thus restoring MUD compliant behavior. Thus, the switch becomes resilient to controller failures, with the failure mode being to allow communication.

However, there is another source of potential disruption that must be addressed: Because the source and destination MAC addresses are classified using two tables, it is possible that the source MAC address classification rule exists in the table, while the destination MAC address classification rule has not yet been inserted into the next table. If the MUD rules have been inserted already, this will result in dropped packets in the MUD rules table until the destination table is populated, because the fall through action for Source MAC - classified packets that do not match a MUD ACE rule is to drop the packet.

We address this issue by defining reserved metadata classifications as follows:

- UNCLASSIFIED: The MAC address does not belong to any known MUD URL. For example, if the packet is emitted with a source address belonging to a laptop, for which no MUD rules exist, then its source MAC address is UNCLASSIFIED.
- UNKNOWN: The MAC address has been sent to the controller and is pending classification. The default rule that is installed when the switch connects to the controller sends the packet to the controller on IP match and stamps the packet with metadata of UNKNOWN.

The classification tables each have rules that send the packet up to the controller while setting the corresponding metadata (for source or destination MAC) to UNKNOWN and forwarding the packet to the next stage. The MUD rules table has rules that permits packets that are UNKNOWN in source or destination MAC classification to proceed to the next stage. The scheme is as shown in Figure 5.

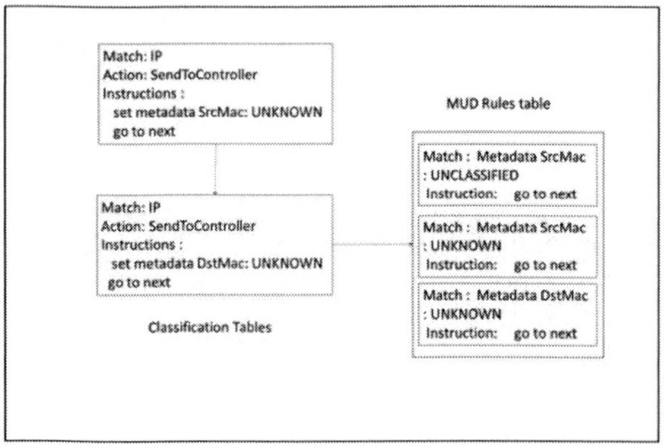

Figure 5. Temporary classifications label added to prevent blocking of flow pipeline during configuration.

On *PacketIn*, the controller pushes flow rules to correctly classify the packet. Because these packet classification rules are pushed at a higher priority than the default send to controller rule in the classification tables, the metadata will change from UNKOWN to the actual classification determined by the controller when the flow rule is installed. In the meanwhile, the pipeline is not blocked.

This "eventually compliant" mode of operation avoids packet drops and provides controller failure resiliency; however, there some limitations: (1) A few packets that violate the MUD rules could get through prior to the classification rule being installed at the switch. This could result in a temporary violation of the ACEs. (2) TCP direction enforcement for short flows, which depends upon detection of TCP SYN flags and correct classification of MAC addresses, is not possible to enforce at the switch until a flow rule that classifies the packet is installed. We quantify these limitations in the next sections.

IV. IMPLEMENTATION

Our implementation [4] uses the OpenDaylight (ODL) SDN controller [5]. The configuration information for the system, which includes the MUD file and ACLs file are presented as north-bound API, are generated using the ODL YANG tools. The association between MUD URL and MAC can be configured directly or inferred by the controller by examining interactions between IOT devices and the DHCP server. For the performance measurement experiments, we directly configured the MAC to MUD URL association.

V. EMULATION EXPERIMENTS

To measure scalability of the implementation, our experimental scenario on MiniNet [6] consisted of 100 devices on one switch all belonging to the same manufacturer randomly exchanging messages. A device randomly picks another device and sends 10 pings, then sleeps randomly with an exponentially distributed average sleep time of 5 seconds. Our goal is to measure the memory scaling as the idle timeout of flow rules is altered. The following chart shows sum of the maximum number of rules in the source and destination classification tables for different values of the idle timeout.

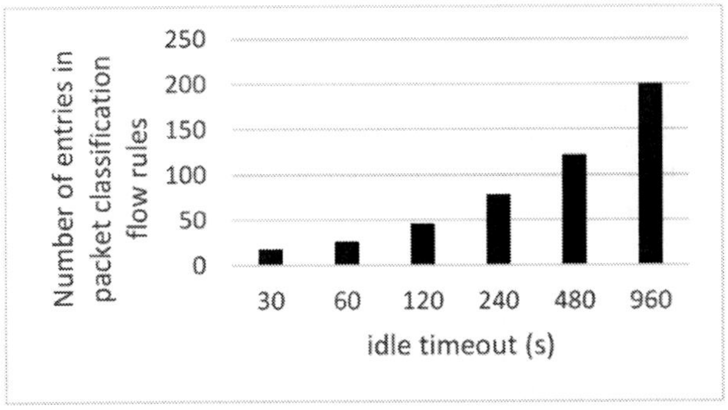

Figure 6. Packet Classification tables size variation with idle timeout. The MUD Rules table is a constant size and has infinite timeout.

In all cases, it is possible to implement the system with just a few rules in the classification table at the expense of an increasing number of *PacketIn* events processed at the controller.

To quantify the overhead involved with *PacketIn* processing under load, we measured the number of packets seen at the controller per burst of packets sent by varying the idle timeout settings for the packet classification rules. The results are shown in Figure 7. The maximum number of *PacketIn* events per burst of pings reaches a maximum of about 6 packets with the classification flow idle timeout set to 15 seconds – 6 packets are processed at the controller under these load conditions before the flow is pushed to the switch. The time it takes for the flow to appear at the switch is the window within which ACE violations can occur in the Relaxed ACL model and is hence significant. Measurements on an actual switch are presented next.

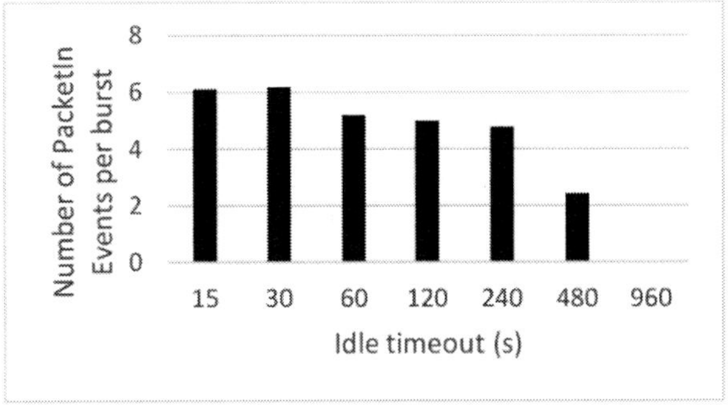

Figure 7. Maximum Number of packetIn events (observed at the controller) per burst of packets.

VI. MEASUREMENTS ON AN OMNIA TURRIS ROUTER

To measure how well our implementation would perform on commercially available hardware that may be a part of a home or small business, we tested our implementation an Omnia Turris [7] router that supports OpenVSwitch [8]. Raspberry Pi devices were used for load generation.

We installed a MUD Profile using the DHCP mechanism which allows the device to be accessed on port 80 from any machine on the local network. The device can access www.nist.gov on port 443. All other access is denied. The baseline performance of the router was measured. Relaxed ACLs were used to install the flow rules. Then, using iPerf [9], we measured the bandwidth with the MUD rules installed under different scenarios. This gives an indication of the overhead involved with MUD rule processing. As previously described, relaxed ACLs give us some advantages i.e., resilience to controller failures and reduced latency for packets that do not violate ACLs. However, packets may get through in violation of an ACL until the time a packet classification rule is pushed to the switch and appears in the switch table as a flow. How many packets get through before further communication is blocked? We used iPerf to perform an experiment where the device initiates an outbound connection with a peer on the local network and sends packets to it. As the "attempted bandwidth" is increased, more packets make it through the pipeline before being blocked, reaching a maximum of about 3 MB total leakage before the flow rules are applied, as shown in Figure 8.

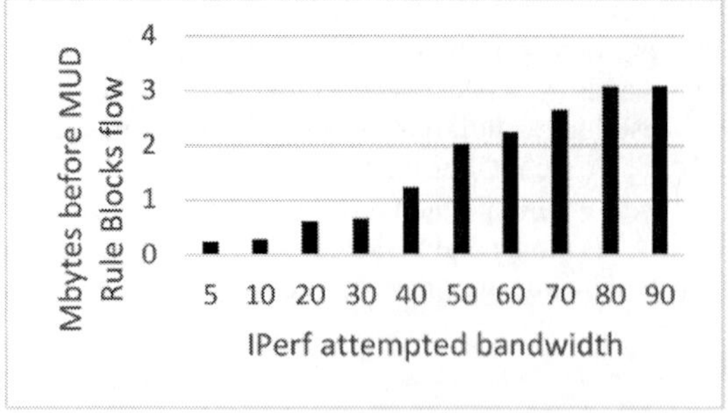

Figure 8. Relaxed ACL TCP packet leakage before ACL application. This is the amount of data that gets through before iperf stops.

Thus, if devices are expected to communicate infrequently and in short bursts, it is better to use the strict ACL model. Otherwise, it is possible that the communication may complete before the MUD ACE flow rules intervene.

Finally, we measured the overhead of strict ACLs on connection establishment. We initiate a connection from a local network resident device to a server accepting connections on port 80 on the MUD-compliant IOT device and measure the overhead in TCP connection establishment with and without relaxed ACL support over 100 attempts. The results are summarized in Table 1.

TABLE I. MAX TCP CONNECTION ESTABLISHMENT TIME FOR STRICT AND RELAXED ACLs

ACL Model	Max Connection establishment time (s)	Standard deviation (s)
Relaxed	0.002	.0003
Strict	2.0	.15

Significantly worse performance for strict ACL is caused by packets being dropped before flow rules are pushed. Dropping packets when the TCP connection is being established adversely impacts the connection establishment time. Note that this phenomenon only occurs when the rule is first installed because of the round trip to the controller before the installation of the rule.

VII. Conclusion

In this paper we presented the design and implementation of the MUD standard on OpenFlow switches, thereby demonstrating its implementation feasibility – even on limited memory devices. Our design is model driven, resilient to controller failure and allows for dynamic re-configuration. Our design uses $O(N)$ flow rules for N distinct MAC addresses seen at the switch.

An open question is how to set the idle timeout for the flows. Our timeout policy for the experiments described in this paper was to set the timeout the same for all devices – which makes sense in this case given a homogenous communication pattern with equal probability that a randomly selected pair of MAC addresses will communicate. In general, the communication between devices and between devices and its controller or host is not likely to be uniform. To achieve best utilization of the switch flow table memory, the idle timeout should be set high for MAC addresses that have a high probability of being referenced and set low for MAC addresses that have a low probability of being referenced [10]. It would be useful to extend the MUD standard to provide hints for communication frequency and length of communication burst for different MUD ACEs so that the controller can use this information to optimize timeouts and pick the appropriate management strategy on the classification flow table.

Our future work includes setting timeouts adaptively and combining MUD with an IDS to develop a comprehensive enterprise security architecture.

References

[1] E. Lear, R. Droms, and D. Romascanu, "Manufacturer Usage Description Specification," Internet Engineering Task Force Work in Progress, Jun. 2018. https://datatracker.ietf.org/doc/draft-ietf-opsawg-mud/ [Accessed: March 2019]

[2] Open Networking Foundation, "OpenFlow Switch Specification, Version 1.5.1 (Protocol version 0x06)", https://www.opennetworking.org/software-defined-standards/specifications/ [Accessed: March 2019]

[3] A. Hamza, H. H. Gharakheili, and V. Sivaraman, "Combining MUD Policies with SDN for IoT Intrusion Detection," in Proceedings of the 2018 Workshop on IoT Security and Privacy, 2018, pp. 1–7.

[4] nist-mud - NIST SDN MUD implementation, https://github.com/usnistgov/nist-mud [Accessed: March 2019]

[5] OpenDaylight, SDN Controller https://www.opendaylight.org [Accessed March, 2019]

[6] MiniNet - An instant Virtual Network on Your Laptop. http://www.mininet.org [Accessed: March 2019]

[7] Omnia Turris https://omnia.turris.cz/ [Accessed: March 2019]

[8] OpenVSwitch: Production Quality Multilayer, Open Virtual Switch., https://openvswitch.org Sep-2018. [Accessed: March, 2019]

[9] J. Dugan, S. Elliott, B. Mah, J. Poskanzer, and K. Prabhu, "iPerf - The ultimate speed test tool for TCP, UDP and SCTP." https://iperf.fr [Accessed: March 2019]

[10] A. Vishnoi, R. Poddar, V. Mann, and S. Bhattacharya, "Effective switch memory management in OpenFlow networks," Proc. 8th ACM Int. Conf. Distributed Event-Based Systems, 2014, pp. 177-188.

Future NetworkArchitectures of Networking of Everything

Hyun-Kook Kahng
Electrical & Information Engineering
Korea University
Sejong, Republic of Korea
e-mail: eekahng@korea.ac.kr

Suyeon Kim
Department of Industry Cooperation
Keimyung University
Daegu, Republic of Korea
e-mail: sykim388@gmail.com

Seong-Soon Joo
ETRI
Daejeon, Republic of Korea
e-mail: ssjoo@etri.re.kr

Sweung-Won Cheung
Hanwha Techwin
Pankyo, Republic of Korea
e-mail: csw1988@gmail.com

***Abstract*—Currently, even though various and advanced networks, such as 4G/5G and IP based networks are available, there is very limited choice of networking in real communication depending on which Internet Service Provider (ISP) is selected by a user. On the Internet, there is no place to inquire about the physical address without DNS (Domain Name Service), which is a centralized service. Nowadays, there are social networks where users share their profiles including name, phone number, email address, even their information about private life. In this paper, we propose an architecture to integrate conventional networks and social networks, so that any user can find a destination without any centralized service by referring to the social network in which every device participates and shares their private information. Furthermore, we believe this concept can be extended beyond communications. In the context of Internet of Things (IoT), if those things are members of social networks, they can perform more advanced tasks, such as collaborative works. We focus on networking issues to integrate various networks, such as transparent networks, things social networks, and things centric networks, in which smart devices participate to provide advanced network services to smart things or thing-users, especially from the IoT perspective, through the conceptual model of Networking of Everything.**

Keywords-NoE; Transparent Network; PDN; Semantic Web; RDF; OWL.

I. INTRODUCTION

There are many different types of networks on the market, such as mobile telecommunication networks, IP-based data networks, etc. However, the networking principle has not changed. Even though multiple networks are available to the same device, the device of a user has no choice but to access the predetermined (pre-contractual) network, since each network is usually operated by different providers. Secondly, even though a device can access two or more different networks, this is done manually (even though now this is possible, network access is still limited). Thirdly, users have to know the address and its format of the device providing the target service. And lastly, at this time, especially in the current Internet, only IP address-routing is the service provided by ISPs, regardless of the service type. In other words, the user has to know everything: what kind of services is available, what is the name of service in each network, who from which network can provide it, how can he access the network, etc. It is already known that current networking cannot support meaningful and rich Internet of Things (IoT) service.

In the IoT, things are supposed to be intelligent, and the thing will be a user of the network which is called a thing-user in Networking of Everything (NoE). While the conventional device is allocated only an Internet address, which is connected to a specific access network on the Internet via Dynamic Host Configuration Protocol (DHCP), thing-users in NoE join thing-user social networks (defined in [4]) to share not only their names or addresses, but their capabilities, context, communicative motivation, experiences, and intentions of collaborative work with others, and then socializes to interact with other thing-users autonomously. The thing-users produce not only the digitalized information but also the varieties of reactions based on the socialized decision. The thing-user may describe its communicative motivation and convey intended meanings to other thing-users or thing-user groups using a mutually understood language such as semantic Web languages with Resource Description Framework (RDF), Ontology Language (OWL) and Extensible Markup Language (XML). The thing-user will discover a thing (or groups) which will provide a service from the thing-user community.

The Future Network (FN)-NoE also focuses on networking issues to integrate diverse networking techniques to provide the users' service requirements mentioned above: transparent networking, dynamic virtual networking, as well as social networking. Social networking is to find a target thing or things. Transparent networking is to interconnect various networks. Lastly, dynamic virtual networking, called Proximity Defined Network (PDN), is to define a temporary working space where thing-users can collaborate for the requested service.

In this paper, we show that the FN-NoE eventually provides the thing-user centric communication service that discovers and coordinates things to perform a collaborative work among the socialized things located autonomously within a space. The architecture and functional procedure of FN-NoE are presented in Sections II and III, respectively. We show a brief application in Section IV and conclude in Section V.

II. STATE OF ART

In recent years, the influence of the Internet has been increasing rapidly and powerfully. This seems to be due to the following factors. First, the performance of networks is becoming very powerful. Giga Internet or 5G network is no longer a dream, but a reality. Second, it is the evolution of the Web which is the most familiar to the users. The World Wide Web Consortium (W3C) extended the Web so that information is given well-defined meaning, better enabling computers and people to work in cooperation. Third, the spread of social networks has created new human relationships. Online social networking technologies enable individuals to simultaneously share information with others.

However, these attempts have faced unexpected problems, as follows. As the Internet with good performance became more widespread, IoT, which was built on the Internet, was introduced, and this resulted in a variety of devices that would become the rapid evolution of IPv4 addresses. Secondly, the semantic Web makes Web content machine understandable. However, it was found that there are too many jobs to describe everything in RDF format. Thirdly, the online-social networks also show some problems like private information disclosure.

At this stage, we have to consider how to integrate these three elements to maximize the advantage and minimize the disadvantages. In IoT, we consider a social network with only machines, or things with semantic Web which understand each other. The things will share information and can verify each other by exchanging WebIDs [6]. The content of semantic Web will be very limited information about predetermined network services; no privacy disclosure. Thus, this new Networking of Everything means the integration of the semantic Web network to communicate with network devices, social networks to share the information of network devices, and conventional networks for data transfer.

III. ARCHITECTURE

The infrastructure for the FN-NoE is constructed with the core networks, the access networks, and the regional networks. The core network and the access networks are evolved from the current networks and provide the connections to the users and the transparent connections between the regional networks, which is a virtual network to provide logical access to an intelligent socialized thing-user.

The FN-NoE can be operated over either existing legacy networks or future networks [1]. A NoE terminal located in a certain space connects to an access network and is connected

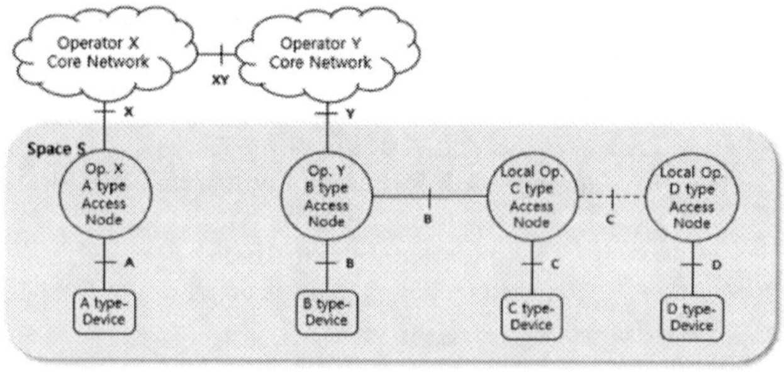

Figure 1. FN-NoE operated over existing legacy networks.

to another NoE terminal through the core networks.

The core networks between NoE terminals may be operated by different network operators and the switching and routing scheme applied to the core networks may be different. The access network is managed by the core network operator and differentiated with the type of access links and access procedures. The access network may have a local network managed by the local private owner as a subnetwork. The local network may have a local network underneath.

Figure 1 shows, excluding thing-user social network, a reference network model where multiple NoE terminals located in a certain space are connected to each other. There is an NoE terminal connected to the A type access network of the core network managed by operator X.

The FN-NoE provides (1) a transparent end-to-end connection between NoE terminals connected to heterogeneous access networks, and according to the preferred connection, (2) a thing-to-thing connection for coordinating NoE terminals autonomously. The required information for coordinating the access network in a certain space to establish a transparent connection is maintained at each NoE terminal. The NoE terminal may share the coordination information with the NoE terminals located within the same space directly or exchange in the regional virtual switch, as shown in Figure 2. The detailed information about the coordinated networking layer will be explained in the next section.

The regional networks are overlaid to the core network and the access networks. The regional networks are formed by the NoE terminals and the NoE virtual switches.

To provide transparent end-to-end connections between the NoE terminals and autonomous coordinated thing-to-thing connections among the NoE terminals, the FN-NoE

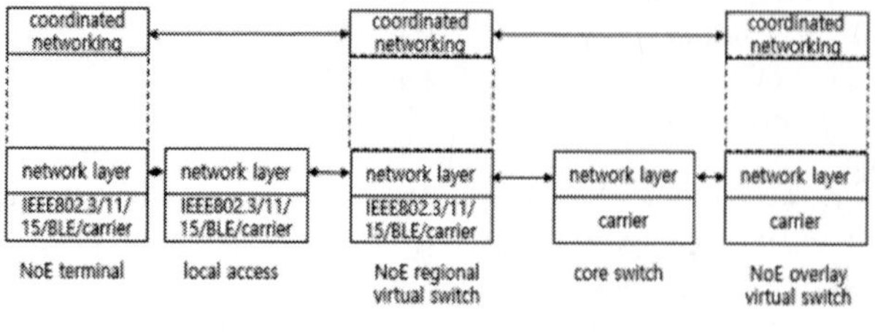

Figure 2. An example of connections in the FN-NoE

specifies following: How to manage a NoE terminal, regional virtual switch, and the overlay virtual switch? How to form a thing-user social community? How to share experience with thing-users? How to discover a thing or thing-user for collaborating? How to establish a transparent connection between the NoE terminals? And how to establish coordinated connections among the NoE terminals?

The coordinated networking layer of the FN-NoE is composed of capability blocks, as shown in Figure 3.

- **The NoE terminal resource and capability profile management** block maintains the profile and the status of the NoE terminal's resources and skill set. This block manages the status of the NoE terminal, regional virtual switch, and overlay virtual switch.
- **The NoE terminal social networking** block performs the process of forming or disbanding a social group. This block controls a NoE terminal to join or leave a social group. This block controls a NoE terminal to publish or subscribe an experience sharing with a social group. The control protocols between the NoE terminal social networking blocks are defined at the reference point R1.
- **The coordinated experience management** block maintains the coordinated networking experienced by the NoE terminal and by the NoE terminals of joined social groups. This block searches the experience base to match a request from a NoE terminal or a social group.
- **The coordinated peer discovery** block performs the process of discovering the NoE terminal to be a peer NoE terminal or the NoE terminals to form a collaborative work group. This block searches a proximal NoE terminal from a social group or hands over the discovery to the regional virtual switches or overlay virtual switches. The control protocols between the coordinated peer discovery blocks are defined at the reference point R2.
- **The transparency networking control** block manages the process of selecting preferred access networks and establishing a transparent end-to-end connection. The control protocols between the transparency networking control blocks are defined at the reference point R3.
- **The thing-user centric networking control** block manages the process of socializing a thing-user and establishing a thing-to-thing connection. The control protocols between the thing-user centric networking control blocks are defined at the reference point R4.

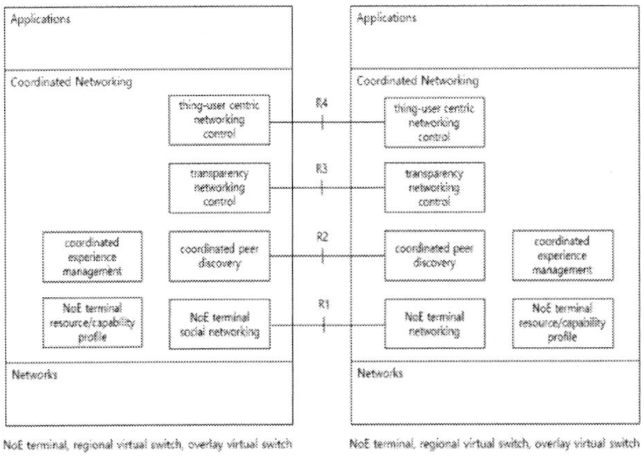

Figure 3. Reference model of the FN-NoE

IV. FUNCTIONAL PROCEDURE

The FN-NoE is composed of two main blocks: Networking of Heterogeneous Networks (NHN), which can be implemented with legacy networks, and Proximity Defined Networks (PDN) which is formed during the thing-user centric communication period

In Figure 4, nodes (or thing-users) are in the scope of three different types of access networks, i.e., heterogeneous. They may or may not communicate with each other. However, if those networks are transparent, then each device with different skills can communicate and collaborate to provide a service to a specific human-user or thing-user.

Any node like a switch, a virtual switch, a regional (virtual) switch or a network agent can be a thing-user if it can use the FN-NoE service.

A. Thing-user social network

In Figure 4, usually when a node (which is just legacy node) accesses the local network 1, it can communicate with a node in network 3 if a node knows its destination network address (or name) and networks should be interconnected via intermediate nodes. When the networks are physically located too far away, it is a very time-consuming job.

However, when thing-user 1 (very smart node) in Figure 4 joins an appropriate social network 1 depending on its profile and objectives, it can locate the exact thing-user in network 3, not by network- dependent routing algorithm, but by context-aware social networking, as shown in Figure 5.

By this thing-user social networking, a transparent networking service is provided to the thing-user, which is only identified by a profile or name (not network address).

Of course, if it can not find its social group, it itself must create and post it to the regional post and/or the global post, if needed, to announce it to others.

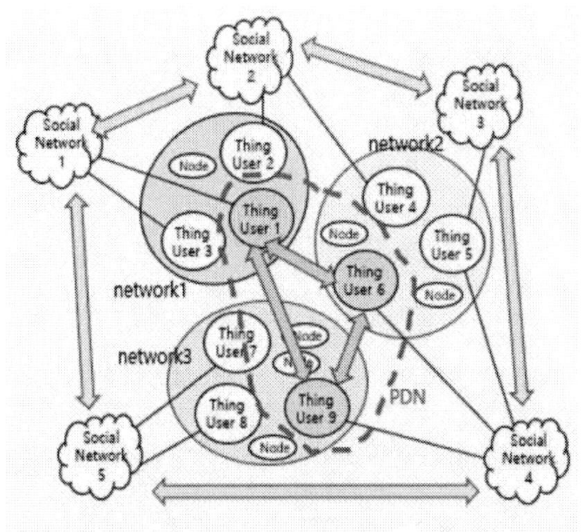

Figure 4. FN-NoE conceptual model

Note that even though the matter to create, find, and maintain the social networking is out of scope of this work, they are key procedures to be defined in other documents.

B. Transparent end-to-end connection

The FN-NoE allows a NoE terminal to select appropriate access networks according to the preferred connection and to establish a transparent end-to-end connection between the NoE terminals. The FN-NoE defines the coordinated networking layer located at the OSI application to provide transparent end-to-end connections between NoE terminals and autonomous coordinated thing-to-thing connections. The coordinated networking layer supports the NoE terminal to be socialized for sharing the coordination experience and for performing context-based discovery and establishing a connection.

The regional virtual switch supports a NoE terminal for discovering an appropriate access network and provides access network to establish a transparent connection. The overlay virtual switch performs a hierarchical peer-to-peer overlay switching for exchanging coordination information between regional virtual switches to provide a transparent end-to-end connectivity between the NoE terminals.

C. Proxmity defined network

Figure 6 shows that when a thing-user locates its destination thing-user or thing-user group, using thing-user social networking, it explains its profile or objectives, and then requests collaboration from its counterpart thing-user(s) in PDN, as shown in Figure 4. If it needs additional thing-users, then it will request to find more thing-user(s) in the near social group, recursively.

PDN is a sort of temporary virtual network in which a group of thing-users collaborate with each other autonomously during the thing-user central communications.

D. Thing-user centric communication

The thing-user centric communication service is accomplished over PDN, which is based on thing-user social

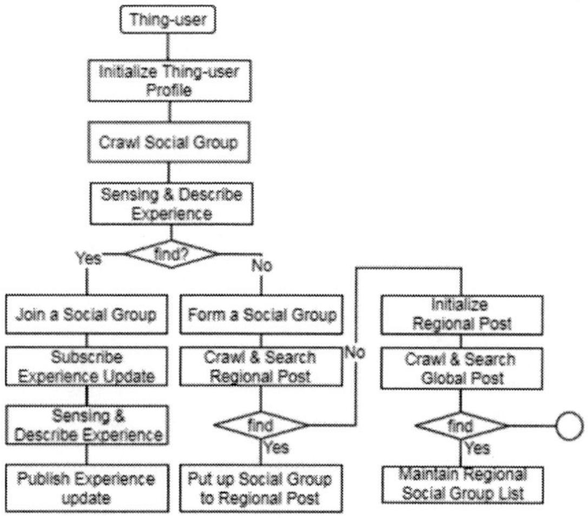

Figure 5. Functional procedure of thing-user social networking

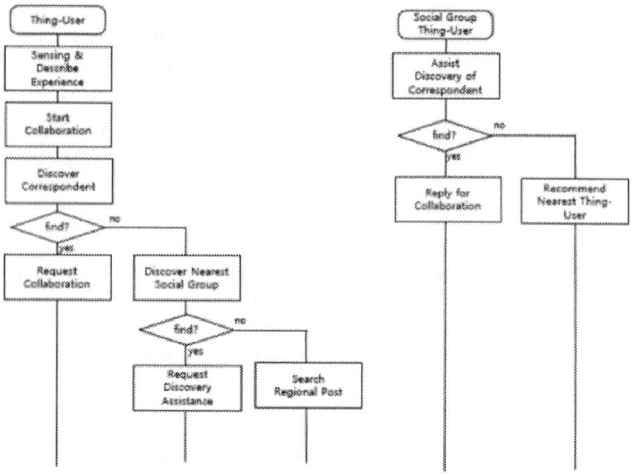

Figure 6. Functional procedure of Proximity Defined Networking

networking. The thing-user communicates with another thing-user or a thing-user group in PDN by conveying the intended meaning, which describes the communication motivation, and experience on a specific task by ontology-based thing-user language. The thing-user discovers a communication party, relying on the assistance of thing-users of a thing-user social group, requests to introduce a thing-user who may be the communicative correspondent or might know the communicative correspondent until it meets the right communication party. The social assistance is accepted upon the trust and reputation of a thing-user acquired in a social group. Currently, in our application, the trust and reputation can be achieved with WebID and semantic inference.

V. APPLICATION

In this section, we briefly introduce an application which was built over a very preliminary NoE architecture [5], namely, an autonomous collaboration system of smart things using accumulated experience knowledge achieved by semantic inference with RDF database.

In Figure 7, smart delivery service with a drone having smart thing's structure is shown as one of services over the autonomous collaboration system.

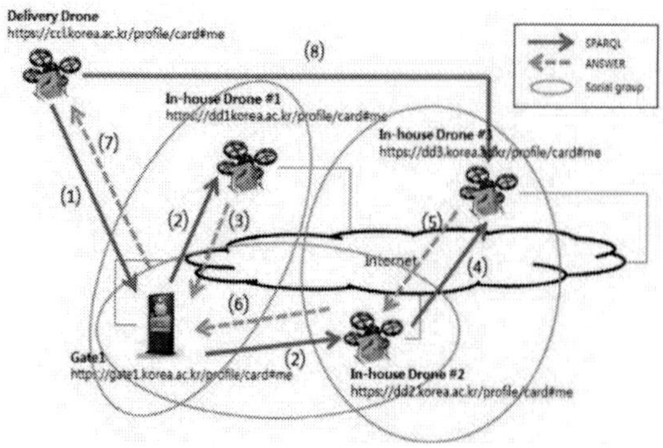

Figure 7. Example of collaborative service over NoE

If all Smart Things have Basic Identity Information (BII) and use semantic technology, the Internet can become the world of Smart Things, which has built up many social networks. Semantic technology provides a way to utilize the new Web application of many Smart Things connected to the Internet. In this paper, we show a mailing and delivery collaboration system among drones as a specific task of spatial autonomous collaboration where Smart Things collaborate using semantic technology, such as SPARQL (a semantic query language for Database) [7]. If a Smart Thing has BII composed of a Web server address, WebID, and endpoint address, and can query SPARQL for a purpose, it shows how spatial autonomous collaboration is possible in intelligent Web without special environment or Artificial Intelligence (AI). The delivery drones that come with the mail look for collaborative in-house drones using BII, Identification Process (IDP), and SPARQL semantic techniques based on the Default Response Rules (DRR).

Smart Thing updates the BII of collaborators in TDB-Experience knowledge after collaboration. It accumulates a collaborative experience and expands its social network. The delivery drones which experienced collaborations with company drones # 3 were able to deliver mail more quickly and accurately by utilizing their experience knowledge when the same task occurred. Thanks to the accumulated experience knowledge, it is possible to process the same thing more quickly and accurately in the future.

VI. Conclusion and Future Work

Networking of Everything (NoE) refers to the process capable to provide FN-NoE services, such as transparent network service, thing-user social network service, and thing-user centric communication service to the thing-users who participate in the FN-NoE. In other words, the distributed social networking of thing-user devices will provide thing-user centric service which is supported by the intelligence and semantic knowledge of the thing-user.

The given application is implemented and verified under the assumption that a delivery social network has already been established. Depending on the purpose, how to establish and dismiss the social network over FN-NoE would be one of our future works.

Problems related to the NoE were defined in ISO/IEC TR 29181-9 in 2017. Even though this paper is a very preliminary stage for its solution, enhanced work on NoE is to be proposed as International Standards on NoE architecture and its companion protocols.

Acknowledgment

This work was supported by the project "Standardization of Networking of Everything Architecture and Protocols" funded by KEIT (No. 20002532).

References

[1] J. Day, "Patterns in Network Architecture. A return to Fundamentals", Prentice Hall, 2008.

[2] T. Berners-Lee, "Linked-Data-Design Issues" [Online]. Available from: https://www.w3.org/DesignIssues/LinkedData.html

[3] S. Joo and H. Kahng, ISO/IEC TR 29181-9, Future Network-Problem statement and requirements-Part 9: Networking of Everything.

[4] S. Tramp, "Distributed Semantic Social networks: Architecture, Protocols and Applications", Doctoral thesis from Universitat Leipsig, 2014.

[5] C. Lee, S. Cheung, S. Joo, and H. Kahng, "Design and Implementation of Autonomous Collaboration System of Smart Things using accumulated Experience knowledge", IEEE/ICACT2019, Phoenix Park, Pyeongchang, Korea. Feb 17-20, 2019.

[6] A. Sambra, H. Story, and T. Berners-Lee, "WebID 1.0 – Web Identity and Discovery", [Online] Available from: https://dvcs.w3.org/hg/WebID/raw-file/tip/spec/identity-respec.html

[7] B. DuCharme, "Learning SPARQL", Second Edition, June 2013, ISBN 978-1-449-37143-2

Review of an ANFIS Methodology-Based Stock Market Prediction System

Manal Alghieth
Faculty of Computer, Information Technology
Qassim University,
Qassim, Saudi Arabia
Email: mgietha@qu.edu.sa

Abstract—**Stock market prediction is of immense interest to trading companies and buyers due to high profit margins. The majority of successful buying or selling activities occur close to stock price turning trends. This makes the prediction of stock indices and analysis a crucial factor in the determination whether the stocks will increase or decrease the next day. This paper describes an Adaptive Network based Fuzzy Inference System (ANFIS) and critically analyses its ability to improve prediction in Yahoo stock data. At present, the focus of research is on the improvement of prediction with low false prediction via the hybridization and extension of existing methodologies. The research results presented a low Mean-Square-Error (MSE) in both testing and validation processes.**

Keywords- Adaptive Network-Based Fuzzy Inference System (ANFIS); Prediction; Time series Stock market prediction; Yahoo! stock data.

I. INTRODUCTION

Stock price forecasting has long been a focus of intelligent soft computing techniques to improve the predictability of financial systems [1]. Due to rapidly changing trends in current global financial markets and the ongoing commercial uncertainties, accurate forecasting of time-based financial trends has become increasingly important. Stock market forecasting provides the investors with a general overview of the changing tendency of the stock markets. Based on the forecasts, the investors can make timely decisions on buying or selling stocks under bargains and avoid financial losses. A wide range of techniques applicable to stock market forecasting have been reported in the literature which are not just limited to econometric modelling but includes Artificial Intelligence (AI) – based soft-computing techniques- as well [2]. Indeed, Artificial Neural Networks (ANN) and Fuzzy Inference Systems (FIS) are two well-known paradigms used in time-series design and prediction, and have their own strength and weaknesses in the forecasting of future data based on a finite set of previous time-based trends [3].

Research in fuzzy logic has drawn substantial attention during the past two decades and has now become a robust paradigm for the prediction of nonlinear and uncertain systems from a wide range of real-world domains including signal data mining [4], information retrieval [5], finance [6] and various real-world forecasting systems including stocks, resource demand and supply, power requirement, and sensor networks [7]-[10]. Despite a continued and high demand of this soft-computing technique, a number of limitations can be associated to it. FIS generally require a great deal of human intervention to accurately and realistically predict certain situations, which induces a high chance of human-based error in the system. Moreover, the increase in the system variables increases substantially the complexity of the system.

The majority of real-world forecasting systems cover application areas that require the knowledge of historic values to be incorporated into the model. This is because the outcome crucially depends upon historic data. Share prices, electricity consumption and weather forecasts are a few examples of such systems. Statistical Analysis (SA), ANN, Case Based Reasoning (CBR), FIS, Decision Trees (DT) and Support Vector Machines (SVM) are examples of a number of soft-computing and machine learning methodologies that are frequently used to implement time-series-based forecasting systems. A comprehensive review of applications of these techniques to financial time-series share market forecasting can be consulted in [38]. This review revealed ANNs to be the most frequently used technique in the financial forecasting sector followed by rough set (RS) theory, CBR, OR, FIS and SVM techniques. At present, the focus of research is on the improvement of prediction with low false prediction via the hybridization and extension of existing methodologies.

ANNs generally operate over an undefined dataset where, when subjected to training data, the technique learns from irregularities and thereby creates its own set of rules. The methodology heavily emphasises on comprehensiveness of data and, unlike fuzzy logic, is well known for its ability to withstand noisy data and outliers [11]. The methodology has the ability to predict missing, sparse or low-quality values, which makes it suitable for financial systems that meets with uncertain data. Moreover, this methodology is well known for its ability to handle input variables in parallel and thus it allows large datasets to be efficiently handled. These characteristics make ANN unique in its ability to generalise over a diverse range of input/output data pairs, making it an ideal candidate to replace the human-based expert rule-generation in fuzzy systems. Yet, this paradigm still has its own disadvantages in that over-training may result in unstable prediction capabilities. This shortcoming is generally overcome by dividing the dataset into three groups of training, test and validation sets where the algorithm is stopped if its error margin repeatedly increases over a consecutive number of iterations.

II. LITERATURE REVIEW

A. *Prediction Systems in Literature*

Time-series is regarded as a sequence of stochastic variables whose behaviour depends upon a number of real-world factors or dependent variables that decide the values of the next variables ahead of time based on past trends [12]. A number of soft-computing prediction methodologies have been reported in the literature, which are generally classified as statistical or AI–based domains type. Time-series analysis provides tools to select models that are then used to predict future events as a statistical time-series problem. These statistical predictions are based on the notion that the observations are based on a probability distribution function. Supporting and hybrid models are extensively reported in the literature to improve the forecasting performance via ANN classifiers [13] and network data flow prediction [14], signal synthesis [15], independent component analysis [16], locally linear embedded (LLE) in multivariate analysis [17] and logistic regression [18]. These statistical modelling algorithms are generally limited on the number of variables used and also tend to demonstrate increasing computational complexities with larger datasets. This is the reason why the majority of these models are used in conjunction with supporting soft-computing techniques including self-organising feature maps [19], Linear and Multiple Discriminant Analysis (LDA/MDA) [20], learning-vector quantization [21], case-based-reasoning, rough-sets, linear and quadratic programming and Support Vector Machines (SVM) [22].

Despite the multitude of techniques available, the scope of this research focuses on two predominant AI paradigms in a bid to improve the overall prediction accuracy of the underlying system. As mentioned earlier, ANNs are known for their capabilities to understand and predict patterns in serial data whereas the FIS provides a platform to embed expert human knowledge thereby improving the overall prediction accuracy of uncertain, real-world systems. Based on their limitations and strengths, the next two subsections present their current state-of-the-art in order to elaborate further on various avenues of improvement.

B. *Fuzzy classifiers in time-series-based financial forecasting*

A tri-classifier clustering approach was implemented by Chang et al. [23] as a fuzzy neural network approach which segmented training data into historical clusters in an apparent bid to reduce the training overhead and predict short-length cases via a larger 5-yearly dataset. The approach claimed improved outcomes when compared to the proposed ANFIS methodology based on the forecasted Root-Mean-Squared-Errors (RMSE). Li et al. [24] presented a genetic particle swarm clustering methodology combined with a fuzzy c-means algorithm in a bid to use gradient method to improve the overall accuracy. Similar to other hybrid time-series systems, this methodology also presented high execution times when subjected to larger and multi-dimensional datasets.

A number of direct neuro-fuzzy approaches have been reported in literature with Tung et al. [25] using financial covariates, Yoshida [26] utilising the Black-Scholes formula, Castillo and Melin [27] reporting via fractal dimensions and Tang and Chi [28] using ROC analysis with Logit performance to improve time-series prediction with promising improvements.

The Taguchi method has been used in a number of forecasting investigations [23], [29]. The focus has predominantly been on the utilization of Grey Relational Analysis (GRA) and the utilization of Grey Extreme Learning Machine (GELM) technique against General Back Propagation Neural Networks (GBPN) methods. The methodologies have also been used to predict the most optimal number of neural parameters for improved prediction rate. However, there is a consensus that an increase in the optimization parameters for these algorithms to control hidden nodes, layers and activation functions generally result in a reduced overall performance of the system being optimised.

C. *Neural Systems in time-series-based financial forecasting systems*

As discussed earlier, ANNs are known to improve prediction accuracies of time-series-data forecasting systems in financial and other trading applications. Their ability to generalise in the presence of noisy feature sets and outliers makes them ideal for share market price prediction, asset allocation and portfolio change forecasting.

Martinetz et al. [30] compared an unsupervised technique based on K-means clustering against methodologies including Kohonen-maps, K-means and Maximum-entropy. The classifier presented outstanding minimization in vector quantization coding distortion error and a faster convergence at a controllable cost of higher computational effort. ANNs were initially employed by Connor et al. [31] with outliers "softly" removed from the data when the training was performed over the "outlier-filtered" data. This technique substantially improved the prediction accuracy of the system. However, in large-scale real-world systems, it is generally impractical to use "pre-training" clustering techniques for outlier removal. Moreover, there is a high probability that such a technique may also eliminate valid feature samples from the database as well. In order to address this issue, a hybrid ANN technique was proposed by Castillo and Melin [27] via a neuro-fuzzy technique. The technique regulated the fuzzy membership functions by means of a single-layer feed-forward neural network. The outcome of this work was far superior than the one obtained with generalised regression-based models. A similar work by Zhang and Berardi [32] utilised varied ANN structures over varied data partitions via varied initial random weights, random architectures and variable data and reported a considerable accuracy over conventional neural architectures.

Research has lately moved into the analysis of noisy chaotic time-series prediction. According to Soofi and Cao [33] chaotic and non-linear time series prediction has a significant effect on the economic and financial time series prediction. This is particularly prevalent in stock market prediction where the nonlinear feature data is normally marred by excessive noise. Leung et al. [34] addressed the optimum prediction of noisy time-series data via a Radial Basis Function (RBF) neural network classifier, where the issue of generalization against a large dataset was tackled using a "cross-validated sub-space" method to identify a suitable number of hidden neurons to efficiently handle noise within the datasets. Recently, in-architecture neural network updates have been explored with Goh [35] creating a neuron-level hyper-plane to separate noise from genuine feature samples. This technique, when combined with the nonlinear subspace, creates an optimal RBF predictor for variable signal-to-noise ratios (SNR).

Improvements in the neural architecture also involve the utilization of the so-called "recurrent" ANN (RPNN) that facilitates long-term prediction [36] and local linear and wavelet-based transforms [37]. Additionally, generalised regression-based ANN, counter-propagation technique, neural adaptive resonance classifiers, CART DT, TreeNet-based data mining and random forests have also been used [38].

III. DESIGN AND ANALYSIS

FIS can be classed as of Mamdani type or Takagi-Sugeno Kang (TSK) type. Mamdani FIS is mostly used in practice, although TSK FIS is well known for its computational efficiency and compactness, and it derives a set of rules from input/output training data pairs. Indeed, an important aspect of TSK FIS is its crisp outcome, which significantly reduces its computational complexity when compared to its Mamdani counterpart. A typical TSK FIS rule is given below:

$$i : IF\ x\ is\ A_i\ and\ y\ is\ B_i\ THEN\ f_i = p_i(x) + q_i(y) + r_i \quad (1)$$

where i stands for the rule number, A_i and B_i are corresponding fuzzy sets to each linguistic label domain, f_i is the output set covered by the fuzzy rule in the fuzzy region and p_i, q_i and r_i are the design parameters.

In the equation (1), the values for parameters p_i, q_i and r_i are obtained by training input/output pairs via an ANN.

First order TSK FIS can be defined and visualised as a moving pointer that moves linearly in an outer space based on the value of the antecedent variables. As each rule in the FIS database is associated to the input variables, the TSK FIS is suitable for systems requiring interpolation of multiple linear inputs. A Sugeno system interpolates linear gains from multiple input parameters that would be applied across the input space. This gives a Sugeno system a smooth curve-based change, which is very close to real-world conditions. For instance, due to input-space interpolation, a Sugeno model demonstrates a Gaussian transition between various states. A real-world example of this phenomenon can be that of a temperature control and monitor mechanism in a boiler system where a Sugeno type controller is used to adjust power levels when temperature changes. Instead of defining heat conditions as Very High, High, Medium, Low and Very Low, a Sugeno system can actually interpolate the intermediate values to show an asymptotic decline or incline from very hot to very cold conditions (Matlab, R2014b).

A. *FIS rule-base generation via subtractive clustering and grid-partitioning*

Expert engineers with in-depth knowledge of the underlying domain generate FIS rules, either when a good database is not available or does not cover the whole modelling scenario. However, in order to generate a comprehensive rule-base that portrays the exact relationship between the input/output feature sets, the variable space must be efficiently clustered.

In a fuzzy c-means clustering algorithm, each data point belongs to each of the clusters based on some degree of membership. Therefore, the closer a point is to the mean position of a cluster, the higher its membership to that cluster is. For instance, the weight of a person may be attributed to two different clusters of individuals with one cluster classified as those being obese and the other being of average weight. Based upon a specific data point's (person's) weight's distance to the centre point of both of these clusters, the data points membership could be 0.33 Obese and 0.67 Average_Weight, effectively assigning him/her to belong predominantly to an Average_Weight cluster.

In the time-series-based stock value prediction case, rules are drawn from multiple variables including opening, high, low and trading volume values. These variables can be bound to the input-space via a number of partitioning methodologies including grid [39], tree [40] and scatter partitioning [41]. Grid-based clustering is generally deemed appropriate for systems with low number of membership functions and input variables. This is primarily due to the fact that the methodology's computational complexity increases exponentially with the increase in the number of membership functions and input variables (Mathworks, 2014b).

A complete FIS with the proposed two input variables, trade volume (ϑ_t) and stock value (δ_t) at a time-instance t, and three membership functions, namely LOW, MEDIUM and HIGH consists of a total number of 9 rules. In general, a complete FIS with p input variables, each one with its domain divided into $N_1, \ldots, N_p$ fuzzy labels, will consists of the following number of rules (2):

$$N_1 * N_2 * \ldots * N_p \quad (2)$$

When all input variables are associated the same number of linguistic labels (N) then the total number of rules possible is p^N, and therefore the number of rules will increase exponentially with respect to the number of input variables and the number of linguistic labels. To reduce the number of rules, alternative techniques such as subtractive clustering was proposed on the basis of a single-pass algorithm for number of cluster and centre estimation [42].

B. Formulation of a neuro-fuzzy approach for financial time-series estimation:

The proposed system implements a neuro-fuzzy approach where the ANN technique is used to tune the FIS parameters. The resultant methodology is widely known as an Adaptive Network based Fuzzy Inference System (ANFIS), which utilises training feature data to induce fuzzy rules via neural training-based weight adjustment.

A wider framework for the proposed TSK ANFIS to predict stock prices is shown in Figure 1, where each layer is further explained below:

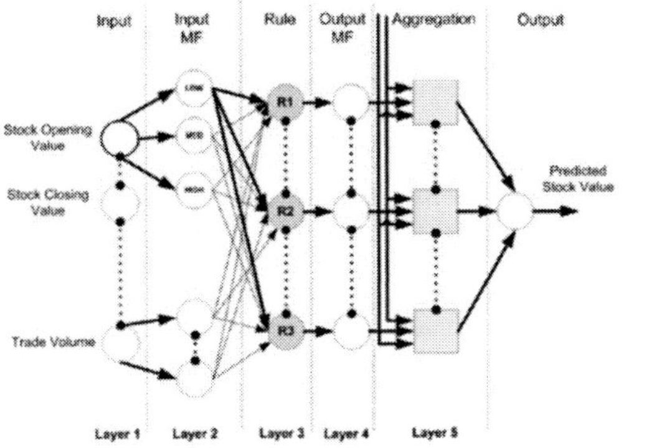

Figure 1. The design of a proposed TSK FIS based ANFIS framework utilising 4 input variables, respective input membership functions, rules and aggregation as hidden layers and output stock prices as the predictive outcome.

Layer – 1: Calculation of membership values for the premise parameter

The nodes in this layer are adaptive and the node output is the extent up to which the given input fulfils the underlying (associated) linguistic variable associated with this node as per the following expression:

$$\mu\, A_i(x_1) = 1 \Big/ 1 + \left|x_1 - {c_i}/{a_i}\right|^{2b_i} \quad (3)$$

where x_1 is the input to the node and a, b, c are adjustable factor variables termed as premise parameters. The layer outputs the membership values of the premise part where an ANN back propagation algorithm is used during the learning stage. The premise parameters are used to define membership functions that are generally fine-tuned via a Gradient-Descent method. As the subsequent values of the parameters change, the linguistic term's membership function $\mu\, A_i(x_1)$ changes as well. That is, the closer a parameter is to a certain membership, the clearer its association to a certain group is. In other words, the membership grade of a fuzzy set specifies the degree up to which the given input satisfies the quantifier. As shown in Figure 2 as the value of the parameters change between parameters a_1, a_2 and a_3, its membership projection (see y axis) changes between 0 and 1.

In the proposed stock price prediction problem, if closing price at time instance t is δ_t^i, which is an input variable with three membership values of HIGH, MEDIUM and LOW, then the three nodes are kept in the Layer – 1 and denoted via various membership function types.

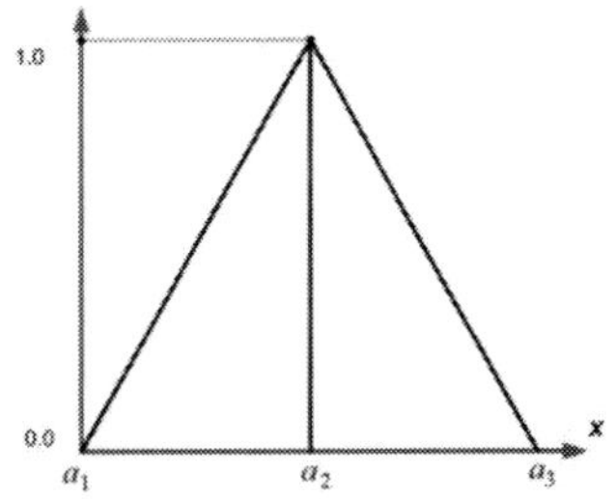

Figure 2. A triangular membership function used for prediction.

For the proposed case of close, low, open and volume variables, the membership functions can be formulated as follows:

$$\mu_{(\delta,v,X)} = \begin{cases} 0,\ x < a_1 \\ x - {a_1}/{a_2} - a_1, a_1 \le x \le a_2 \\ a_3 - {x}/{a_3} - a_2, a_2 \le x \le a_3 \\ 0, x > a_3 \end{cases} \quad (4)$$

As an example, if the value of x = 3.5 then its membership value would be 0.75, which is calculated as follows:

$$x - {a_1}/{a_2} - a_1 = 3.5 - {2}/{4} - 2 = {1.5}/{2} = 0.75$$

Layer – 2 : The fuzzification layer

In Layer – 2, the nodes are kept fixed with each expressing one linguistic variable (e.g., MEDIUM) mapped to one input variable in layer 1. The output at this layer is a membership value specifying the extent up to which an input variable belongs to a specific set. This extent is also regarded as the firing strength of the rules, and it is obtained by multiplying the input signals from the preceding layer (ANFIS 2013):

$$\omega_1 = \mu\, A_i(x_1)\mu\, B_i(x_2) \quad (5)$$

For instance, for a FIS containing 3 rules with each containing membership values (See calculation shown previously in Layer 1) as Rule 1: if $x\ is\ A1\ and\ y\ is\ B1\ then\ f1 = p1x + q1y + r1$ $\omega_1 = 0.75 \times 0.67 = 0.5025$. Similarly, for assumed Rule 2: if $x\ is\ A2\ and\ y\ is\ B2\ then\ f2 = p2x + q2y + r2$ $\omega_2 = 0.25 \times 0.33 = 0.0825$ and Rule 3: if $x\ is\ A3\ and\ y\ is\ B3\ then\ f3 = p3x + q3y + r3$ $\omega_3 = 0.25 \times 0.3 = 0.075$. Based on the rule firing values, rule 1 will fire as it has the highest weight value.

A complete Layer – 2 with 4 variables and three linguistic labels each will require a total of $3^4 = 81$ rules. The rule strength is calculated where a clustering algorithm decides the initial number and type of membership function to be allocated to each of the variable type.

Layer – 3: Rule-strength normalization:

The output to this layer, represented by a fixed number of nodes, is the rule's antecedent part that is the firing strength of the fuzzy rule in its normalised form represented as a $t-\text{norm}$. The ith node in this layer calculates the ith rule's firing strength ratio to the firing strength of the sum of all rules as follows (ANFIS 2013).

$$\bar{\omega}_i = \frac{\omega_i}{\sum_{j=1}^{R}\omega_j} \qquad (6)$$

where ω_i is the firing strength of the ith rule computed in the previous Layer – 2. Following-up from the previous 3-rule example, the normalization (for Rule 1) is as follows:

$$\bar{\omega}_1 = \frac{\omega_1}{\sum_{j=1}^{3}\omega_j} = \frac{0.5025}{0.5025 + 0.0825 + 0.075} = \frac{0.5025}{0.66} = 0.7613$$

Layer – 4: The Rule-Consequent Layer

The nodes in this layer are not fixed and adaptively change where, for every i^{th} node, a linear function is computed whose coefficients are adapted by an error function. The error function is a multi-layer feed-forward neural network as described below:

$$\overline{\omega_i} * f_i = \overline{\omega_i} * (p_i x_1 + q_i x_2 + r_i) \qquad (7)$$

where $\overline{\omega_i}$is the weight output of the input layer (Layer – 2), whereas p_i, q_i, r_i are the parameter set where i represents various the total inputs to the system. These parameters are also called the "consequent parameters" where at this stage the overall subsequent output is computed by summing all the input signals. Thus, the final output for the given input in Layer-1 will be:

$$\sum_i \overline{\omega_i} f_i = \sum_i \omega_i f_i \Big/ \sum_i \overline{\omega_i} \qquad (8)$$

Clearly (8) demonstrates the ability of a multivariate time-series system based on a sliding-window.

IV. "YAHOO" CASE STUDY

The Yahoo dataset is regarded as a standard stock dataset and it is widely used as a benchmark to evaluate a wide range of machine learning algorithms. The sample stock data to explain the underlying concept was downloaded from Yahoo! Finance [43]. The data contains a daily trading of stock volume and prices from 12/04/1996 to 31/08/2012 consisting of the following five parameters:

- Open (share price)
- Low (share price)
- High (share price)
- End-of-day Close (share price)
- Volume (trade volume in US$)

The data is extracted for adaptive neuro-fuzzy training based on a sliding-window operation: Based on the single-step (one-day) sliding window operation, a feature vector containing a set of input vectors and the output (closing value) will be obtained in a row-wise fashion. Each row represents a single day prediction based on the previous 'n' number of days.

This study uses experimental data from Yahoo Finance to evaluate the performance of the proposed methodology. The closing, low and high stock values for the entire duration are shown in Figure 3, which shows substantial fluctuations in stock market values during the daily operating hours. This measures a significant justification for the utilization of all the four (i.e., close, low, high and adj close) values in classifier training in addition to the trading volume measure. The justification lies in the fact that the opening stock price of a share may substantially change by the end of the trading day and may therefore change the closing stock price drastically.

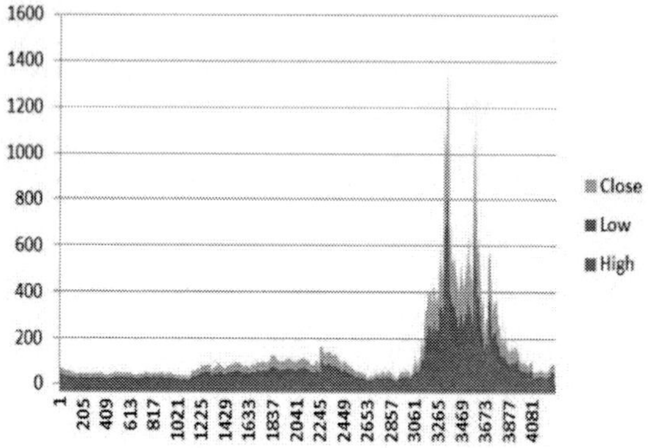

Figure 3. Closing, low and high share value limits during the entire 18-year duration of the stock market data.

The system was trained against the AForce.Neuro neural computation library with extensions made to the AForge.Fuzzy computations library for the hybridised implementation of the ANFIS framework. The training was based on a 10-day-delay with 10 neurons via a nonlinear autoregressive classification [44]. The data was divided into three randomly selected groups with training, testing and validation data selected at 75%, 15% and 15%, respectively. The 75-15-15 is a standard machine learning training practice used in research that was adopted from standard Matlab ANN toolbox (Matlab, 2014a). It must be noted that validation data group was only used to measure network generalization where the training was halt if the generalization stopped improving for at-least 5 consecutive epochs. An epoch in ANN terminology is the completion of a single training iteration leading either to the termination of the training sequence or the start of the next iteration based upon the criteria set in the initialization stage of the training process. The data division left 17980 target time steps of data for training, and 3853 days each for validation and testing purposes. The non-linear auto-regression for this training is described by the equation given below where d = 10 days (Mathworks, 2014c):

$$y(t) = f(y(t-1), y(t-2), \ldots, y(t-d)) \quad (9)$$

Equation (9) shows a sliding window operation based upon previous d=10 values to predict share prices on the 10th day.

The algorithm was run over a range of randomly selected data combinations and generated promising regression outcomes particularly over test and validation data, as shown in Figure 4. A regression value closer to 1 means a close regression relationship between outputs and targets whereas a value closer to zero shows a poor correlation and therefore a poorly trained system.

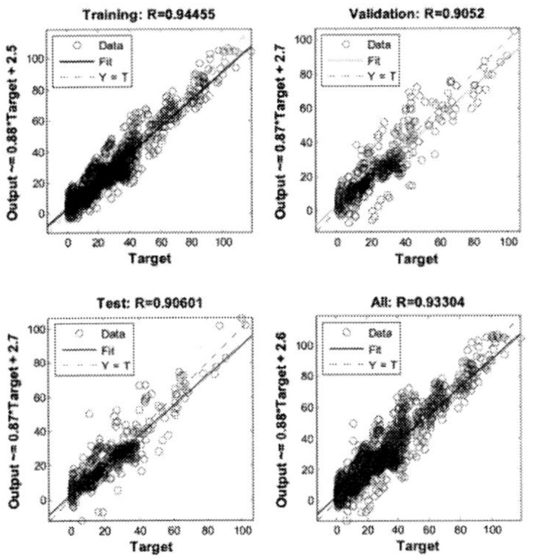

Figure 4. High regression closure values depicting a robustly trained ANN classifier.

The validation performance plotted during the 20-epochs training cycle generated a low Mean-Square-Error (MSE) pattern, which also demonstrates an optimally converged network. Indeed, Figure 5 demonstrates the ability of the underlying training sequence to have improved the overall actual-to-predicted Mean-Square-Error (MSE). The best prediction outcome was shown to be from training data. This is obvious due to the fact that training sequences are already used and known to the system, which is a clear indication of why the overall training error is lower when compared to validation. The highest validation MSE is attributed mainly to the fact that it is obtained when the trained classifier is used against unseen data. On top of it, validation is also used to terminate the training sequence when it sees 5 consecutive MSE increments in continuous epochs. The test performance is still better than the remaining two datasets. This may be attributed to the fact that test sequences generally see a trained classifier and do not tend to see an uncertain classifier which is being trained.

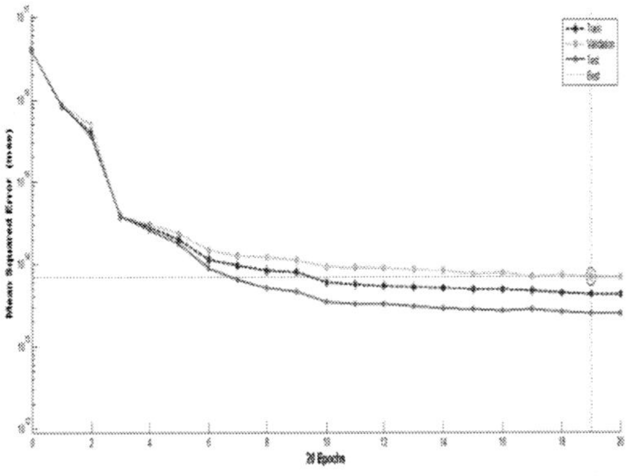

Figure 5. Validation MSE performance during network training.

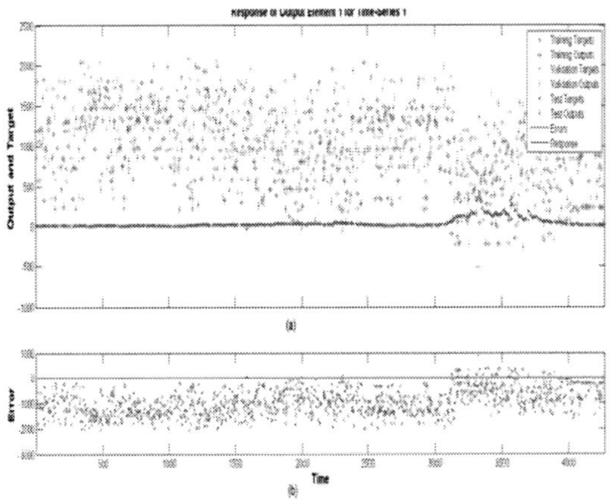

Figure 6. (a) Output and target plot of testing (red markers) and validation data (blue markers) and (b) the respective error plot.

The overall system outcome presents outstanding classification accuracy as evident from Figure 6. The markers for both '.' and '*' represent the target and output comparison for both validation (blue) and test data (red). In Figure 6, the majority of error values can be seen during the 2006 global recession time (see right-most part of Figure 6 (a). Nonetheless, the majority of correct classifications are shown as test values, which demonstrate the viability of this classifier to predict stock data. A sparse spread shows outstanding neural classification accuracy. A sparse error basically indicates a better-trained classifier, which is expected to demonstrate higher prediction accuracy when subjected to unseen data sequences. The overall accuracy of the system was evaluated against two standard testing methodologies of k-fold and jack-knife-based techniques with k = 5. The overall accuracy of these measures is shown in TABLE 1. The k-fold validation randomly divided unseen data into 5 unique sets out of which 4 were used for localised training, testing and validation. Once trained, the trained classifier was then used against a totally unseen (5th) dataset with the prediction outcome recorded. In the next cycle, "group 2" was used as a baseline group against a classifier trained on group 1, 3, 4, 5. The overall accuracy is shown in TABLE I. Nonetheless, the overall system accuracy provides a promising venue for the underlying system to be further improved and extended.

TABLE I. OVERALL ANFIS PREDICTION ACCURACY BASED ON 5-FOLD CROSS-VALIDATION:

Group	5-fold validation (%)
1	92.71
2	85.71
3	92.87
4	89.54
5	88.95
Average	89.956

V. CONCLUSION

This work particularly evaluated the most commonly employed soft-computing paradigms in stock market prediction that include fuzzy logic and neural networks. An in-depth analysis of the current state-of-the-art introduced significant potential in the utilization of hybridised classification systems. The proposed approach utilised the generalization capabilities of neural networks to improve the automated rule-generation capability of Adaptive Network based Fuzzy Inference System (ANFIS) framework. The approach utilised data from Yahoo stock data to train a 10-day-delay back-propagation algorithm that converged with a very promising value greater than 0.8.

The large dataset generated by Yahoo contained a total of 4281 days comprising of an estimated 11 years. In order to evaluate the overall consistency of reporting, the proposed technique employed a data evaluation technique which presented a rounded identification accuracy of 90% with k-fold validation. Despite the promising prediction outcome, the technique could still be improved with a varied number of neurons, activation functions, training algorithm types, number of neurons and the induced training delay. It was envisaged that an improvement in these values can be brought-in via a number of existing optimization techniques. As discussed in the literature review, genetic algorithms, particle swarm optimization, tabu-search and other similar optimization algorithms can be employed to induce an automated, hill-climbing heuristic for the methodology to further improve the system outcome.

REFERENCES

[1] Y. Chen, "Classifying credit ratings for Asian banks using integrating feature selection and the CPDA-based rough sets approach," Knowledge-Based Systems, 26, pp. 259-270, 2012.

[2] L. Dymowa,"Soft computing in economics and finance," Springer, 2011.

[3] E. Blandis, and R. Simutis,"Using Principal Component Analysis and Neural," Network for Forecasting of Stock Market Index. Bizinesa augstskola Turiba SIA, Riga, 2002.

[4] D. Zhu, X. Wang, and R. Ren, "Heuristics R and D projects portfolio selection decision system based on data Mining and fuzzy logic," Intelligent Computation Technology and Automation (ICICTA), 11-12 May, pp. 118-121, 2010.

[5] H. Yih-Jen, "A new method for fuzzy information retrieval based on fuzzy hierarchical clustering and fuzzy inference techniques." Fuzzy Systems, IEEE Transactions on, v. 13, n. 2, p. 216-228, 2005. ISSN 1063-6706.2005.

[6] M. A. Lee and M. H. Smith, "Handling uncertainty in finance applications using soft computing", Uncertainty Modeling and Analysis and Annual Conference of the North American Fuzzy Information Processing Society, Proceedings of ISUMA - NAFIPS, Third International Symposium on 17-19 September, pp. 384-389, 1995.

[7] Y. A. Hiemstra, "Stock market forecasting support system based on fuzzy logic," System Sciences, pp. 281-287, 1994.

[8] M. Ben Ghalia and P. Wang, "Intelligent system to support judgmental business forecasting: the case of estimating hotel room demand," Fuzzy Systems, IEEE Transactions on v. 8, n. 4, pp. 380-397, 2000.

[9] D. Qiaolin, T. Jing, and L. Jianxin, "Application of new FCMAC neural network in power system marginal price forecasting," Power Engineering Conference, IPEC, 29 November – 2 December, pp. 1-57, 2005.

[10] G. Ollos and R. Vida, "Adaptive Event Forecasting in Wireless Sensor Networks," Vehicular Technology Conference (VTC Spring), IEEE, 15-18 May, pp. 1-5, 2011.

[11] T. Liu, "Optimizing mining association rules based on Artificial Neural Network," World Automation Congress (WAC), 24-28 June, pp. 1-4, 2012.

[12] N. Balakrishnan, "Methods and applications of statistics in business, finance, and management science," Hoboken, NJ: Wiley, 2010.

[13] R. Kozma, M. Kitamura, M. Sakuma, and Y. Yokoyama, "Anomaly detection by neural network models and statistical time series analysis," Neural Networks, IEEE World Congress on Computational Intelligence 27 June -2 July, pp. 3207-3210, vol.5., 1994.

[14] K. Huang, Z. Qi, and B. Liu, "Network anomaly detection based on statistical approach and time series analysis," Advanced Information Networking and Applications Workshops, Waina 26-29 May 2009, pp. 205-211, 2009.

[15] H. Akaike, "Use of statistical models for time series analysis," Acoustics, Speech, and Signal Processing, IEEE International Conference on ICASSP '86, pp. 3147-3155, April 1986.

[16] E. Oja, K. Kiviluoto, and S. Malaroiu, "Independent component analysis for financial time series," Adaptive Systems for Signal Processing, Communications, and Control Symposium, IEEE, pp. 111-116, 2000.

[17] Z. Dazhuo, L. Jinxia, and M. Wenxiu, "Clustering based on LLE for financial multivariate time series," management and service science, 20-22 September, pp. 1-4, 2009.

[18] Q.-Z. Li and W.-C. Shi, "Research in financial risk prediction on biochemical industry of China listed companies," Management Science and Engineering (ICMSE) 20-22 September, pp. 1517-1521, 2012.

[19] F. E. H. Tay and L. J. Cao, "Application of support vector machines in financial time series forecasting," Omega-International Journal of Management Science, v. 29, n. 4, pp. 309-317, 2001.

[20] J. Keyes, "Financial services information systems," Boca Raton: Auerbach, 2000.

[21] L. S. Lopes, N. Lau, P. Mariano, and L. M. Rocha, "Progress in Artificial Intelligence," 14th Portuguese Conference on

Artificial Intelligence, EPIA 2009, Aveiro, Portugal, October 12-15, 2009.

[22] L. Yuling, G. Haixiang, and H. Jinglu, "An SVM-based approach for stock market trend prediction," Neural Networks (IJCNN), 4-9 August, pp. 1-7, 2013.

[23] P. Chang, C. Liu, and C. Fan, "Data clustering and fuzzy neural network for sales forecasting: a case study in printed circuit board industry," Knowledge-Based Systems, v. 22, n. 5, pp. 344-355, 2009.

[24] C. Li, J. Zhou, P. Kou, and J. Xiao, "A novel chaotic particle swarm optimization based fuzzy clustering algorithm. Neurocomputing", 83, pp.98-109.2012.

[25] W. L. Tung, C. Quek, and P. Cheng, "GenSo-EWS: a novel neural-fuzzy based early warning system for predicting bank failures," Neural Networks, v. 17, n. 4, pp. 567-587, 2004.

[26] Y. Yoshida, "The valuation of European options in uncertain environment," European Journal of Operational Research, v. 145, n. 1, pp. 221-229, 2003.

[27] O. Castillo and P. Melin, "Hybrid intelligent systems for time series prediction using neural networks, fuzzy logic, and fractal theory," IEEE Transactions on Neural Networks, v. 13, n. 6, pp. 1395-1408, 2002.

[28] T. C. Tang and L. C. Chi, "Predicting multilateral trade credit risks: comparisons of Logit and Fuzzy Logic models using ROC curve analysis," Expert Systems with Applications, v. 28, n. 3, pp. 547-556, 2005.

[29] F. L Chen, and T. Y Ou, "Sales forecasting system based on Gray extreme learning machine with Taguchi method in retail industry." Expert Systems with Applications, 38(3), pp. 1336-1345.2011.

[30] T. M. Martinetz, S. G. Berkovich, and K. J. Schulten, "Neural-gas network for vector quantization and its application to time-series prediction," IEEE Transactions on Neural Networks, v. 4, n. 4, pp. 558-569, 1993.

[31] J. T. Connor, R. D. Martin, and L. E. Atlas, "Recurrent neural networks and robust time-series prediction," IEEE Transactions on Neural Networks, v. 5, n. 2, pp. 240-254, 1994.

[32] G. P. Zhang and V. L. Berardi, "Time series forecasting with neural network ensembles: an application for exchange rate prediction," Journal of the Operational Research Society, v. 52, n. 6, pp. 652-664, 2001.

[33] A. S. Soofi and L. Cao, "Modelling and forecasting financial data: techniques of nonlinear dynamics," Boston, Mass.: Kluwer Academic Publication, 2002.

[34] H. Leung, T. Lo, and S. C. Wang, "Prediction of noisy chaotic time series using an optimal radial basis function neural network," IEEE Transactions on Neural Networks, v. 12, n. 5, pp. 1163-1172, 2001.

[35] C. K. Goh and K. C. Tan, "Evolutionary multi-objective optimization in uncertain environments: issues and algorithms," Berlin: Springer-Verlag, 2009

[36] M. Han, J. Xi, S. Xu, and F. Yin, "Prediction of chaotic time series based on the recurrent predictor neural network," IEEE Transactions on Signal Processing, v. 52, n. 12, pp. 3409-3416, 2004.

[37] Y. Chen, B. Yang, and J. W. Dong, "Time-series prediction using a local linear wavelet neural network," Neurocomputing, v. 69, n. 4-6, pp. 449-465, January 2006.

[38] P. R. Kumar and V. Ravi, "Bankruptcy prediction in banks and firms via statistical and intelligent techniques - a review," European Journal of Operational Research, v. 180, n. 1, pp. 1-28, 1, 2007.

[39] H. Ishibuchi and T. Nakashima, "A study on generating fuzzy classification rules using histograms," pp. 132-140 vol.1, 21-23 April 1998.

[40] Y. JaeHung, andI. K Sethi, "Design of radial basis function networks using decision trees." Neural Networks, pp. 1269-1272 vol.3. Nov/Dec 1995.

[41] H. Shinn-Ying, "Design of accurate regressions with a compact fuzzy-rule base using an evolutionary scatter partition of feature space." Systems, Man, and Cybernetics, Part B: Cybernetics, IEEE Transactions on, v. 34, n. 2, p. 1031-1044. ISSN 1083-4419, 2004.

[42] S. A. Chiu, "Cluster extension method with extension to fuzzy model identification. Fuzzy Systems,". IEEE World Congress on Computational Intelligence, Proceedings of the Third IEEE, pp. 1240-1245, vol. 2, June 1994.

[43] Yahoo (2014) Yahoo Inc. stock data YAHOO [Online] Available at <https://uk.finance.yahoo.com/q/hp?s=YHOO> [Accessed: 20/06/2014].

[44] S. A Yusuf, D. J Brown, A. Mackinnon, R. Papanicolaou "Application of dynamic neural networks with exogenous input to industrial conditional monitoring," Neural Networks (IJCNN), The 2013 International Joint conference, pp.1, 8, 4-9 Aug. 2013.

Techniques to Improve a Flow Diffusion Algorithm for Folded Clos Networks

Satoru Ohta
Department of Electrical and Computer Engineering, Faculty of Engineering
Toyama Prefectural University
Imizu, Japan
e-mail: ohta@pu-toyama.ac.jp

***Abstract*—Folded Clos networks (FCNs) are important as topologies for data center networks. To achieve high performance with an FCN, it is necessary to establish a routing method that uniformly diffuses flows between links. To satisfy this requirement, a previous study proposed a method, called the "rebalancing algorithm," which is a distributed algorithm based on locally obtainable information. An advantage of this method is that the number of flows on a link is upper bounded by a theoretically derived constant. Therefore, the link load does not grow heavier than this bound when using the rebalancing algorithm. This paper presents two techniques to improve the rebalancing algorithm. Applying these techniques, the algorithm can more uniformly diffuse flows. In addition, when these techniques are employed, the upper bound on the number of flows remains valid. The effectiveness of the two techniques is confirmed via computer simulations.**

Keywords—network; algorithm; routing; data center; packet.

I. INTRODUCTION

The importance of data center networks is obvious because most popular information services are provided via data centers. Therefore, it is essential to establish topologies for high performance data center networks. To satisfy this requirement, studies on data center networks have been performed based on several topologies including the Clos network [1], fat-tree [2], DCell [3], and BCube [4]. Of these, the Clos network is a particularly interesting topology because it can achieve high throughput for arbitrary traffic patterns. Therefore, various data center networks based on the Clos network topology have been implemented and operated [1][5]–[7].

A Clos network is a three-stage non-blocking switching network originally investigated by Charles Clos in 1953 [8]. In data center network applications, the network appears in the form of a folded Clos network (FCN). An FCN is essentially equivalent to a three-stage network; however, it is constructed by folding the corresponding three-stage Clos network at its center.

To apply an FCN to data center networks, the routing of a packet is important. Inadequate routing may cause load imbalances between the links. Such imbalances may cause traffic congestion and degrade the performance. Meanwhile, if the load is uniformly distributed between the links, an FCN can achieve high throughput by fully utilizing the bandwidth of every link.

As a routing method, several past studies [6][7][9] have employed the idea of forwarding a packet to a randomly selected route. This method is rational to some extent because it uniformly distributes the average number of flows between the links. However, with this method, the load on a given link may grow excessively large with a substantial probability. Consequently, due to heavily loaded links, traffic congestion may occur. Such congestion degrades the network performance. As pointed out in [10], this problem may become critical for big data applications, which require high bandwidth transmission. Therefore, it is important to develop a routing algorithm that diffuses the traffic load more uniformly than random routing.

Meanwhile, a routing algorithm for an FCN should be executable in a distributed manner to decrease the processing overhead and handle frequent route decisions. In addition, the algorithm should work without global information of the entire network to eliminate the communication overhead associated with gathering information. Routing can be performed on either a per-packet basis or a per-flow basis. This study examines a method based on per-flow routing because packet reordering is unavoidable for per-packet routing.

Reference [11] presented two distributed algorithms that diffuse flows in FCNs. Using computer simulations, it was shown that these methods more uniformly diffuse flows than random routing. These methods are called the rebalancing algorithm and the load sum algorithm. Of the two, the rebalancing algorithm works with information that is locally obtainable at the source switch of a flow. Meanwhile, the load sum algorithm is less practical due to the communication overhead between switches, even though it performs better with respect to load equality. Therefore, if the rebalancing algorithm is improved to more uniformly diffuse flows, a more practical and efficient algorithm will be obtained.

This paper presents techniques to improve the rebalancing algorithm with respect to load equality. These techniques are based on information that is locally obtainable at the source switch of a flow. The first technique modifies the algorithm to more evenly distribute the uplink loads. The second technique focuses on the fact that the algorithm has a process for scanning middle switch indices for routing and rerouting. Therefore, with the second method, the order of scanning the middle switch indices is determined so as to uniformly diffuse flows.

An advantage of the rebalancing algorithm is that an upper bound is theoretically derived for the number of flows on a link. When using the presented improvement techniques, this upper bound is not affected. Therefore, the worst-case link load is limited as in the case where these techniques are not applied. The effectiveness of the two techniques is confirmed via computer simulations.

The remainder of the paper is organized as follows. In Section II, FCN is explored. Section III reviews related work. Section IV explains the rebalancing algorithm, which is investigated for improvement. Two modification techniques are presented in Section V. The effectiveness of the techniques is evaluated in Section VI. Finally, Section VII concludes the paper.

II. Folded Clos Network

A Clos network is a three-stage switching network originally investigated by Charles Clos [8]. An FCN is essentially equivalent to a three-stage Clos network. However, an FCN is constructed by folding the three-stage network at its center. An example of an FCN is shown in Figure 1.

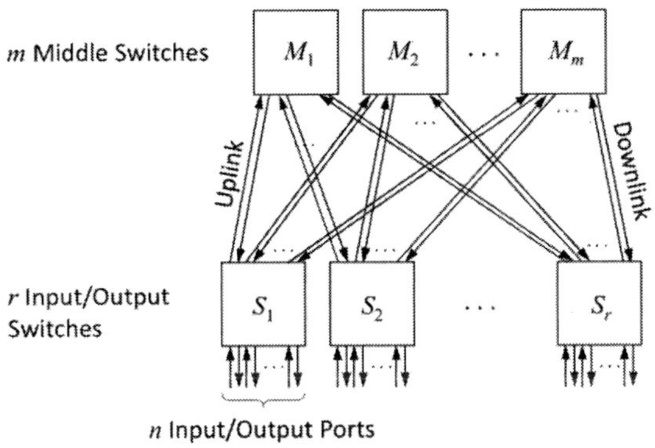

Figure 1. An example of a FCN.

As shown in Figure 1, an FCN is constructed from r input/output switches S_1, S_2, …, S_r that are connected by m middle switches M_1, M_2, …, M_m via links. Each middle switch is connected to every input/output switch via an uplink and a downlink. An uplink is set from an input/output switch to a middle switch, while a downlink is set in the reverse direction.

Because a middle switch is connected to every input/output switch, a packet can reach its destination switch from an arbitrary middle switch via a downlink. Therefore, the source switch can transmit a packet to the destination switch via any middle switch. However, the traffic load on an uplink or downlink depends on the routing at the source switch. If the routing is inadequate, traffic congestion occurs. This degrades the performance. Congestion is avoided if the traffic is evenly diffused between the uplinks and downlinks in an FCN. Therefore, it is important to establish a routing method that is executed at the source switch of a packet.

This paper assumes that routing is performed on a flow basis. A flow is a packet stream identified by a set of fields in the packet header. A frequently used field set is {*source address, destination address, protocol, source port, destination port*}, which is associated with an IP socket. Needless to say, other field sets can also be used as flow identifiers. If a fixed route is assigned to a flow, packet reordering does not occur. This is advantageous because packet reordering leads to throughput degradation. This paper considers the case where the FCN connects many hosts and processes via its $N = nr$ input/output ports. In this situation, many concurrent flows exist between ports.

III. Related Work

A common idea for diffusing traffic in an FCN is to route a packet to a randomly selected middle switch. This idea, called Valiant load balancing, was employed in [6] and originally presented in [12]. Reference [9] explores the method of computing routing table entries from indices of switches and host identifiers. This is equivalent to randomly assigning route flows using the output of a hash function fed with switch indices and host identifiers. The architecture reported in [7] employs a per-packet adaptive routing mechanism as well as per-flow deterministic routing. For the deterministic routing, flows are diffused to random middle switches via a hash function fed with input ports and destinations.

The idea of randomly routing flows is rational to some extent because the average number of flows is balanced between the links. However, the worst-case load on a certain link can grow excessively large with substantial probability. This may cause traffic congestion and degrade the performance, e.g., via the packet latency or network throughput. The adaptive routing proposed in [10] may reduce this disadvantage of random routing. Initially, this method semi-randomly selects routes for the flows at the source switches. Then, the destination switches identify bad links, which are excessively loaded by this initial routing. Then, the destination switches notify the source switches of the flows, passing the bad links as bad flows. With this notification, the source switches to reroute the bad flows. The rerouting is repeated until there are no bad links. In [10], the convergence of the rerouting was evaluated using an analysis based on Markov chain models and computer simulation. Unfortunately, it is not clear theoretically how many times the flows should be rerouted to eliminate all the bad links in the worst case. It is also unclear whether bad links are definitively removed by the method of [10]. Due to these difficulties, this method may not be practical.

Reference [11] presented two flow-based routing methods that more uniformly diffuse flows than random routing. With these methods, a flow is routed (or rerouted) at its source switch in a distributed manner. One of these methods is the rebalancing algorithm, which runs using locally obtainable information. The other method is the load sum algorithm, which requires communication between the source and destination switches. The simulation results show that these methods both outperform random routing. It is also shown that the load sum algorithm more uniformly diffuses flows than the rebalancing algorithm. The simulation result reported in [11] shows that every flow equality metric is smaller for the load sum algorithm than for the rebalancing algorithm. However, the load sum algorithm may be inefficient with respect to the communication overhead between switches, particularly in the case of short-duration flows. Namely, the traffic amount exchanged by a short-duration flow may become comparable to or smaller than that by the communication between switches. This is very inefficient. From this viewpoint, the rebalancing algorithm is likely more practical. By improving this method with respect to the uniformity of the flow diffusion, it is thought that the rebalancing algorithm will become advantageous.

IV. REBALANCING ALGORITHM

This paper presents techniques to improve the rebalancing algorithm presented in [11]. This algorithm is actually a packet stream version of the method shown in [13]. The algorithm assumes that the route of a newly generated flow is determined when its first packet arrives at the input switch. It may not be easy to strictly implement such a mechanism with currently available technologies. However, it is important to investigate potentially implementable methods that perform better than conventional routing.

This section explores some definitions, identifies local information, and details the algorithm.

A. Definitions

Throughout the paper, the following variables are employed.

- $F(i, j, k)$: the number of flows that go through a source switch S_i, a middle switch M_j, and a destination switch S_k $(1 \le i, k \le r, 1 \le j \le m)$.
- $U(i, j)$: the number of flows on the uplink set from S_i to M_j.
- $D(j, k)$: the number of flows on the downlink set from M_j to S_k.

Obviously, $U(i, j)$ and $D(j, k)$ are related to $F(i, j, k)$ as follows:

$$U(i, j) = \sum_{k=1}^{r} F(i, j, k), \quad (1)$$

$$D(j, k) = \sum_{i=1}^{r} F(i, j, k). \quad (2)$$

The algorithm is described using these variables.

B. Locally obtainable information

For data center network applications, flows may be generated and completed very frequently in the FCN. For such a situation, the routing of a flow should be executed in a distributed manner because the load offered by frequent route decisions will become excessively heavy for concentrated computations. In addition, it is impractical to perform communication between switches. This is because there may be very short flows that consist of only a few packets. As described in Section III, it is clearly inefficient to exchange packets between switches for the routing of such short flows. Therefore, the route of a flow should be decided at its source switch using locally obtainable information.

An input/output switch is able to obtain the headers of the packets, which arrive from its input port and are forwarded to middle switches. From these headers, the switch can identify the flows to which the packets belong. Because the switch decides the routes for the flows as the source, it can count how many flows go to each middle switch. Therefore, $U(i, j)$ can be managed at the source switch S_i. Moreover, the switch can also extract the destination switch of the flows from the packet headers. Using this information, the source switch S_i will be able to count $F(i, j, k)$ as well. However, $D(j, k)$ is not known at S_i because flows from switches other than S_i may enter the downlink to S_k.

Suppose that a new flow is generated and that its source switch is S_i. Then, assume that S_i can detect the arrival of a new flow. This is possible by comparing the flow identifiers to the routing table. It is also possible for S_i to detect the completion of a flow by timeout. Therefore, S_i can launch routing or rerouting processes at a flow arrival or completion.

C. Basic algorithm

The pseudocode for the rebalancing algorithm [11] is described in Figure 2.

```
Algorithm rebalancing
// α: a positive integer
if a new flow arrives at switch S_i and its destination is S_k then
        Find J such that F(i,J,k) ≤ F(i,j,k) for any j (1 ≤ j ≤ m);
        Route the flow to M_J;
        F(i, J, k):= F(i, J, k) + 1;
end if
if a flow passing through source S_i and destination S_k is completed
then
        M_x:= the middle switch that the completed flow was routed
        through;
        Find J such that F(i,j,k) ≤ F(i,J,k) for any j (1 ≤ j ≤ m);
        if F(i,J,k) − F(i,x,k) ≥ α then
                Find a flow that goes through M_J and S_k;
                Reroute the flow to M_x;
                F(i, J, k):= F(i, J, k) − 1;
        else F(i, x, k):= F(i, x, k) − 1;
        end if
end.
```

Figure 2. Rebalancing algorithm [11].

As shown in Figure 2, the algorithm decides the route for a new flow so as to decrease the difference between the $F(i, j, k)$s for a fixed pair of i and k. In addition, if the difference between the $F(i, j, k)$s exceeds a constant α by the flow completion, a flow is rerouted so as to decrease this difference. As a result, the rebalancing algorithm has the following property.

Property: *With the rebalancing algorithm,*

$$F(i, j, k) \le F(i, j', k) + \alpha, \quad (3)$$

for $1 \le j, j' \le m,\ 1 \le i, k \le r.$

Proof: This property is proved via induction on the flow arrival and completion events. Assume that (3) holds after the K-th event. Then, for a new flow arrival between S_i and S_k, $F(i, J, k)$ increases by 1 and the other $F(i, j, k)$s are unchanged. Meanwhile, $F(i, J, k)$ is not larger than $F(i, j, k)$ for an arbitrary value of j prior to the flow arrival. Therefore, $F(i, J, k)$ is not larger than $F(i, j, k) + 1$ for any j after the flow arrival. This means that (3) holds after the flow arrival event. If a flow that goes through S_i, M_x, S_k is completed, $F(i, x, k)$ decreases by 1. Therefore, if $F(i, J, k)$ is the maximum of the $F(i, j, k)$s, the difference between $F(i, J, k)$ and $F(i, x, k)$ may exceed α. However, if this happens, the algorithm reroutes a flow from M_J to M_x. Then, $F(i, x, k)$ does not change due to the flow completion and the maximum of the $F(i, j, k)$s does not increase. Therefore, (3) holds after the flow completion. Consequently, (3) is valid after the $(K + 1)$-th event. Under the initial state, no flows exist in the network, and therefore the $F(i, j, k)$s are 0 for all i, j, and k. This satisfies (3). Therefore, the property is proved.

□

An advantage of the rebalancing algorithm is that an upper bound exists for the number of flows on an uplink or downlink. Let f_0 denote the maximum number of flows given to an input or output port. Then, as shown in [11],

$$U(i, j) \le \frac{nf_0 - \alpha(r-1)}{m} + \alpha(r-1)\text{, and} \tag{4}$$

$$D(j, k) \le \frac{nf_0 - \alpha(r-1)}{m} + \alpha(r-1) \tag{5}$$

The above equations are derived from (3). The proof of the bound is detailed in [11]. Due to this characteristic, it is assured that the load on a link does not grow extremely heavy.

In the rebalancing algorithm, the parameter α determines the frequency of rerouting as well as the uniformity of flow diffusion. If α is smaller, flows will be more frequently rerouted and more uniformly diffused. If α is large, rerouting never occurs. In this case, flows are diffused via the route decision when they arrive at their source switches. Unfortunately, if rerouting is omitted by setting α to a large value, the number of flows on a link can become considerably large in the worst case. However, simulation results show that the algorithm works well even without rerouting. Following [11], a rebalancing algorithm that omits the rerouting process is referred to as a "balancing algorithm" hereafter.

V. Modification Techniques

This section presents two modification techniques to improve the load equality of the rebalancing algorithm. These techniques add criteria to select the middle switch index J in steps 2 and 8 of the algorithm. However, they do not change the conditions that $F(i, J, k)$ and other $F(i, j, k)$s should satisfy. Therefore, (3) holds even if these techniques are applied. Consequently, the upper bound shown by (4) or (5) is unchanged by these techniques.

A. *Uplink flow diffusion*

The algorithm described in the previous section uses $F(i, j, k)$ and the events of flow arrival and completion in the local information. Therefore, of the available local information, $U(i, j)$ remains unused. Even though the rebalancing algorithm decreases the difference between the $F(i, j, k)$s for a particular pair of i and k, the uplink load $U(i, j)$ is not necessarily uniformly distributed. In step 2 of the rebalancing algorithm, the middle switch M_J is selected such that $F(i, J, k)$ will be the minimum of the $F(i, j, k)$s. In this process, there may be two or more candidates for J. Suppose that we select J from the candidates so that $U(i, J)$ will be the minimum of the candidates. Then, flows will be more uniformly distributed between the uplinks. This does not necessarily improve the load equality between the downlinks. However, the performance will at least be improved for the uplinks.

Similarly, flow diffusion via rerouting can also be modified using $U(i, j)$. In step 8 of the algorithm, M_J is selected such that $F(i, J, k)$ will be the maximum of the $F(i, j, k)$s. Suppose that there are two or more such indices J. Then, it is possible to use the index that maximizes $U(i, J)$. We refer to this modification using $U(i, j)$ as "modification 1."

B. *Start index for scanning the middle switches*

The order of searching for index J in steps 2 and 8 also affects the performance of the rebalancing algorithm. Assume that J is scanned in the order of 1, 2, …, m in step 2. Then, a smaller index is more likely to be selected as J. Therefore, $F(i, j, k)$ will be larger for a smaller index j with a high probability even though the differences between the $F(i, j, k)$s are bounded by α for fixed i and k. According to (1) and (2), this implies that $U(i, j)$ and $D(j, k)$ will also tend to be larger for a smaller value of j. To avoid this unbalance between $U(i, j)$ and $D(j, k)$, the scanning of J should start from a different index depending on k for a fixed value of i. Similarly, the start index should differ depending on i for a fixed value of k. In addition, the start index should be evenly distributed between 1, 2, …, m for different values of i or k. To satisfy this requirement, let us examine the following start index j_s:

$$j_s = (i + k)\lceil m / r \rceil. \tag{6}$$

In the above equation, the term $\lceil m/r \rceil$ is necessary to evenly distribute j_s between 1, 2, …, m for the case of $m \ge 2r$. In step 2 of the algorithm, the index was scanned in the order of $j_s, j_s + 1, j_s + 2, \ldots$, if the index reaches $m + 1$, it wraps to 1.

For step 8 of the algorithm, it was found from simulation results that the index should be started from $(j_s + m) \bmod m$ and then decreased. If the index reaches 0, it wraps to m. The reason for this scheme is explained as follows. This scheme aims to generate the situation where $F(i, j_s, k)$ is not less than $F(i, j_s + 1, k)$, $F(i, j_s + 1, k)$ is not less than $F(i, j_s + 2, k)$, and so on. To maintain this situation, it is favorable to select J from later elements of the sequence j_s, $j_s + 1$, $j_s + 2, \ldots$, $(j_s + m) \bmod m$ because $F(i, J, k)$ decreases due to rerouting.

The employment of the start index stated above is called "modification 2" hereafter.

VI. EVALUATION

The effectiveness of the improvements was evaluated using computer simulations. The simulations examined the rebalancing and balancing algorithms to which modifications 1 and 2 were applied. For comparison, the original rebalancing and balancing algorithms reported in [11] were also evaluated. In the rebalancing algorithm, the parameter α was set to 1.

In the simulations, the following two network models were employed:

- FCN1: $r = 48$, $m = n = 24$, and
- FCN2: $r = 24$, $m = n = 48$.

The parameters used for FCN1 are the same as those found in the model examined in [10]. Thus, it is considered that the parameters are adequate to simulate a realistic network. FCN2 was also examined to assess the algorithm behavior for a different topology with the same scale.

The degree of the load equality was estimated using the following metrics, which were also used in [11]:

- Maximum: the maximum number of flows in the links at a certain measurement time,
- Variance: the variance in the flow numbers in the links at a certain measurement time, and
- Bad links: the number of links, in which the number of flows exceeds a threshold C.

The threshold for bad links, C, was set to 105. This value was slightly larger than the average number of flows under the given traffic condition. The values of the above metrics will be smaller if the flows are more uniformly diffused.

A flow was generated by opening a socket between the hosts a and z. These hosts are connected to two randomly selected input/output switches. By opening a socket, two flows are generated for the direction from a to z as well as for the reverse direction.

Reference [6] reports that an average machine has ten concurrent flows in a real-world data center. By aggregating the traffic from 10 such machines, the average number of flows will be 100 for a port of each input/output switch. This situation was simulated by the following traffic model. The interval of opening sockets was randomly determined by an exponential distribution with an average of 0.001 s. The duration of a socket was also a random value according to an exponential distribution with an average of 57.6 s. For this traffic condition and the network models, the average number of flows in the network was estimated to be 100.

The sockets were opened 2×10^6 times. The metrics were measured every 1 s in the period from 401 s to 1900 s. The system was considered to be in equilibrium during this period. The averages of the metrics were computed from the measured data.

The simulation was performed by a custom event-driven simulation program. Thus, any existing simulation platform was not employed. The program was built using C language, and compiled by gcc 4.8.5. The simulation was performed on a Core i3/16GB RAM PC, which runs on CentOS 7.

The simulation result for the rebalancing algorithm and FCN1 is summarized in Table I. Table II shows the result for the balancing algorithm and FCN1.

TABLE I. RESULT FOR THE REBALANCING ALGORITHM AND FCN1.

Algorithms	Maximum	Variance	Bad Links
Original Version	111.678	10.838	122.841
Modification 1	111.085	7.348	66.934
Modification 2	109.942	9.254	92.203
Modifications 1 & 2	110.347	6.848	56.835

TABLE II. RESULT FOR THE BALANCING ALGORITHM AND FCN1.

Algorithms	Maximum	Variance	Bad Links
Original Version	113.537	14.796	187.919
Modification 1	112.617	9.666	102.452
Modification 2	110.869	11.413	126.949
Modifications 1 & 2	112.437	9.411	98.201

Tables I and II show that the load equality is successfully improved by modifications 1 and 2. As shown in the tables, every metric decreased when applying the modifications. In particular, modification 1 effectively improved the variance and bad links metrics. Therefore, this modification is effective even though it does not affect the equality between the $D(j, k)$s. The improvement due to modification 2 is not large in comparison to that due to modification 1. However, every metric also gets smaller when using modification 2. By applying both modifications 1 and 2, the best result was obtained for the variance and bad links metrics. Particularly, the improvement in the bad links metric is obvious. This implies that the number of flows is concentrated into a narrow range for most links.

Tables III and IV list the results for FCN2. Table III shows the case of the rebalancing algorithm, while Table IV shows the case of the balancing algorithm.

TABLE III. RESULT FOR THE REBALANCING ALGORITHM AND FCN2.

Algorithms	Maximum	Variance	Bad Links
Original Version	106.827	4.223	10.817
Modification 1	106.493	2.989	5.363
Modification 2	105.829	3.650	5.768
Modifications 1 & 2	106.014	2.767	3.319

TABLE IV. RESULT FOR THE BALANCING ALGORITHM AND FCN2.

Algorithms	Maximum	Variance	Bad Links
Original Version	107.517	5.049	19.756
Modification 1	107.138	3.544	9.947
Modification 2	106.255	4.176	9.428
Modifications 1 & 2	107.016	3.439	8.553

Tables III and IV show that every metric decreases due to the modifications for the case of FCN2 as well. This implies that the modifications will be effective in general for various networks with different parameters. It also confirms that the definition of j_s is adequate for modification 2 because other definitions do not necessarily yield such a result.

In a comparison of the rebalancing and balancing algorithms, we find that the former is always superior to the latter for any case. However, the rerouting performed by the rebalancing algorithm may cause packet reordering, which may decrease the throughput. Meanwhile, the proposed modifications considerably improve the load equality of the balancing algorithm, which does not perform rerouting. Therefore, a practical solution is to use the balancing algorithm including the proposed modifications.

VII. Conclusion and Future Work

This paper investigated techniques to improve the rebalancing algorithm [11], which diffuses flows in an FCN. The first technique decreases the difference between the uplink loads by adding a criterion to decide on the middle switch used in the routing or rerouting processes. In addition, it was inferred that the load equality depends the order of the scanning of the middle switch indices. Based on this, the second technique decides the start index for scanning so as to balance the loads. The two techniques were applied to the rebalancing algorithm as well as the balancing algorithm and evaluated using computer simulations. Here, the balancing algorithm is a version of the rebalancing algorithm that is modified to omit the rerouting process. The results show that the presented techniques successfully improve the load equality.

Further study is necessary in the future to determine how the load equality provided by the presented techniques affects the packet-level performances such as the packet latency. The implementation of these techniques is also an important future work. Nevertheless, it is concluded that the rebalancing and balancing algorithms become more practical when employing the presented techniques.

References

[1] F. Hassen and L. Mhamdi, "High-capacity Clos-network switch for data center networks," in proc. ICC 2017, paper NGNI07-1, pp. 1–7, Paris, France, May 2017.

[2] Z. Guo and Y. Yang, "On Nonblocking Multicast Fat-Tree Data Center Networks with Server Redundancy," IEEE Trans. on Computers, 64, 4, pp. 1058–1073, Apr. 2014.

[3] C. Guo et al., "DCell: a scalable and fault-tolerant network structure for data centers," in proc. ACM SIGCOMM '08, pp. 75–86, Seattle, WA, USA, Aug. 2008.

[4] C. Guo et al., "BCube: a high performance, server-centric network architecture for modular data centers," in proc. ACM SIGCOMM '09, pp. 63–74, Barcelona, Spain, Aug. 2009.

[5] N. Farrington and A. Andreyev, "Facebook's data center network architecture," in proc. 2013 Optical Interconnects Conference, pp. 49–50, Santa Fe, NM, USA, May 2013.

[6] A. Greenberg et al., "VL2: a scalable and flexible data center network," Communications of the ACM, 54, 3, pp. 95–104, Mar. 2011.

[7] S. Scott, D. Abts, J. Kim, and W.J. Dally, "The BlackWidow high-radix Clos network," in proc. ISCA '06, pp. 16–28, Boston, MA, USA, June 2006.

[8] C. Clos, "A study of nonblocking switching networks," Bell System Technical Journal, 32, 2, pp. 406–424, Mar. 1953.

[9] M. Al-Fares, A. Loukissas, and A. Vahdat, "A scalable, commodity data center network architecture," in proc. SIGCOMM '08, pp. 63–74, Seattle, WA, USA, Aug. 2008.

[10] E. Zahavi, I. Keslassy, and A. Kolodny, "Distributed adaptive routing for big-data applications running on data center networks," in proc. ANCS '12, pp. 99–110, Austin, Tx, USA, Oct. 2012.

[11] S. Ohta, "Flow diffusion algorithms based on local and semi-local information for folded Clos networks," in proc. ICESS 2018, pp. 46–54, Takamatsu, Japan, Nov. 2018.

[12] L. G. Valiant, "A scheme for fast parallel communication," SIAM J. Computing, 11, 2, pp. 350–361, May 1982.

[13] S. Ohta, "A simple control algorithm for rearrangeable switching networks with time division multiplexed links," IEEE J. on Selected Areas in Communications, SAC-5, 8, pp.1302–1308, Oct. 1987.

Crowdsourced Misuse Detection in Dynamic Spectrum Sharing Wireless Networks

Debarun Das
School of Computing and Information
University of Pittsburgh
Pittsburgh, USA
Email: ded59@pitt.edu

Taieb Znati
School of Computing and Information
University of Pittsburgh
Pittsburgh, USA
Email: znati@pitt.edu

Martin Weiss
School of Computing and Information
University of Pittsburgh
Pittsburgh, USA
Email: mbw@pitt.edu

Pedro Bustamante
School of Computing and Information
University of Pittsburgh
Pittsburgh, USA
Email: pjb63@pitt.edu

Marcela M. Gomez
School of Computing and Information
University of Pittsburgh
Pittsburgh, USA
Email: mmg62@pitt.edu

J. Stephanie Rose
School of Computing and Information
University of Pittsburgh
Pittsburgh, USA
Email: jsr67@pitt.edu

***Abstract*— This paper proposes a spectrum enforcement framework by mobile, crowdsourced agents, who work in collaboration with a trustworthy infrastructure. To address the scarcity of spectrum, the Federal Communications Commission (FCC) mandated dynamic sharing of spectrum among the different tiers of users. The success of spectrum sharing, however, relies on the automated enforcement of spectrum policies. While most works in the past focus on automating spectrum enforcement before an actual harm has occurred, we focus on *ex post* spectrum enforcement, which happens during/after the occurrence of a potentially harmful event, but before/after an actual harm has occurred. The chief challenge here is to ensure *efficient ex post* enforcement. In order to achieve this, we focus on attaining maximum coverage of the region of enforcement, ensuring reliable and accurate detection of violation, and exploring a methodology to select *qualified* crowdsourced agents, called volunteers. We ensure maximum coverage of the given area of enforcement by proposing to divide it into regions using the Lloyd's algorithm and solving the enforcement problem by a divide and conquer mechanism over the entire area. We determine qualification of volunteers based on their likelihood of being in a region, over a given time interval and on trust, which is based on their *behavior* over the past. Finally, we use a non-incentive-based algorithm to select qualified volunteers for every region in the given area. We simulate the enforcement framework in CSIM19 (C++ version) and analyze the performance of the proposed volunteer selection algorithm over the area of enforcement.**

Keywords- volunteer; sentinel; ex post enforcement; crowdsourced spectrum monitoring; volunteer selection.

I. INTRODUCTION

With the exponential increase in use of wireless services, the demand for additional spectrum is steadily on the rise. In order to address this potential spectrum scarcity problem, the Federal Communications Commission (FCC) proposed Dynamic Spectrum Access (DSA), wherein licensed frequency bands when idle, are utilized by unlicensed users. In April 2015, the FCC adopted a three-tiered spectrum sharing infrastructure that is administered and enforced by Spectrum Access System (SAS) [1]. This architecture consists of Incumbents in tier 1, Priority Access Licensed (PAL) devices in tier 2 and General Authorized Access (GAA) devices in tier 3. Incumbents, in general, include military radars, fixed satellite service Earth stations and several of the Wireless Broadband Services (3650 – 3700 MHz) [2]. The SAS ensures that the spectrum is always available to the incumbent users when and where needed. The next level of access is provided to the users who buy PAL for a given location and period of time (usually for a three-year term). The remaining spectrum can then be used by devices having GAA. These devices have no protection from interference. They must, however, protect incumbents and PALs, while accessing spectrum [2].

As spectrum sharing becomes more intense and more granular with more stakeholders, we can expect an increasing number of potentially enforceable events. Thus, the success of spectrum sharing systems is dependent on our ability to automate their enforcement. The three key aspects of any enforcement regime are: the timing of enforcement action, the form of enforcement sanction and whether the enforcement action is private or public [3]. This paper focuses on detection of spectrum misuse. Thus, the key aspect of enforcement action for our consideration, is the timing of enforcement. Timing of an enforcement can be either *ex ante* (before a potentially "harmful" action has occurred) or *ex post* (after a potentially "harmful" action has occurred, but potentially before or after an actual "harm" has been done) [4]. The *ex ante* and *ex post* enforcement effects are inextricably linked. For example, if the *ex ante* rules and processes are sufficiently strong then *ex post* harms may be prevented before they occur. Also, certain types of *ex ante* rules may be easier to monitor and hence lower the cost of enforcement. Even strong *ex ante* rules may require *ex post* enforcement; for example, licensing approval for equipment is usually based on a prototype or pre-production unit, but compliance of production units may require some kind of policing. Till date, more significance has been given on automating *ex ante* enforcement of usage rights. As an example, the TV White Spaces database systems essentially work by preventing users with subordinate rights from using spectrum when and where other users with superior rights are operating [5]. This concept has been extended in the new Citizens Broadband Radio Service (CBRS) to a SAS that is designed to distinguish the three classes of user types discussed previously [2].

We observe that both SAS and CBRS have well-developed mechanisms to avoid interference but provide no support for addressing interference when it occurs. As we consider *ex post* enforcement approaches, the need to detect enforceable events, gather information about these events and adjudicate claims based on rules and evidence becomes important. In this paper, we focus on the detection of an interference event, or RF signal energy that is caused by a malicious user. The primary challenge is to ensure efficient *ex post* spectrum enforcement. In order to address this challenge, this paper proposes an enforcement framework that aims to achieve a) maximum coverage of the entire area of enforcement, b) an accurate, reliable and feasible detection of an event of violation, c) use of an effective method for hiring and deploying detecting agents. By employing a hybrid infrastructure of crowdsourced and trusted, dedicated resources, we aim to ensure "optimal" detection of spectrum access violation in Dynamic Spectrum Sharing Wireless networks. The major contributions of this paper are:

a) *Region Coverage*: We use a clustering algorithm to organize the area into smaller sized "regions" in order to ensure more manageable detection of violation
b) *Crowdsourced Detection*: We explore a mechanism to select crowdsourced detecting agents (called volunteers) for ensuring that a spectrum violation is detected with high probability of accuracy and efficiency.
c) *Volunteer Selection*: We develop a framework to assess the *qualification* of a volunteer across two dimensions - location likelihood and trust, to select volunteers using a non-incentive-based algorithm to ensure "optimal" quality of spectrum enforcement.

The paper is organized in the following manner. Section III of the paper discusses about the enforcement framework. Section IV discusses about the crowdsourced monitoring methodology, with a focus on the parameters that qualify a volunteer for selection and the appropriate volunteer selection mechanism. Section V discusses about the experimental setup and the results we obtained from applying the proposed volunteer selection algorithm. Finally, we conclude the paper and discuss about future works in Section VI.

II. Related Works

Jin *et al.* [20] introduces the first crowdsourced spectrum misuse detection for DSA systems. Dutta and Chiang [13] discusses about crowdsourced spectrum enforcement for accurate detection and location of spectrum enforcement. Salama *et al.* [22] proposed an optimal channel assignment framework for crowdsourced spectrum monitoring, where volunteers are assigned to monitor channels based on their availability patterns and are awarded with incentives in return. Li *et al.* [23] models the spectrum misuse problem as a combinatorial multi armed bandit problem to decide which channels to monitor, how long to monitor each channel, and the order in which channels should be monitored. Several incentive-based crowdsourced spectrum sensing works have been done over the past few years. Yang *et al.* [7] studied two incentive based crowdsourcing models, where a Stackelberg Equilibrium was computed in the platform-centric model, and a truthful auction mechanism was proposed under the user-centric model. Zhu *et al.* [14] proposes an incentive-based auction mechanism to improve fairness of bids by taking into consideration the effects of malicious competition behavior and the "free-riding" phenomenon in crowdsourcing services. Lin *et al.* [6] takes the Sybil attack into consideration for incentive based crowdsourced spectrum sensing. The works [11] and [12] propose frameworks for crowdsourced spectrum sensing without violating the location privacy of mobile users. Contrary to the formerly proposed spectrum monitoring approaches, which rely exclusively either on large deployment of physical monitoring infrastructure [8]-[10] or on crowdsourcing, we believe that spectrum misuse and access rights violations can be effectively prevented by using trusted infrastructure, composed of a central DSA Enforcement Infrastructure and a minimal number of mobile, wireless devices with advanced trust and authentication capabilities, augmented with an opportunistic infrastructure of wireless devices with various software and hardware capabilities. Moreover, in contrast to the usual methodologies, we explore the use of a non-incentive-based methodology for selection of volunteers to ensure maximum coverage of enforcement area and accurate detection of spectrum violations.

III. Enforcement Framework

The main challenge in the design of a hybrid infrastructure stems from the fact that it is not easy to determine where and how the resources are to be mobilized, given the non-deterministic nature of mobile devices' *behavior.* It is equally difficult to determine how collaboration between these devices must take place to ensure swift detection and response to spectrum misuse and access rights violation. To address this, we broadly follow a crowdsourced monitoring infrastructure, supported by sentinel-based monitoring and a central DSA Enforcement Infrastructure.

A. System Model

The entire area of enforcement R is divided into smaller regions, with an Access Point AP_r, associated with every $r \epsilon R$. Authorized users, who are legitimate Secondary Users (SUs) gain access to an available channel through the local AP_r in r. On the contrary, malicious users are unauthorized transmitters who intrude on spectrum by illegitimately using spectrum frequencies in r that they have not been authorized to use by the local AP_r. Some of the authorized users volunteer to monitor a given channel for access violation, in addition to accessing the spectrum to transmit their own data. Such volunteers are mobile agents who can monitor radio access behavior within their neighborhood and detect anomalous use of spectrum. To carry out spectrum monitoring practices, volunteers incur transmit power consumption cost and bandwidth consumption cost.

As shown in Figure 1, the system model further consists of a central DSA Enforcement Infrastructure, which consists of a set of Volunteer Service units VS_r for every $r \in R$, a Volunteer Selection Unit and a DSA Database. A volunteer $v \epsilon V$ in $r \in R$ registers itself to the VS_r associated with r. A VS_r stores and updates volunteer attributes over the entire period of enforcement. The Volunteer Selection Unit uses the latest attributes of all the volunteers in a VS_r to select volunteers for monitoring a given channel in r over the next epoch of enforcement. The DSA Database maintains a channel-user occupancy list, for the entire area of enforcement R. The information contained in the DSA Database is used to identify the channels and their respective authorized users in R. Finally, the system model consists of a set of sentinels S' who monitor a given channel in r at random intervals to verify the detection results reported by the volunteers and to prevent selection of volunteers who have unreliable behavior.

B. *Coverage of Region*

To ensure maximum coverage of an area R for enforcement, we follow a divide and conquer method. We propose to divide the entire area R into smaller regions and then focus on solving the enforcement problem for a single region $r \in R$. This in turn can be used for solving the problem for the whole R. For division of R into regions, we propose the employment of the Voronoi algorithm [15]. Initially, we assume that the volunteers in V are randomly distributed over R and the access points are spread uniformly over R. For each volunteer $v \in V$, its corresponding Voronoi region r consists of every volunteer in the Euclidean plane whose distance to the local AP_r is less than or equal to its distance to any other AP_r [15]. However, the Voronoi algorithm may not produce regions that are of equal size. This is a disadvantage because it may result in some of the regions to have an undersupply of volunteers over time, which in turn may result in possible loss in detection of spectrum violation. Thus, we propose to apply a relaxation to the Voronoi algorithm, called the Lloyd's Algorithm [16], which produces uniformly sized convex regions, and thus improves the probability of a fair distribution of volunteers over all regions. The number of regions in R is equal to the number of access points in R.

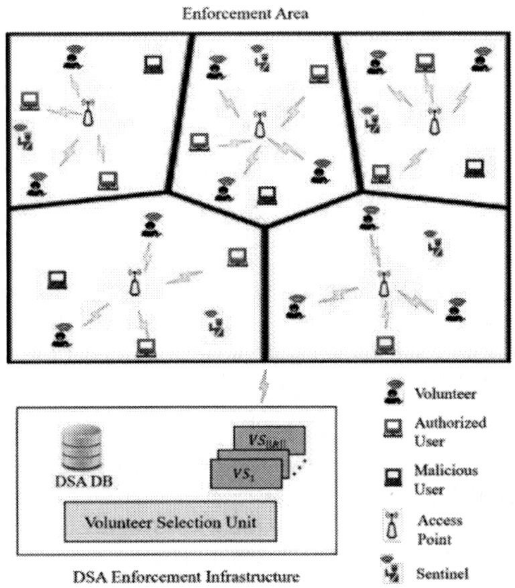

Figure 1. System Model.

IV. CROWDSOURCED SPECTRUM MONITORING

A volunteer $v \in V$ is associated with the following parameters: Serial Number of the sensing device S_v used by v and its location $L_{v,t}$ at time t. While S_v can be used to uniquely identify a volunteer, the location $L_{v,t}$ allows the VS_r of the DSA Enforcement Infrastructure to estimate whether v will be available to monitor a given channel in r in the future.

As shown in Figure 2, we divide the total enforcement time into a set of intervals called the Monitoring Intervals, MIs. Each MI is further divided into a set of n sub-intervals called the Access Unit Intervals (AUIs). One AUI is defined as the smallest interval over which a user, intruder or legitimate, can accomplish useful work. It is used as the interference monitoring interval by the selected volunteers to determine access violation or legitimacy. A new set of volunteers is selected at the end of every MI by the Volunteer Service unit VS_r associated with region r. Volunteer selection in r is primarily based upon twofold parameters of trust and location likelihood of a v in r.

A. *Trust*

The trust of a volunteer v is determined by its past behavior. The behavior of a volunteer v is chiefly determined by its accuracy in detection of spectrum violation. At the end of every AUI i, a volunteer v reports the observed state $\Phi_{i,v,r}$ of a channel c_r that it monitors, over i. The state of a channel c_r can be either a) violated, when c_r is being used by a malicious transmitter b) not violated, when c_r is either idle, i.e., when no user, authorized or malicious, uses c_r or safe, i.e., when c_r is used by an authorized transmitter. The necessary ground truth required for calculating accuracy of interference detection by v in r is acquired from the observed state $\Phi_{j,s,r}$ of c_r by a sentinel $s \in S'$ that monitors c_r at a random AUI j. A sentinel s is a trustworthy agent who helps in verifying volunteer detection result and helps to identify unreliable volunteers. As shown in Figure 2, a sentinel s monitors c_r in r at a random interval j,which is not known to the volunteers. This helps us to calculate the behavior $b_{i,v,r}$ of v in r at AUI i by using (1) given below.

$$b_{i,v,r} = \begin{cases} 1, & \Phi_{i,v,r} = \Phi_{j,s,r} \\ 0, & \Phi_{i,v,r} \neq \Phi_{j,s,r} \end{cases}, \forall i = j \quad (1)$$

As shown in (1), the behavior of a volunteer $b_{i,v,r}$ at i in r is assigned to zero when there is a mismatch in the observed state of c_r, between v and s.This can be because a) v makes a false detection, b) v lies about the true result, or c) s makes a false detection, d) s lies about the true result. However, for this paper, we assume that s is trustworthy and never makes a false detection or lies about a true result. An AUI when both v and s monitor channel c_r is called a matching interval. We aggregate $b_{i,v,r}$ over all the matching intervals to find the trust $T_{v,r}$ of v in r, by calculating the arithmetic mean $T_{v,r}$, given by (2),

$$T_{v,r} = \frac{1}{m}\sum_{p=1}^{m} b_{p,v,r} \quad (2)$$

where p is a matching interval and m is the total number of matching intervals over all the monitoring intervals observed so far.

B. *Location Likelihood*

In order to efficiently support detection of channel violation in a region r, volunteers who are most likely to reside a major proportion of time in r after a visit to r, must be given preference. For this purpose, the VS_r estimates the fraction of time that a volunteer v stays in r after its current visit to r. As shown in Figure 3, after the $(j)^{th}$ visit of v to r, we measure its $(j-1)^{th}$ sojourn time, $S_{j-1,v,r}$, in r as the difference between its $(j-1)^{th}$ departure time, $dep_{j-1,v,r}$ from r and its $(j-1)^{th}$ arrival time, $arr_{j-1,v,r}$ in r. Furthermore, we calculate the $(j-1)^{th}$ return time of v in r, $R_{j-1,v,r}$, as the difference between $arr_{j,v,r}$ and $arr_{j-1,v,r}$. As given by (3), this enables us to calculate the proportion of time, $P_{j-1,v,r}$, that v resided in r on its previous $((j-1)^{th})$ visit to r, as the ratio of $S_{j-1,v,r}$ to $R_{j-1,v,r}$. Based on this information, the VS_r estimates the proportion of time that v is likely to stay in r before its jth departure from r, as an exponentially smoothed average, given by (4).

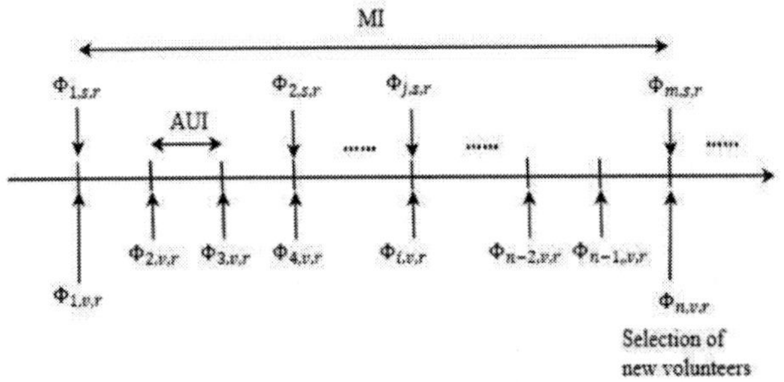

Figure 2. Observations $\Phi_{i,v,r}$ by volunteer v after every AUI and $\Phi_{j,s,r}$ by sentinel s after random AUIs, for the 1st MI.

$$P_{j-1,v,r} = \frac{S_{j-1,v,r}}{R_{j-1,v,r}} \quad (3)$$

$$\tilde{P}_{j,v,r} = \alpha . P_{j-1,v,r} + (1-\alpha). \tilde{P}_{j-1,v,r}. \quad (4)$$

In order to estimate the smoothed average, $\tilde{P}_{j,v,r}$ more accurately, smoothing factor α is computed as:

$$\alpha = c\frac{E^2_{j-1,v,r}}{\sigma_{j,v,r}}. \quad (5)$$

where $0 < c < 1$, $E_{j-1,v,r} = P_{j-1,v,r} - \tilde{P}_{j-1,v,r}$ is the prediction error, and $\sigma_{j,v,r}$ is the average of the past square prediction errors on visit j. $\sigma_{j,v,r}$ can be expressed as follows:

$$\sigma_{j,v,r} = c. E^2_{j-1,v,r} + (1-c). \sigma_{j-1,v,r}. \quad (6)$$

Moreover, at any given time t, the location $L_{v,t}$ of volunteer v enables us to estimate the likelihood of v to stay in r over the next monitoring interval, MI, based on the assumption that the likelihood of v to stay in r decreases as the displacement between $L_{v,t}$ and the centroid O_r of r increases. This is expressed by the separation factor, $Y_{t,v,r}$, given by (7) as follows:

$$Y_{t,v,r} = \gamma_1 e^{-\gamma_2 d(L_{v,t}, O_r)}. \quad (7)$$

where $0 < \gamma_1, \gamma_2 < 1$, are parameters defined by the system and $d(L_{v,t}, O_r)$ is the displacement between $L_{v,t}$and O_r. Since $Y_{t,v,r}$ is exponential, so we empirically select values of γ_1 and γ_2 to avoid high variance in the values of $Y_{t,v,r}$ across all the volunteers.

Hence, the location likelihood, $L_{v,r}(MI)$ of v in r at time t over the next MI, is given by a function f of the parameters, $\tilde{P}_{j,v,r}$ of the latest (j^{th}) visit of v in r and $Y_{t,v,r}$,. We observe

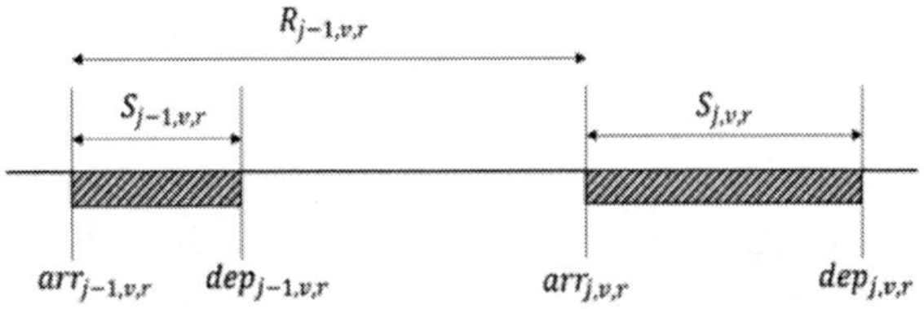

Figure 3. Sojourn time $S_{j,v,r}$ and Return time $R_{j,v,r}$ of volunteer v after its jth visit to region r.

that since $R_{j-1,v,r} > S_{j-1,v,r}$ and $0 < \alpha < 1$, so $0 < \tilde{P}_{j,v,r} < 1$. Similarly, since $d(L_{v,t}, O_r) \geq 0$, so $0 < Y_{t,v,r} \leq 1$. As weighting the parameters by linear regression requires large amount of data and preferential weighting is hard to establish as it usually requires an expert opinion on the importance of an individual parameter relative to the overall composite parameter [17], so we assign equal weights to the parameters $\tilde{P}_{j,v,r}$ and $Y_{t,v,r}$. Finally, we define function f as the product of parameters $\tilde{P}_{j,v,r}$ and $Y_{t,v,r}$ as given by (8) below.

$$L_{v,r}(MI) = \tilde{P}_{j,v,r} \times Y_{t,v,r} \tag{8}$$

C. Selection of volunteers

From the set of volunteers, V, in total area of enforcement, R, the VS_r associated with r in the DSA Enforcement Infrastructure selects k_r qualified volunteers to monitor r at the beginning of every MI. This is determined by the estimated Qualification $Q_{v,r}(MI)$ of a volunteer v to monitor the associated channel c_r in r over the next MI, given by (9), defined below.

$$Q_{v,r}(MI) = g(T_{v,r}, L_{v,r}(MI)) \tag{9}$$

As shown in (9), $Qualification\ Q_{v,r}(MI)$ of a v in r is given as a function g of its location likelihood $L_{v,r}(MI)$, over the next MI, and trust $T_{v,r}$. Since $L_{v,r}(MI)$ and $T_{v,r}$ represent the measurement of two different parameters, we normalize both the parameters by using the min-max normalization technique [17]. We apply equal weighting to the two parameters since the other two widely used weighting methods of linear regression and preferential weighting are cumbersome due to the requirement of large amount of data and of expert opinion on preference, respectively [17]. We aggregate $L_{v,r}(MI)$ and $T_{v,r}$ in function g, using a) multiplication, b) addition, c) geometric mean, d) arithmetic mean and compare the performance of using different aggregation methods in Section V.

This work focuses on spectrum enforcement over a single channel in a region. However, it can be extended to deal with multiple channels in a region by selecting volunteers to cover additional channels. We also assume that a volunteer v can be hired to monitor more than one region over the next MI as v is mobile and can potentially cover multiple regions over a given MI. The Volunteer Selection Unit of the DSA Enforcement Infrastructure builds a centralized $||V||$-by-$||R||$ matrix $\Psi_{V,R}$, using the values of volunteer attributes from the VS_r associated with every region $r \in R$. The matrix $\Psi_{V,R}$ is a volunteer-region qualification matrix that contains the qualification values $Q_{v,r}(MI)$ of all $v \in V$ for every $r \in R$. The Volunteer Selection Unit selects k_r volunteers dynamically from V based on the qualification values of all $v \in V$ for r, using Algorithm 1.

For the volunteer selection Algorithm 1, we use the volunteer-region qualification matrix $\Psi_{V,R}$ to select qualified volunteers for every $r \in R$ (line 1). At the end of a MI (line 3), the Volunteer Selection Unit gains access to the qualification values of all $v \in V$ for r from $\Psi_{V,R}$ and stores them in a list Q_r (line 4). If the number of volunteers to be selected in r, k_r is 1, then we use the classic secretary algorithm [18] to select the most qualified volunteer dynamically, with constant probability. In a classic secretary algorithm, we observe the first $||Q_r||/e$ qualification values to determine a *threshold* and then select the first of the remaining volunteers, whose qualification value is above the threshold [19]. However, if $k_r > 1$, we select volunteers dynamically by using a variant of the multiple-choice secretary algorithm, which proceeds as follows. We draw a random sample m_r from a binomial distribution $Binomial(||Q_r||, \frac{1}{2})$, from which we select up to $\lfloor k_r/2 \rfloor$ volunteers recursively (lines 8-13). We keep appending the selected volunteers in set $V_{S,r}$. If m_r is greater than $\lfloor k_r/2 \rfloor$, then we set l_r to $\lfloor k_r/2 \rfloor$, otherwise we set l_r to m_r. Next, we set a $threshold$, which is the l_r^{th} largest qualification value in the sample of first m_r qualification values. After this, we select every volunteer with qualification value greater than $threshold$, till we select a maximum of k_r volunteers (lines 16-20) [19]. We apply this algorithm for selection of volunteers in every $r \in R$. The expected total qualification value of the k_r volunteers selected by Algorithm 1 is at least $(1 - \frac{5}{\sqrt{k_r}})$ times the total qualification value of the top k_r volunteers [19].

V. Experiments And Results

We simulate the enforcement framework by using the C++ version of the CSIM19 simulation engine. For simplicity, we

Algorithm 1 Selection of Volunteers

```
1: Maintain matrix Ψ_{V,R} that stores qualification values ∀v ∈
   V, ∀r ∈ R, list of selected volunteers V_{S,r}, ∀r ∈ R
2: for all r ∈ R do
3:   if t = MI then
4:     Q_r ← Ψ_{V,R}[r]
5:     if k_r = 1 then
6:       Run Classic Secretary Algorithm
7:     else
8:       m_r ← Binom(||Q_r||, 1/2)
9:       if m_r > ⌊k_r/2⌋ then
10:        l_r ← ⌊k_r/2⌋
11:      else
12:        l_r ← m_r
13:      Recursively select upto l_r volunteers
14:      B_r ← descending_sort(Q_r[1], ..., Q_r[m_r])
15:      threshold ← B_r[l_r]
16:      for i ← m_r + 1, ..., ||Q_r|| do
17:        if Q_r[i] > threshold and ||V_{S,r}|| < k_r then
18:          V_{S,r} ← V_{S,r} ∪ v
19:        else
20:          Reject v
```

Figure 4. Algorithm for selection of volunteers.

divide the entire area of enforcement R (of total area 500,000 sq. units) into two regions of equal area. This work can, however, be easily extended to deal with more regions. With the assumption that 1 sq. unit is equivalent to 1 sq. meter and by taking the average population density of Pittsburgh (2,140/sq. km) [21], we calculate the total population (1,070 people) in the area of enforcement. A random fraction of people from the total population are chosen as volunteers (equals 183 volunteers). Volunteers are initially placed at random positions within R and they change their positions with a random speed from the range 0-70 m/s at a random direction after every fixed interval of time. The maximum speed of a volunteer is chosen higher than the usual speed limit of a vehicle in a city in order to compensate for the limited simulation time. Additionally, we assume that every volunteer uses a sensing device with maximum battery capacity of approximately 7 Wh and that the battery discharges at the rate of 1 J/s for a random time interval drawn from an exponential distribution of the mean active time interval of 100 s. After every active time interval, we assume that the device remains idle for a random time interval drawn from an exponential distribution of the mean idle time interval of 10 s. The simulation runs till the battery of the sensing device used by every volunteer is exhausted, i.e., for 5665 AUIs. Each AUI is equivalent to 5 seconds and one MI is equivalent to 5 AUIs. We select $\gamma_1 = 1$ and $\gamma_2 = 0.01$ for the separation factor $\Upsilon_{t,v,r}$ of v with respect to r. Since $\Upsilon_{t,v,r}$ is exponential, so we empirically decide the value of the γ_2, which is the coefficient of $d(L_{v,t}, O_r)$ from (7), to avoid high variances in the qualification values of volunteers. Since we did not notice significant difference in the results for different values of α, we determine the value of α empirically as 0.1 for the sake of simplicity in implementation. Finally, we assume that $k_r = k$ for every $r \in R$.

Primarily, we evaluate two performance metrics – the *hit ratio* and the *accuracy of detection*. In a monitoring interval MI, if a volunteer v selected for monitoring r is in r at the beginning of an AUI in the given MI, then it is a *hit*, otherwise it is a *miss* for the AUI in the given MI. This is according to the assumption that a selected volunteer v can successfully monitor a channel c_r in r over an AUI only if v resides in r over the given AUI. The *hit ratio* of a region $r \in R$ over a given MI measures the ratio of the number of *hits* of all the selected volunteers to the sum of the number of *hits* and the number of *misses* of all the selected volunteers in r. Figure 5 compares the mean *hit ratio* of all the regions over the entire duration of simulation, by using the proposed Algorithm 1 and the Random algorithm for different ranges of k. The Random algorithm selects k volunteers randomly from the total set of volunteers V. For this experiment, the qualification $Q_{v,r}(MI)$ of a volunteer v for region r is equal to its location likelihood $L_{v,r}(MI)$. We observe that Algorithm 1 has a better mean *hit ratio* than the random algorithm for all the ranges of k. However, the mean *hit ratio* by applying Algorithm 1 decreases consistently (from 0.91 for k =1-20% of $||V||$ to 0.57 for k = 20-40% of $||V||$) with the increase in k because the proportion of *qualified* selected volunteers reduces as the value of k increases. The error bars in Figure 5 represent the mean standard deviation of the mean *hit ratio* across all regions, which decreases from 0.22 for k =1-20% of $||V||$ to 0.101 for k = 80-100% of $||V||$, using Algorithm 1 and decreases from 0.19 for k =1-20% of $||V||$ to 0.06 for k = 80-100% of $||V||$, using the Random algorithm. This type of behavior is attributed to the fact that a balance is approached between the proportions of *qualified* and *unqualified* selected volunteers as the value of k increases.

We assume that every volunteer monitors the channel in r with a probability of successful detection p_v, drawn randomly from a uniform distribution in the range of $0 + \delta$ to $0.5 + \delta$ (with $\delta = 0.1$) and that a sentinel in r monitors the channel with the probability of successful detection of

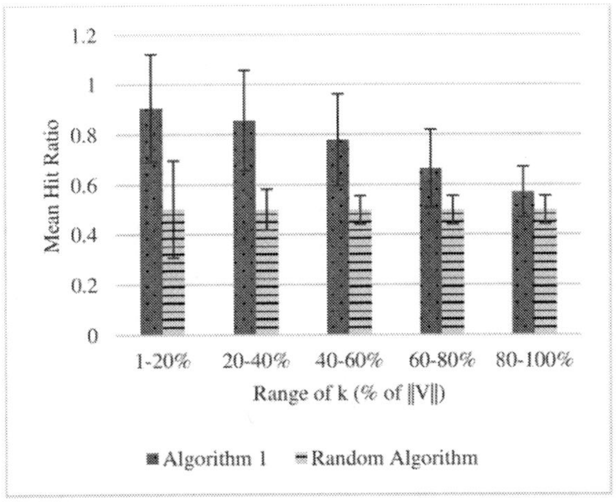

Figure 5. Comparison of the mean *hit ratio* of selecting volunteers by using Algorithm 1 and the Random algorithm.

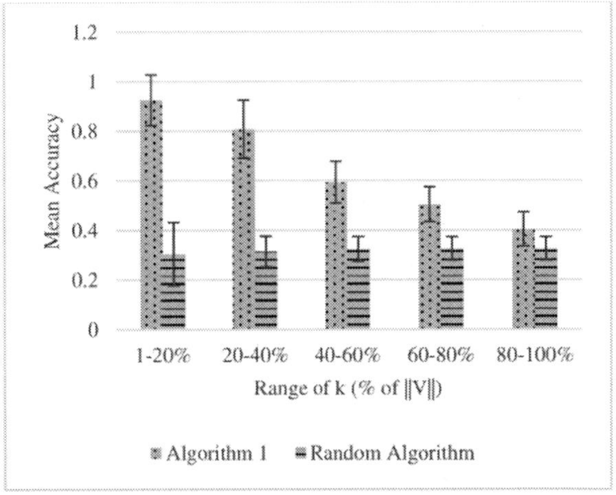

Figure 6. Comparison of the mean accuracy of detection by selecting volunteers using Algorithm 1 and Random algorithm.

0.5. The observed detection value of a v at the end of an AUI is a random sample taken from a binomial distribution of 100 trials with a probability of success equal to p_v. Similarly, the observed detection value of a sentinel $s \in S'$ at the end of an AUI is a random sample from a binomial distribution of 100 trials with a probability of success equal to 0.5. If the observed detection values of a v and s in r are both either greater than or lesser than an empirically selected threshold value of 42, then the detection by v is considered accurate. Figure 6 compares the mean accuracy of detection of the selected volunteers over all the MIs between Algorithm 1 and the Random algorithm for varying ranges of k. For this experiment, the qualification $Q_{v,r}(MI)$ of a volunteer v for region r is equal to its trust $T_{v,r}$. We observe that Algorithm 1 performs better than the Random algorithm for all the ranges of k. The mean accuracy of detection decreases consistently (from 0.92 for k = 1-20% of $||V||$ to 0.403 for k = 80-100% of $||V||$) with the increase in k because of the decrease in the fraction of *qualified* volunteers in r as k increases. The uniform distribution of p_v for all $v \epsilon V$ ensures that the mean standard deviation in accuracy of detection across all regions decreases from 0.103 for k =1-20% of $||V||$ to 0.069 for k = 80-100% of $||V||$, using Algorithm 1 and decreases from 0.13 for k =1-20% of $||V||$ to 0.05 for k = 80-100% of $||V||$, using the Random algorithm.

Finally, in Figure 7, we compare the mean *hit ratio* and the mean accuracy of detection by using different data aggregation methods to aggregate the trust $T_{v,r}$ and location likelihood $L_{v,r}(MI)$ of v to calculate it's qualification $Q_{v,r}(MI)$ using (9) for region r over the next MI. For this experiment, we select volunteers using Algorithm 1 for k = 1-20% of $||V||$. We observe that by using the aggregation methods of sum and arithmetic mean, we obtain a mean accuracy value (equals 0.86) higher than the mean *hit ratio* (equals 0.76). On the contrary, we observe that the mean accuracy value (equals 0.78) is lower than the mean *hit ratio* (equals 0.85) when we use the data aggregation methods of product and geometric mean. Also, we observe that the results we obtain by using sum and arithmetic mean are similar. Likewise, we get similar results for both product and geometric mean. This would help us to decide about the proper aggregation method to use based on the requirements of the system for efficient spectrum enforcement.

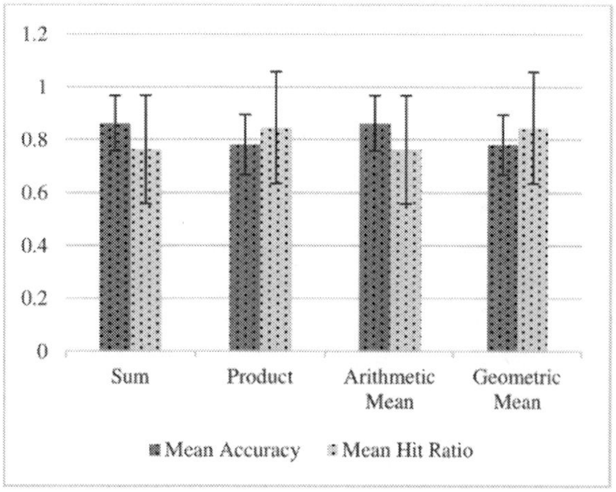

Figure 7. Comparison of the mean hit ratio and mean accuracy of detection by selecting volunteers using Algorithm 1 with different aggregation methods to calculate $Q_{v,r}(MI)$ of volunteer v in r for k = 1 to 20% of $||V||$.

VI. CONCLUSION

In this paper, we discuss about a spectrum enforcement framework based on a crowdsourced monitoring infrastructure, supported by sentinel-based monitoring and a central DSA Enforcement Infrastructure. The objective is to maximize coverage of the area of enforcement and to ensure reliable detection of spectrum access violation by selecting *qualified* volunteers. We propose to maximize the coverage of the region of enforcement by following a divide-and-conquer mechanism wherein we divide the area of enforcement into smaller regions, by applying the Lloyd's algorithm, which is a relaxation to the Voronoi algorithm. Every small region in the enforcement area is responsible for its own spectrum enforcement, which in turn ensures enforcement of the entire area. The qualification of a volunteer for the upcoming time interval is decided by its likelihood to stay in the region over the next monitoring interval and by its trust. We use a variant of the multiple-choice Secretary algorithm to select volunteers dynamically based on their qualifications to monitor a region. We observe that this non-incentive-based volunteer selection algorithm performs better than a non-incentive-based algorithm that selects volunteers randomly for spectrum monitoring.

We plan to extend this work to explore different mechanisms to select volunteers for multi-channel spectrum enforcement. We further plan to explore different statistical and machine learning based mechanisms to determine the trust and location likelihood of volunteers in the enforcement area.

ACKNOWLEDGMENT

This work was sponsored in part by the National Science Foundation through grants 1265886, 1547241, 1563832, and 1642928.

REFERENCES

[1] Federated Wireless. *Citizens Broadband Radio Service (CBRS) Shared Spectrum: An Overview.* [Online]. Available from: http://federatedwireless.com/wp-content/uploads/2017/03/CBRS-Spectrum-Sharing-Overview-v3.pdf.

[2] Federal Communications Commission. *3.5 GHz Band / Citizens Broadband Radio Service.* [Online]. Available from: https://www.fcc.gov/wireless/bureau-divisions/broadband-division/35-ghz-band/35-ghz-band-citizens-broadband-radio#block-menu-block-4.

[3] E. Schlager and E. Ostrom, "Property-Rights Regimes and Natural Resources: A Conceptual Analysis," Land Econ., vol. 68, no. 3, 1992, pp. 249–262.

[4] Shavell, Steven. "The Optimal Structure of Law Enforcement." The Journal of Law & Economics, vol. 36, no. 1, 1993, pp. 255–287. JSTOR, www.jstor.org/stable/725476.

[5] A. Gopinathan, Z. Li, and C. Wu, "Strategyproof auctions for balancing social welfare and fairness in secondary spectrum markets," 2011 Proc. IEEE INFOCOM, 2011, pp. 3020–3028.

[6] J. Lin, M. Li, D. Yang, G. Xue, and J. Tang, "Sybil-proof incentive mechanisms for crowdsensing," in IEEE INFOCOM 2017, pp. 1–9.

[7] D. Yang, G. Xue, X. Fang, and J. Tang, "Crowdsourcing to Smartphones: Incentive Mechanism Design for Mobile Phone Sensing," in Proceedings of the 18th Annual International Conference on Mobile Computing and Networking, 2012, pp. 173–184.

[8] M. B. H. Weiss, M. Altamimi, and M. McHenry, "Enforcement and spectrum sharing: A case study of the 1695-1710 MHz band," in 8th International Conference on Cognitive Radio Oriented Wireless Networks, 2013, pp. 7–12.

[9] D. Yang, X. Zhang, and G. Xue, "PROMISE: A framework for truthful and profit maximizing spectrum double auctions," in Proceedings - IEEE INFOCOM, 2014, pp. 109–117.

[10] R. Chen, J.-M. Park, and J. H. Reed, "Defense Against Primary User Emulation Attacks in Cognitive Radio Networks," IEEE J.Sel. A. Commun., vol. 26, no. 1, Jan. 2008, pp. 25–37.

[11] X. Jin, R. Zhang, Y. Chen, T. Li, and Y. Zhang, "DPSense: Differentially Private Crowdsourced Spectrum Sensing," in Proceedings of the 2016 ACM SIGSAC Conference on Computer and Communications Security, 2016, pp. 296–307.

[12] X. Jin and Y. Zhang, "Privacy-Preserving Crowdsourced Spectrum Sensing," IEEE/ACM Trans. Netw., vol. 26, no. 3, Jun. 2018, pp. 1236–1249.

[13] A. Dutta and M. Chiang, ""See Something, Say Something" Crowdsourced Enforcement of Spectrum Policies," IEEE Trans. Wirel. Commun., vol. 15, no. 1, Jan. 2016, pp. 67–80.

[14] X. Zhu, J. An, M. Yang, L. Xiang, Q. Yang, and X. Gui, "A Fair Incentive Mechanism for Crowdsourcing in Crowd Sensing," IEEE Internet Things J., vol. 3, no. 6, Dec. 2016, pp. 1364–1372.

[15] F. Aurenhammer, "Voronoi diagrams—a survey of a fundamental geometric data structure", ACM Comput. Surv., vol. 23, no. 3, Sep. 1991, pp. 345–405.

[16] Q. Du, M. Emelianenko, and L. Ju, "Convergence of the Lloyd Algorithm for Computing Centroidal Voronoi Tessellations," SIAM J. Numer. Anal., vol. 44, no. 1, Jan. 2006, pp. 102–119.

[17] B. Talukder, K. W. Hipel, and G. W. vanLoon, "Developing Composite Indicators for Agricultural Sustainability Assessment: Effect of Normalization and Aggregation Techniques," Resources, vol. 6, no. 4, 2017.

[18] Gautam Kamath. *Advanced Algorithms, Matroid Secretary Problems.* [Online]. Available from: http://www.gautamkamath.com/writings/matroidsec.pdf.

[19] R. Kleinberg, "A Multiple-choice Secretary Algorithm with Applications to Online Auctions," in Proceedings of the Sixteenth Annual ACM-SIAM Symposium on Discrete Algorithms, 2005, pp. 630–631.

[20] X. Jin, J. Sun, R. Zhang, Y. Zhang, and C. Zhang, "SpecGuard: Spectrum misuse detection in dynamic spectrum access systems," 2015 IEEE Conf. Comput. Commun., 2015, pp. 172–180.

[21] Pittsburgh Population. (2018-06-12). [Online]. Available from: http://worldpopulationreview.com/us-cities/pittsburgh/.

[22] A. M. Salama, M. Li, and D. Yang, "Optimal Crowdsourced Channel Monitoring in Cognitive Radio Networks," in IEEE Global Communications Conference, GLOBECOM, Singapore, December 4-8, 2017, pp. 1–6.

[23] M. Li, D. Yang, J. Lin, M. Li, and J. Tang, "SpecWatch: A framework for adversarial spectrum monitoring with unknown statistics," Comput. Networks, vol. 143, 2018, pp. 176–190.

Distributed Detection of Tor Directory Authorities Censorship in Mexico

Gunnar Eyal Wolf Iszaevich
Instituto de Investigaciones Económicas, UNAM
Facultad de Ingeniería, UNAM
Mexico City, Mexico
Email: gwolf@gwolf.org

***Abstract*—The Tor network relies on individuals to set up relays for it to operate. Campaigns have in the past been successfully made to invite more people to join, and the network currently consists of close to 6,500 relays, spread globally. Although the Latin American region has many characteristics that make it natural to expect a wide participation in Tor, it has lagged behind most of the world in its Tor activity — Both considering client usage and participation as relays. This study focuses on the difficulties the Mexican user community has faced in setting up Tor relays, and presents how -and why- we deployed a relatively very simple and unsophisticated network censorship reporting system, as well as the results we have received so far. While this is still considered a work in progress, it has yielded important results as an aide allowing to specify the needed characteristics for potential relays, with a clear, measurable result.**

Keywords: ***ISP*; *Tor*; *Censorship*; *Detection*; *Mexico*.**

I. INTRODUCTION

Anonymity loves company, says the adage. In our networked world, this means that the technical excellence of an anonymity technology is often second in importance to its usability [3], as a great program with very low usability will keep its mass adoption low — and if few people use it, de-anonymizing one of its users becomes easier. Hence, a fundamental concern for any anonymity-providing network is how to get more people to adopt it.

The best known, best studied and most popular anonymization technology is Tor [15]. It provides a low latency network, overlaid over the regular Internet, based on *onion routing* [14]. Tor is a network that relies on volunteers to provide the servers (*relays*) and their respective bandwidth for its operation.

One of the clearest ways people can help the Tor project is by running new relays; several campaigns and proposals have been launched by individuals and organizations asking committed users to set up new relays [6][10][13].

While the campaigns have been successful on a global scale, some regions' participation in the network remains quite low. In April 2017, the Tor Project started its *Global South* working group [9] to increase awareness and participation in the project for users in countries in said regions, be it as users or as participants in the network.

As the time of this writing, the Tor network consists of slightly over 6,300 relay nodes as reported by the Tor Metrics site [12]. As can be seen in Fig. 1, while there was a constrant growth in the number of relays until 2015, the number has since remained fairly stable. Tor Metrics also reports the number of daily users of the network to be close to two million; the Latin American region represents only a tiny percentage, with a combined weight of only 1.53% of the network's users [11].

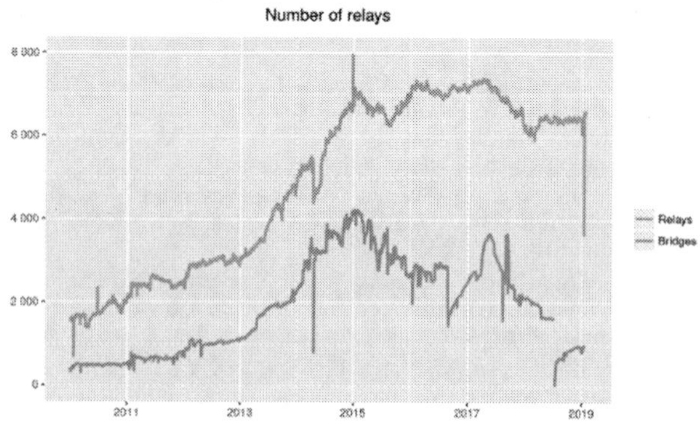

Figure 1. Number of relays and bridges over time, 2010–2019. Source: Tor Metrics [12]

The number of relays is not a core concern for the Tor network, nor is -as can be understood from Fig. 2- its available bandwidth; even though the number of relays available in the last years has not changed, advertised bandwidth has kept an overall increasing trend, and more importantly, consumed bandwidth is kept close to half of it.

However, Tor relatively lacks *diversity*, a fundamental and most desired property to be able to withstand deanonymization attacks by nation-state adversaries [8]. One of the goals of the aforementioned *Global South* group is to promote the installation of Tor relays worldwide.

Tor usage throughout the world is superbly depicted in Graham's 2014 visualization [5]; it shows that in 2014 Mexico had a similar amount of users as Sweden or Austria, a countries with a tenth of Mexico's population — and with a much better record on human rights and freedom of the press. This trend continues, as Tor Metrics reports all said countries in the 10,000 to 15,000 daily users range.

The number of relays ran from each of the aforementioned countries, however, is dozens of times larger than in Mexico. The sum of the factors so far mentioned led us to pursue convincing other sympathizers to set up Tor relays.

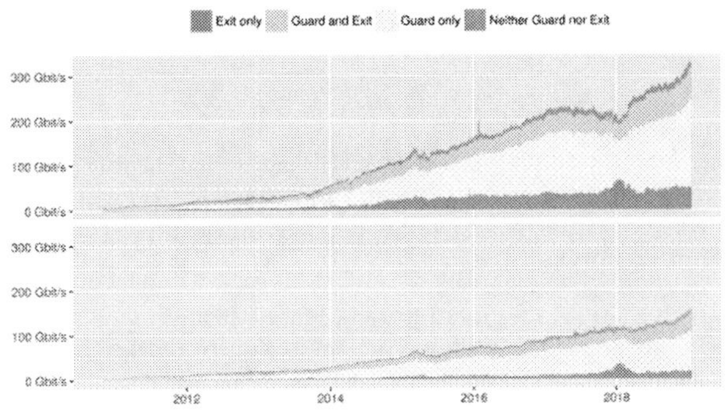

Figure 2. Advertised (above) and consumed (below) bandwidth in the Tor network, 2010–2019. Source: Tor Metrics [12]

While large numbers of relays have never been observed in Mexico, Fig. 3 shows a clear symptom of network censorship: while there was only one stable relay before 2013, in the lapse of a year the number grew (partly due to the aforementioned campaigns) to stabilize between seven and eight relays. However, in late 2015 there is a sharp drop, and while there are some spikes, Mexico's presence was clearly limited.

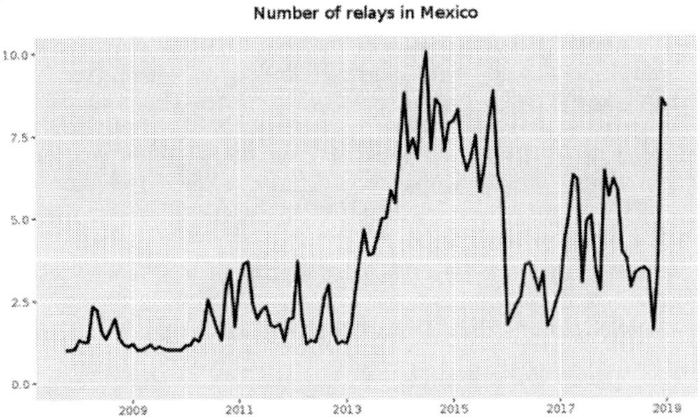

Figure 3. Number of relays in Mexico, 2008–2019. Source: Tor Metrics [12]

Besides anecdotal evidence by several former relay operators, we have found online reports from around the time this censorship was instated [1].

During 2017 and 2018, our project (UNAM/DGAPA/PAPIME PE102718) in consonance with Derechos Digitales' (see Section VI) engaged in promoting further relays, but it wasn't until after we had partial results of the project this article presents that the spike at the end of the graph.

The results we can report so far are, sadly, not that we managed to stop the censorship — but by finding an ISP (Internet Service Provider) amenable to running relay nodes, managed to successfully improve participation. However, with this information documented, we are starting to contact relevant ISPs in order to work legally and socially against their blocking.

II. Network censorship, architecture or policy?

When attempting to set up Tor relays in residential (Digital Subscriber Line, or DSL) connections in Mexico, we found they repeatedly failed to be recognized by the Metrics site. Although we did have some anecdotal evidence pointing towards the ISP blocking connectivity to the Tor directory authorities (DirAuths) [1], we needed further validation to ensure whether this was effectively due to network censorship (and not misconfiguration).

Also, as we were embarking on a project to distribute Raspberry Pi computers donated by the *Derechos Digitales* NGO for volunteers interested in setting up a relay, we felt necessary to do a more thorough review to check the status of the different providers.

We identified the three following points as in need of an answer:

1) Does the ISP *actively interfere* with connections?
   We need to know if there are technical measures *purposefully* set up by the ISP to block connections to Tor.
2) Does the ISP perform *deep NAT* (Network Address Translation) to its customer's networks?
   Due to the scarcity of IPv4 addresses, many ISPs (specially the local ones, or the latecomers to the market) don't provide a network-visible IP address to each user. Instead, several layers of NAT can be traversed on the way to the real network (we have detected up to seven *hops* inside NATted networks). If users cannot be reached from the outside network, there is no way they can set up relays.
3) Does the ISP allow end users to reconfigure their routers and receive incoming connections?
   Even having the necessary network capabilities to reach the user's connection, and allowing unfettered access to the Tor DirAuths, residential-grade routers are usually configured –in good measure for security– to reject any connections not started within the client's network.
   All modern routers have the capability to set up network forwarding for specific ports. Not all ISPs, though, allow the user to configure in this fashion their routers.

Given that item number 3 needs actually reconfiguring network equipment, we decided not to pursue it at this stage.

From the three points mentioned above, although they are all important for the project's goals, only item 1. qualifies as network censorship.

III. Interface description

As we needed to survey different networks countrywide, we decided to make a public call for participation: asking individuals to run some tests for us. We needed to design a simple task which any interested person could easily follow.

We considered adopting preexisting tools for this task, mainly OONI (Open Observatory of Network Interference, see Section IV for further details). However, given that our interest was specific and limited to getting information as to give to potential relay operators (which ISPs would be feasible to set up relays with), we did not consider necessary to design a full application; we decided to request information based on tools readily available in default installations of any general-purpose operating system.

With this in mind, we set up a simple form, reproduced in Fig. 4, collecting only some data about the connection of each probe, and giving instructions to run *traceroute*, either on Unix or Windows-based systems. We request our users to provide the results of running *traceroute* to all of the Tor DirAuths. *Traceroute*, being an ICMP probing tool, has many known shortcomings and many readily available tools would probably do a better job. The criteria for choosing *traceroute* is, again, that it is available and preinstalled in every major operating system.

Figure 4. Interface at http://rutas.priv-anon.unam.mx with the form shown to users when submitting a trace

We acknowledge the main blocker for this form is the means we requested participants to submit their information from: They have to open an interactive terminal, paste into it a long command, wait for a couple of minutes (we have observed run times between one and two minutes from non-censored networks, and between four and six minutes from censored ones) for it to finish, and paste back their results in the browser. We reproduce here the command for Unix systems:

```
for i in 171.25.193.9 86.59.21.38
199.58.81.140 194.109.206.212
204.13.164.118 131.188.40.189
128.31.0.34 193.23.244.244
154.35.175.225 128.31.0.39
199.254.238.52; do traceroute $i;
done
```

It is far from user friendly. This design was chosen due to the limited time and resources we had.

IV. Related work

There are many projects with different scopes aimed at detecting network censorship in the context of Tor participation. Even with this stated level of specificity, this section is far from comprehensive.

OONI [4] is a global project aimed at finding and reporting several instances of network censorship worldwide. OONI operates in a fashion comparable to what Tor does, based on a large amount of *probes* run continuously on hosts provided by volunteers, performing network connections and looking for censorship or filtering evidence in many ways, including tests for Tor connectivity. OONI also has user-friendly applications that can be installed in mobile devices. A major output of OONI's work is the interpretation of the gathered data in a global fashion, often correlating censorship events with news items.

The OONI application, however, includes the probes only for web connectivity, instant messaging, network performance, and middleboxes detection. But even in the server-based probe, Tor connectivity is measured by trying to connect as a client to network. Our tests verify the reachability of the DirAuths, needed for setting up relays, but not for client connections.

Quite probably, we will be able to work with the OONI developers to add DirAuth reachability to their probes. This is a clear next step for our project.

The *traceroute.org* site, set up by Thomas Kernen [7], provides a directory of servers offering a Web form from which they run *traceroute* on behalf of the users. This site has sadly not been updated since 2011, and thus contains many broken links. While the linked sites do provide a valuable resource to network administrators, it does not provide any severs in Mexico, and is thus not suitable for our needs.

The model presented by Danezis [2] has many items compatible with what we try to achieve, but goes to greater lengths to assure a given address is blocked. It also presents a series of user connections to directory servers to detect censorship. While Danezis' model contemplates repeating measurements at time intervals of one week, given the nature of participation and our goal of not installing any software in the participating clients, ours is based on one-shot measurements. Besides, this work is presented as a model, not as a comparable implementation.

Another country-specific project worth mentioning is research on Internet censorship in China [16]. This works has a very different focus than our project's. China is probably, together with Iran the foremost country-level censorship example, and the researchers' approaches are applied in a much bigger scale. Of course, citing said article in no way means that Mexico's censorship is in any way comparable to China's.

The article starts by describing the *Great Firewall of China* at a BGP (Border Gateway Protocol) level, analyzing the conformation of the Autonomous Systems (AS), and explaining where they discovered the different filtering devices and presenting the filtering not as a *Great Firewall*, but as an

Internet Panopticon, with local and peripherial filtering points performing different tasks.

V. Results and Discussion

Throughout five months, we received 79 reports from 12 states (out of 32 in the country). Table I shows the distribution of reported ISPs.

TABLE I. Number of reports received from each of the different available ISPs

ISP	Reports
Telmex	32
Axtel	10
Izzi	7
Total Play	7
AT&T	6
Megacable	4
Alestra	2
UNAM	2
Avantel	1
Bestel	1
Cablevisión	1
Express VPN	1
Maxcom	1
Movistar	1
Nextel	1
Telcel	1

The distribution is close to what we expected, with Telmex (which spans its constituents, Uninet and Infinitum) clearly dominating the scene.

The results are aggregated and presented, one report per row, in a table as the one (partially) shown in Fig. 5; row colors represent the percentage of DirAuths each IP could reach: Red (0-25%), orange (25-50%), yellow (50–75%) and green (75-100%).

Figure 5. Results table. Last octet of all IP addresses has been manually obscured.

By the time this project was started, we knew for a fact that Telmex censored connections to DirAuths; this was confirmed, as most connections report 3 out of 11 successful connections. There are several records showing 0/11 — Given the similarities in them, we believe this to be caused by old modems not properly implementing NAT forwarding support for *traceroute*.

A second interesting finding was the high amount of connections providing sufficient but still not perfect returns — this means, connections where Tor relays could be installed, as they can exceed the 50% mark, but not by much — Most strikingly, the two tested connections at UNAM, Mexico's largest and most important university, can barely withstand being a relay, as they can reach only 55% of the DirAuths. This is another item to verify, both technically (what kind of communications exactly are being censored) and politically (why are they being censored).

Since we managed to systematize the results, we have been inviting prospective relay operators to connect via Axtel, the ISP that has the highest success rate. This has led to the spike at the right of Fig. 3.

VI. Further Work

As for the reasons of the censorship, we have contacted Customer Support for the ISP with the largest market share, Telmex. As it was expected, they denied instrumenting this blocking. We have started contacting the Federal Institute for Telecommunications (IFT) so we can push for a real reply.

As it was said in the Abstract, this article presents a Work in Progress. We still have not analyzed the records to find evidence of *deep NAT*. ISPs, particularly smaller or newer ones, do not do this because of censorship, but because of their limited network resources; nevertheless, their connections are being censored.

Acknowledgement

The author wishes to acknowledge the UNAM/DGAPA/PAPIME PE102718 project for the needed facilities to carry out the activities here presented, as well as Derechos Digitales for its logistical and economical support.

Personal thanks to Vasilis Ververis, for preparing Fig. 3 which, in short, supports the writing of this article.

References

[1] F. Bustillos, *Is tor being blocked by isp? (mexico)*, 2016. [Online]. Available: https://lists.torproject.org/pipermail/tor-relays/2016-January/008491.html (visited on 03/15/2019).

[2] G. Danezis, "An anomaly-based censorship detection system for tor," *The Tor Project*, 2011. [Online]. Available: https://research.torproject.org/techreports/detector-2011-09-09.pdf.

[3] R. Dingledine and N. Mathewson, "Anonymity loves company: Usability and the network effect.," in *WEIS*, 2006. [Online]. Available: https://www.freehaven.net/anonbib/cache/usability:weis2006.pdf (visited on 03/15/2019).

[4] A. Filasto and J. Appelbaum, "Ooni: Open observatory of network interference.," in *FOCI*, 2012.

[5] M. Graham and S. D. Sabbata, "The anonymous internet," Internet Geographies, Oxford Internet Institute, Tech. Rep., 2014. [Online]. Available: http://geography.oii.ox.ac.uk/the-anonymous-internet/ (visited on 03/15/2019).

[6] R. Jansen, N. Hopper, and Y. Kim, "Recruiting new tor relays with braids," in *Proceedings of the 17th ACM conference on Computer and communications security*, ACM, 2010, pp. 319–328. [Online]. Available: http://www.robgjansen.com/publications/braids-ccs2010.pdf (visited on 03/15/2019).

[7] T. Kernen, *Traceroute.org*, 1998–2011. [Online]. Available: http://www.traceroute.org/ (visited on 03/15/2019).

[8] I. R. Learmonth, "Strength in numbers: Measuring diversity in the tor network," Tor Project, Tech. Rep., Dec. 11, 2018. [Online]. Available: https://blog.torproject.org/strength-numbers-measuring-diversity-tor-network (visited on 03/15/2019).

[9] A. Macrina, *Next steps from tor meeting*, Apr. 10, 2017. [Online]. Available: https://lists.torproject.org/pipermail/global-south/2017-April/000000.html (visited on 03/15/2019).

[10] D. McDevitt, "Tor exit relays to be run in libraries: Library freedom project," Open Technology Fund, Tech. Rep., Jul. 9, 2015. [Online]. Available: https://www.opentech.fund/news/tor-exit-relays-to-be-run-in-libraries-library-freedom-project/ (visited on 03/15/2019).

[11] J. Nájera, A. Argüelles, and S. Alcántar, "La internet anónima: Tor en méxico," Enjambre Digital, Tech. Rep., 2018. [Online]. Available: https://tor.enjambre.net/ (visited on 03/15/2019).

[12] T. Project, *About tor metrics*, 2009–2018. [Online]. Available: https://metrics.torproject.org/about.html (visited on 03/15/2019).

[13] R. Reitman, "Tor challenge inspires 1,635 tor relays," Electronic Frontier Foundation, Tech. Rep., Sep. 19, 2014. [Online]. Available: https://www.eff.org/deeplinks/2014/09/tor-challenge-inspires-1635-tor-relays (visited on 03/15/2019).

[14] P. Syverson, R. Dingledine, and N. Mathewson, "Tor: The secondgeneration onion router," in *Usenix Security*, 2004. [Online]. Available: https://www.onion-router.net/Publications/tor-design.pdf (visited on 03/15/2019).

[15] *The tor project*. [Online]. Available: https://www.torproject.org/ (visited on 01/25/2019).

[16] X. Xu, Z. M. Mao, and J. A. Halderman, "Internet censorship in china: Where does the filtering occur?" In *International Conference on Passive and Active Network Measurement*, Springer, 2011, pp. 133–142. [Online]. Available: https://censorbib.nymity.ch/pdf/Xu2011a.pdf (visited on 03/15/2019).

Early Detection of Censorship Events with Psiphon Network Data

Simin Kargar
Psiphon
Washington, D.C.
email: s.kargar@psiphon.ca

Keith McManamen
Psiphon
Toronto, Canada
email: k.mcmanamen@psiphon.ca

Jacob Klein
Psiphon
Washington, D.C.
email: j.klein@psiphon.ca

***Abstract*—Over the past decade, circumvention tools have had a significant impact in ensuring access to censored content and preserving user privacy online. In addition, circumvention network data can be used to detect early indicators of Internet censorship and identify population-level effects of changes in the network environment. Monitoring network traffic for key indicators provides an opportunity to diagnose, analyze, and respond to online censorship events in real time. This paper examines the performance of Psiphon, a free and open source circumvention tool, during blocking events that occured over the past year in Iran, Iraq, and Turkmenistan. The study also offers insight into how Psiphon network data detected early signs of blocking in these examples. Through three case studies, we explore detailed data that were leveraged to improve Psiphon network resiliency during socially and politically critical times in various contexts.**

Keywords-information controls; online censorship; Internet shutdown; circumvention tools; social media blocking; psiphon.

I. Introduction

This study presents analysis of three major censorship events that occurred in 2018 in the context of observable anomalies in discrete time series data from Psiphon network. Psiphon offers free, open source tools that are accessible, easily operated, and trusted worldwide. Psiphon provides recourse to online censorship by routing a user's Internet connection via a distributed global network of servers. Like other Virtual Private Network (VPN) software, an encrypted tunnel is established between the user's device and a Psiphon server, allowing traffic to be transmitted securely and thereby circumvent filtering on censored networks. Although encrypted, VPN traffic tends to have identifiable characteristics and traffic patterns increasingly vulnerable to blocking by deep-packet inspection (DPI) and traffic fingerprinting. Psiphon is designed to mitigate the risk of direct attempts to disrupt network traffic by using sophisticated traffic obfuscation techniques that disguise and vary readily-identifiable features in Internet traffic and provide resilience to fingerprinting. Moreover, a multi-protocol architecture of transports ensures network resiliency in the event that censors successfully fingerprint and block a subset of those protocols. Amid intensifying censorship against VPNs and circumvention tools, the reliability of the Psiphon network has driven widespread adoption in countries that continuously censor the Internet as well as in response to spontaneous censorship events.

Consequently, both in regions where the use of circumvention tools is a persistent need, and where politically-motivated, isolated, and unexpected censorship and network attack events occur, Psiphon has consistently provided a statistically significant snapshot of circumvention tool usage patterns. Disruptions in network performance typically follow social and political contours. They also offer an opportunity to investigate blocking events in real time. Given that the dynamics and internal workings of Internet censorship are highly opaque to media and civil society, this network vantage point provides unique insight into the technical context behind these critical events.

By reviewing case studies from three different contexts, this paper offers a baseline for targeted and strategic blocking events that occurred in response to emerging Internet policy developments and critical socio-political events. The remainder of the paper comprises of the following:

Section II provides an overview of related work in this space. Section 3 explores Psiphon network data of three blocking events from 2018 that occurred in Iran, Iraq, and Turkmenistan with a population-level effect. Section IV discusses how this approach can contribute to the accurate identification of periods of anomalous Psiphon usage as an early warning sign of censorship and targeted Psiphon blocking. Finally, Section V concludes by discussing the implications of anomalies and early detection of online blocking events for Psiphon's ability to rapidly scale and reach populations at the height of critical times. It also offers some direction for future work in this space.

II. Related Work

While circumvention network data remains an underutilized point of analysis, past research in this area has used metrics from the Tor network and quantitative statistical models. The anomaly-based censorship detection system developed by Danezis analyses time series connection data over seven-day periods, flagging an anomaly whenever total Tor connections from a country deviate from the normal distribution of the top 50 Tor-using countries [1]. Wright, Darer, and Farnan refine this methodology to create a multivariate anomaly detection system using principal component analysis, to allow ongoing per-country detection of more nuanced internet filtering events [2]. The latter emphasize the applicability of this approach to usage data of other services, including Psiphon.

While quantitative approaches are robust, one of their limitations is a tendency to be passive towards the changing social and political conditions on the ground. Two noteworthy studies have analyzed Psiphon network data using an events-based methodology. First, in 2013, Psiphon collaborated with the civil society organization ASL19 on an analysis of information controls in Iran during the 2013 Presidential elections, where censors actively endeavoured to disrupt Psiphon network traffic [3]. This study conducted a detailed examination of Psiphon data over a six-month period in the context of evolving developments in Iranian Internet policy and in the political cycle, and effectively formalized this mixed-methods approach to examining the impacts of information controls. Second, in a recent paper using data provided by Psiphon, Deibert, Oliver, and Senft build on the previous study by conducting a comparative analysis of Iranian information control regimes, contrasting tactics used to disrupt the Psiphon network during the 2016 Parliamentary elections with those employed during the prior election blocking in 2013 [4]. Likewise following this mixed-methods approach, the analysis in this study couples network analytics with the evolving sociopolitical dynamics of online censorship to enhance the blocking resilience of Psiphon tools in the unfolding local contexts.

III. Case Studies

Over the past year, Psiphon registered the scale and impact of many online blocking events. Among these, the cases of Iran, Iraq, and Turkmenistan stand out due to their scope and population-level effects. The unprecedented blocking of Telegram and Instagram in Iran in late 2017 and early 2018, and the ostensibly permanent blocking of Telegram in May 2018, brought about a surge in the use of circumvention tools, in particular Psiphon [5]. A crackdown on VPN usage in Turkmenistan between January and April 2018 [6] involved intensified traffic fingerprinting that degraded the general performance of VPNs and other circumvention tools, and shifted the protocol distribution of Psiphon traffic. The government-imposed Internet [7] and social media shutdown in Iraq in July 2018 [8] led to similar surges in the Psiphon usage. Psiphon network data captured noteworthy intricacies of these events.

The following will investigate these cases in further detail to address two main research questions: (1) to what extent does data-based analysis of Internet censorship correspond to the social and political contours of a given society, and (2) how can Psiphon data be applied to develop narratives of Internet censorship in adversarial environments?

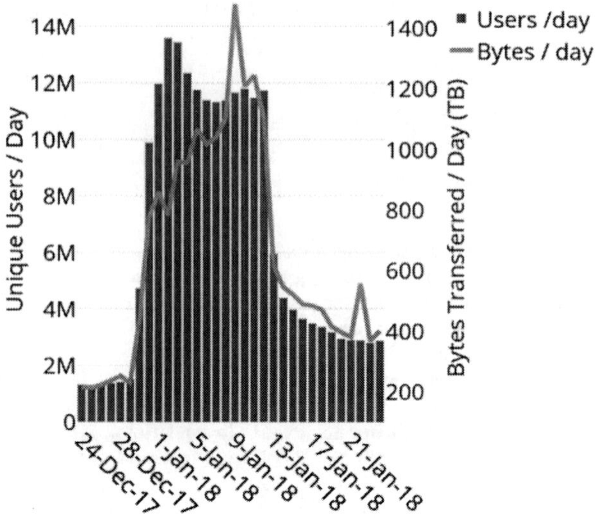

Figure 1. Iran Telegram and Instagram Blocking (Dec 2017-Jan 2018)

A. Iran

For those circumventing Iran's filtering apparatus, Psiphon has been a popular tool since its inception in 2006. Between late December 2017 and the second week of January 2018, anti-government demonstrations broke out across Iran as a reaction to economic grievances. Protesters effectively utilized Telegram and Instagram to organize, which precipitated a temporary ban on both platforms [9]. The government of Iran lifted the ban as the protests subsided [10], but reinstated the ban on Telegram four months later. As Figure 1 indicates, the December 31 disruption of international Internet traffic and the blocking of two popular communication tools resulted in a 600%

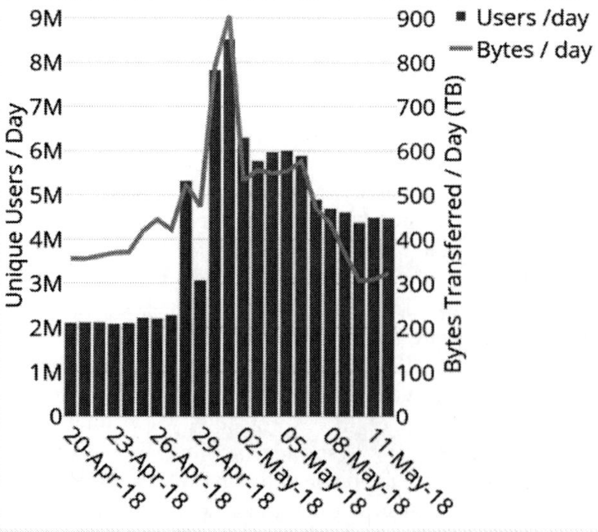

Figure 2. Iran Ban on Telegram Messenger (Apr-May 2018)

surge in Psiphon unique users and network bandwidth usage within 24 hours, and a 900% increase from baseline usage over the next seven days.

In late April 2018, as the permanent blocking of Telegram became imminent, Telegram servers actually faced a major outage that affected users across the UK, Europe, Russia and the Middle East [11][12]. However, concerned users in Iran attributed this problem to Iran's censorship apparatus and turned to Psiphon to restore access to the Telegram network. As Figure 2 indicates, this caused a surge in the Psiphon network on April 28, two days before Telegram was officially blocked in Iran. At the time, Telegram was the most popular messaging application with an estimated 40 million users in Iran [13]. When Iran's judiciary officially announced the ban on April 30, it drove unprecedented adoption of Psiphon on all platforms. The surge peaked at 8.5 million daily unique users, transferring 900 TB across the network. As Iranian authorities confirmed, the broad-scale adoption of circumvention tools, including Psiphon, helped mitigate the intended effects of the blocking orders [14].

B. *Iraq*

On July 9, 2018, protests broke out in the southern Iraqi city of Basra. Citizens took to the streets to demonstrate against widespread unemployment, corruption, and inadequate public services. In the days that followed, the protests spread to several other cities, making this the country's longest and most widespread protest period in recent history [15]. The government responded by declaring a state of emergency and censoring access to major social media platforms Facebook and Twitter, and messaging apps WhatsApp and Viber. Subsequently, reports of complete Internet shutdowns were received from several Iraqi cities, including the capital of Baghdad, on July 14 [16]. Psiphon connections from Baghdad were observed to drop from a rate of 500,000 connections per hour to zero, simultaneously across all ISPs, for the hours the shutdown persisted. This trend was reflected across 15 other Iraqi cities, indicating that a widespread Internet shutdown had been implemented. However, in regions where Internet access was not entirely blocked, such as in the Kurdistan region where Internet Service Providers (ISPs) remain moderately autonomous from central Iraqi authorities, data transfer reflected users circumventing app or site-specific blocking. A second shutdown occurred on July 19, when Psiphon connections from Baghdad decreased by 98% and network bandwidth transfer fell to nearly zero. Initially unconfirmed by news media covering the story, Psiphon data registered a second nationwide Internet shutdown in near-real time after the termination of traffic at the ISP-level, consistent with an intentional service blackout.

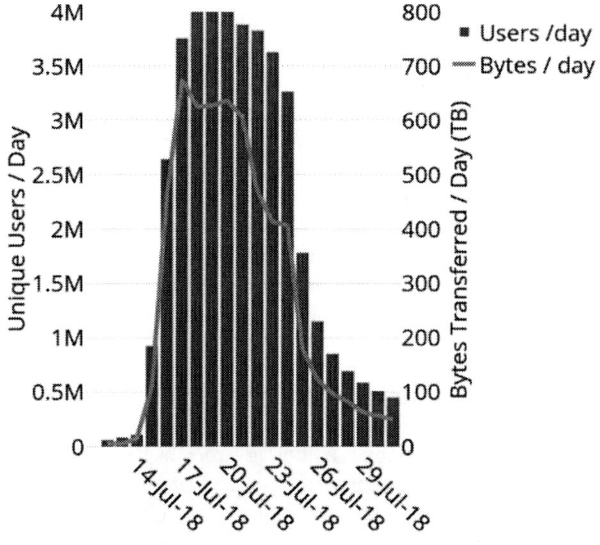

Figure 3. Iraq Social Media Shutdown (Jul 2018)

Soon after the onset of the first nationwide shutdown, Psiphon experienced the beginning of a surge in users as Iraqis turned to the Psiphon network to circumvent the ongoing blocking. Though the nationwide Internet shutdowns were lifted, blocks on specific social media and messaging platforms remained in effect until July 26 [17], driving up demand for circumvention tools. Following the July 19 shutdown, eight of the top ten apps in Iraq's Google Play store were VPNs, with Psiphon holding the top spot [18]. As indicated in Figure 3, Psiphon's user base grew from 50,000 to over 4 million between July 12 and July 20, and elevated usage persisted until the social media blocking was lifted. Since these events, the baseline number of users connecting to Psiphon from Iraq has increased 2.9% on the pre-blocking monthly average.

C. *Turkmenistan*

Beginning in early 2018, the state-owned and only operating ISP in Turkmenistan, TurkmenTelecom, initiated a crackdown on VPNs. Media sources reported that TurkmenTelecom was using newly acquired high-speed DPI filtering technology at scale to identify and block circumvention traffic [19]. As Radio Free Europe's Turkmen service reported, the ISP targeted individual Internet users and notified them that continued use of VPNs or proxy tools would result in disconnection from the Internet [20]. According to research conducted by the OpenNet Initiative, DPI technology has been in use in Turkmenistan since at least 2010 to maintain an extensive blacklist of websites and keywords [21]. More sophisticated traffic fingerprinting based on protocol type was not previously observed at national scale.

Psiphon network data corroborated these early reports and anecdotal claims. Beginning January 23, Psiphon's daily unique users and overall network bandwidth usage consistently decreased over the next 30 days, as indicated in

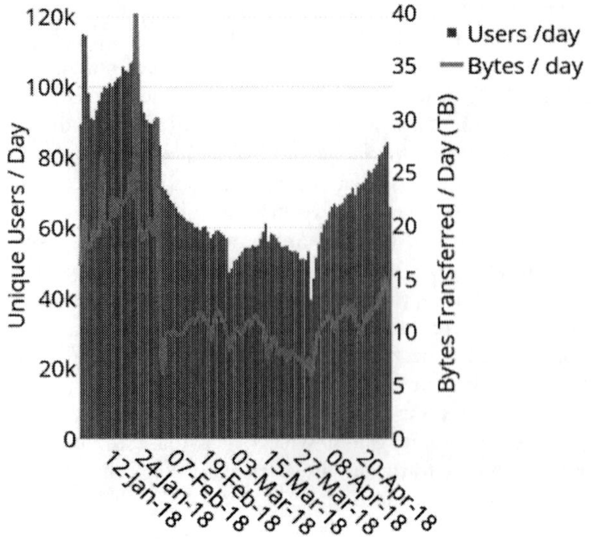

Figure 4. Turkmenistan VPN Filtering (Jan-Apr 2018)

Figure 4. The degradation of directly-connecting protocols in Turkmenistan was also evident in fluctuations in the normal Psiphon network protocol distribution. As shown in Figure 5, direct connections in blue and purple gradually became less viable, resulting in network tactics shifting the balance of traffic to more resilient transport protocols. While redundancy in Psiphon's protocol architecture allowed the network to adapt to enhanced filtering measures, the interference observed against direct connections corroborates reports that general VPN performance was effectively disrupted.

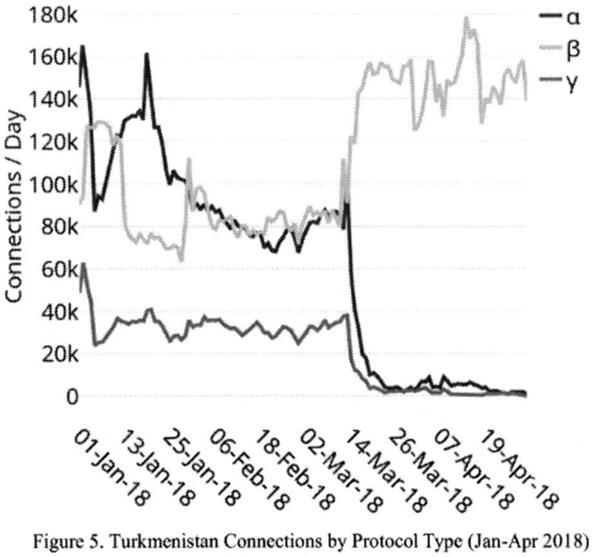

Figure 5. Turkmenistan Connections by Protocol Type (Jan-Apr 2018)

Normal network performance appeared to be restored by August 2018, but similar network interference against direct connections was observed again throughout September and November 2018, and developments remain ongoing.

IV. DISCUSSION

Based on the case studies reviewed herein, our approach can contribute to the accurate identification of periods of anomalous Psiphon usage as an early warning sign of censorship events and, specifically, interference with Psiphon network traffic. Anomalies detected in the Psiphon network data correspond to other indicators of Internet interdiction in countries with a record of policies and tactics adversarial toward Internet freedom [22].

While this analysis demonstrates the strength of a mixed-methods appreach, it is important to acknowledge some future directions for information controls research of this nature. First, technical, quantitative analyses still remain largely decoupled from granular social and political case studies, though the dynamics of Internet censorship involve vast and inextricable dimensions of each. Certainly, the computational methodologies discussed in Section II provide important macro-scale insights that can serve as a focal point for in-depth social scientific research, but often are not intrinsically actionable intelligence for media and civil society advocacy. Second, the event-mapping methodology as applied to selected case studies here can benefit from integration with systematized, automated anomaly-detection on data feeds to allow precise real-time alerting of such events across a broader spectrum of censored countries. Third, looking forward, exploring the application of machine-learning approaches in order to more comprehensively identify the various indicators, even precursors, of critical censorship events to facilitate rapid detection and response is seen as a valuable direction for further research.

As Crete-Nishihata, Deibert, and Senft explain, the study of information controls is a multidisciplinary challenge [23]. Technical measurements are essential but will lead to greater insights into online censorship if we interpret such data with contextual knowledge and social science methods. Performing analysis on real-time filtering events as well as historical filtering behavior provides an opportunity for collaboration with academic researchers, advocacy groups, and the media. This can, in particular, offer insights into the unfolding events in places that do not often receive sufficient media coverage and international attention.

Additionally, partnerships between circumvention tool providers and other stakeholders can support consistent methods of comparing approaches taken by authoritarian regimes to their previous actions in order to further analyze their learning in the realm of online censorship [24]. This will provide a consistent baseline for comparative scholarship and investigations of online censorship cases by academic researchers, advocacy groups, and the media.

V. CONCLUSIONS

Detecting anomalous events within Psiphon data enables us to identify anomalies in the status of Internet freedom globally, and more specifically, in countries with a poor record of securing freedom of expression and access to information. Anomalies in multiple variants such as the number of users, bytes transferred, session duration, and length of establishing connections demonstrate the seasonality in online censorship events. Such data coupled with contextual narratives from users of circumvention tools, media, advocacy groups, and other researchers can significantly enhance our understanding of network disruptions worldwide. Through these examples, we have demonstrated how Psiphon data correspond to imminent, potential, and actual online censorship events on a national or local level. In addition, combining multiple network metrics helps to identify anomalies in Psiphon network performance as an indicator of both degraded domestic Internet performance and direct interference against Psiphon traffic. Applying this knowledge can result in a customized experience of Psiphon services, which is tailored for the unique needs of specific censorship environments, both known and emerging. Comprehensive analysis of anomalies and early detection of online blocking events enhance Psiphon's ability to rapidly scale and reach populations at the height of critical times.

Beyond the technicalities of this approach, the analysis presented herein focused on two types of state actors: (a) those that are known to engage in active filtering, and (b) states that often do not receive significant attention from the media and Internet freedom community. Partnerships between circumvention tool providers and more diverse actors will be conducive to detailed investigations of these cases and will ultimately serve a broader spectrum of stakeholders.

REFERENCES

[1] G. Danezis, An Anomaly-Based Censorship Detection System for Tor", 2011. Retrieved 2019.02.26 from: https://censorbib.nymity.ch/pdf/Danezis2011a.pdf.

[2] J. Wright, A. Darer, and O. Farnan, On Identifying Anomalies in Tor Usage with Applications in Detecting Internet Censorship, Association for Computing Machinery, 2018. Retrieved 2019.02.26 from: https://doi.org/10.1145/3201064.3201093.

[3] ASL19 and Psiphon, Information controls: Iran's presidential elections, 2013. Retrieved 2019.02.26 from: https://asl19.org/cctr/iran-2013election-report/.

[4] R. Deibert, J. Oliver, and A. Senft, Censors Get Smart: Evidence from Psiphon in Iran. Review of Policy Research, e0001, 2019. Retrieved 2019.02.26 from: https://doi.org/10.1111/ropr.12333.

[5] S. Kargar and K. McManamen, Censorship and Collateral Damage: Analyzing the Telegram Ban in Iran, September 2018, Berkman Klein Center Research Publication No. 2018-4. Retrieved 2019.02.26 from: https://dx.doi.org/10.2139/ssrn.3244046.

[6] RFE/RL (Azat Habar), Users of proxy servers in Ashgabat are denied access to the Internet, January 29, 2018. Retrieved 2019.02.26 from: https://rus.azathabar.com/a/29004792.html.

[7] NetBlocks, Study shows extent of Iraq internet shutdown and social media restrictions during protests, July 2018. Retrieved 2019.02.26 from: https://netblocks.org/reports/study-shows-extent-of-iraq-internet-shutdown-and-social-media-restrictions-during-protests-zPyXjzAE.

[8] T. Rami and L. Taha, The Iraqi government turns off the Internet in response to protesters demanding water and electricity, August 2018. Retrieved 2019.02.26 from: https://asl19.org/ar/blog/2018-08-01-iraqi-government-shuts-down-the-internet-in-response-to-protestors-demanding-water-and-electricity.html.

[9] A. Filastò and M. Xynou, Iran Protests: OONI data confirms censorship events (Part 1), January 2018. Retrieved 2019.02.26 from: https://ooni.torproject.org/post/2018-iran-protests/.

[10] Deutsche Welle, Iran unblocks Telegram messenger service shut down during country-wide protests, January 2018. Retrieved 2019.02.26 from: https://www.dw.com/en/iran-unblocks-telegram-messenger-service-shut-down-during-country-wide-protests/a-42141829.

[11] D. Snelling, Telegram DOWN - Popular messaging app not working as major outage confirmed, April 2018. Retrieved 2019.02.26 from: https://www.express.co.uk/life-style/science-technology/952670/Telegram-down-messaging-app-not-working-outage-confirmed-WhatsApp-rival.

[12] Status overview of problems at Telegram, Retrieved 2019.02.26 from: https://downdetector.com/status/telegram/news/212777-problems-at-telegram-2.

[13] A. Vahdat, Iran orders internet providers to block Telegram, April 2018. Retrieved 2019.02.26 from: https://apnews.com/22e81a82289745a49b991bae413e9b71.

[14] R. Faghihi, Iran's conservatives return to Telegram after failed ban, November 28, 2018. Retrieved 2019.02.26 from: https://www.al-monitor.com/pulse/originals/2018/11/iran-telegram-ban-conservative-media-rejoin-tasnim-fars.html.

[15] P. Cockburn, Iraq protests: Demonstrators blame 'bad government, bad roads, bad weather, and bad people', July 17, 2018. Retrieved 2019.02.26 from: https://www.independent.co.uk/news/world/iraq-protests-bad-government-roads-weather-people-haider-abadi-sadr-oil-a8451736.html.

[16] D. Madoury, Internet in Iraq Returns After Two-Day Blackout, July 18, 2018. Retrieved 2019.02.26 from: https://blogs.oracle.com/internetintelligence/internet-in-iraq-returns-after-two-day-blackout.

[17] Middle East Monitor, Iraq lifts ban on social networking sites, July 27, 2018. Retrieved 2019.02.26 from: https://www.middleeastmonitor.com/20180727-iraq-lifts-ban-on-social-networking-sites.

[18] Appbrain analytics dashboard, Retrieved 2019.02.26 from https://www.appbrain.com/.

[19] RFE/RL (Azat Habar), Expert: Turkmen authorities buy spyware for Internet control, March 12, 2018. Retrieved 2019.02.26 from: https://rus.azathabar.com/a/29091514.html.

[20] RFE/RL (Azat Habar), Users of proxy servers in Lebap are faced with the shutdown of the Internet, February 2, 2018. Retrieved 2019.02.26 from: https://rus.azathabar.com/a/29024861.html.

[21] R. Deibert, J. Zittrain, R. Rohozinski, and J. Palfrey, Access Controlled: The Shaping of Power, Rights, and Rule in Cyberspace, Cambridge, MA: MIT Press, p 244, 2010.

[22] A. Shahbaz, Freedom on the Net 2018; The Rise of Digital Authoritarianism, Freedom House, 2018. Retrieved 2019.02.26 from: https://freedomhouse.org/report/freedom-net/freedom-net-2018/rise-digital-authoritarianism.

[23] M. Crete-Nishihata, R. Deibert, A. Senft, Not by Technical Means Alone: The Multidisciplinary Challenge of Studying Information Controls, IEEE Internet Computing, vol. 17, no. 3, pp. 34-41, May-June 2013.